Better Schools:
A Values Perspective

Clive Beck

The Falmer Press
(A member of the Taylor & Francis Group)
New York • Philadelphia • London

UK   The Falmer Press, Falmer House, Barcombe, Lewes, East Sussex, BN8 5DL

USA   The Falmer Press, Taylor & Francis Inc., 1900 Frost Road, Suite 101, Bristol PA 19007

First published 1990

British Library Cataloguing in Publication Data
Beck, Clive
Better schools: a values perspective
1. Schools. Role in society
I. Title
370.19'3
ISBN 1–85000–622–9
ISBN 1–85000–623–7 pbk

Library of Congress Cataloging-in-Publication Data
Beck, Clive
Better schools: a values perspective on education/Clive Beck.
p. cm.
Includes bibliographical references.
ISBN 1–85000–622–9.
ISBN 1–85000–623–7. (pbk.)
1. Education—Aims and objectives. 2. Social values.
I. Title LB41.B39 1990
370.11—dc20   90–16835 CIP

Jacket design by Caroline Archer

Typeset in 10½/13 point Bembo by
Bramley Typesetting Limited, 12 Campbell Court, Bramley, Basingstoke, Hants.

Printed in Great Britain by
Taylor & Francis (Printers) Ltd, Basingstoke

Contents

Introduction

Schools are of great concern to most of us, whether as parents, ordinary citizens or educators. We are often unsure, however, just what their role is and to what extent they are fulfilling it. We do not know whether to complain about them, or gratefully accept them as they are.

The purpose of this book is (a) to identify the *goals* of schooling, and (b) to suggest what *form* of schooling is needed in order to achieve these goals. While schools are already doing a good job in many ways, lack of clarity about objectives hinders them in their task. As John Goodlad has said recently, unless the goals of schools are clearly set forth, 'the specifics designed to teach concepts, skills, and values become the ends rather than the means, obscuring the larger ends.' (John Goodlad. *A Place Called School*, New York: McGraw-Hill, 1984, p. 290.)

The form of schooling, however, must be examined as well as the goals, since the education we aim at and see as 'good' must be feasible. As John Dewey said often, speaking of education and of life in general, our aims must be modified by our experience of reality. The values perspective on schools offered in this book, then, will be concerned with means as well as ends.

A key theme of the book will be the relationship between school and society. Some writers have suggested that reform at the school level is impossible because schools are so strongly influenced by society. It has been said that schools 'reproduce' society, and even that education *is* socialization. While not taking such an extreme position, I will attempt to show that society is one of the major realities that schools must take into account, and that school and societal reform must go hand in hand if significant improvement is to be achieved.

From one point of view, schools deserve much more credit than they currently receive. Their accomplishments are many. They provide a relatively safe, humane and pleasant environment for vast numbers of children. They teach most children to read, write and calculate, and give them an introduction to our intellectual traditions not otherwise available. They reinforce many of the values learned in the home, and foster new outlooks and behaviour needed in the work place and other public settings of pluralistic societies. They offer a range of artistic, cultural and sporting activities, and initiate children into pastimes which bring them pleasure for the rest of their lives. With a minimum of pomp and corruption (contrast them with business and political institutions), schools manage both to care for our children and to give them a solid social, cultural and intellectual grounding. School teachers and other school personnel have reason to feel proud of what they do.

Paradoxically, however, from another point of view the performance of schools might well be described as scandalous. Some of the shortcomings of schooling will be documented in the chapters that follow. But here we might note the two central scandals: first, schools massively deprive children of intellectual and cultural stimulation, teaching with a scope and efficiency considerably less than what is needed; and secondly, schools enormously distort children's perception of social and political reality and of what is ultimately important in life. The first problem is widely recognized: parents and citizens constantly ask, Why aren't our schools more effective? The second problem is less commonly noted, partly because adults share many of the distorted ideas about society and life which schools transmit.

How can one reconcile these two assessments, that schools have a solid record of achievement of which educators can be proud, and that their performance is scandalous? The answer, I believe, lies largely in the close connection between school and society already alluded to. Schools are doing quite well, *under the circumstances.* The results are indeed scandalous in many ways, as indicated, but the causes are embedded in long-standing social and cultural conditions. The problem is largely a societal one; and a broad societal effort is required, with the school as just one of several players. Thus, schools can be proud of what they are doing in the present societal context, but should be spurred on to work with others in bringing about major improvements.

On what basis do we make value judgments of this kind about the ways in which schools are doing well or badly? By what criteria do we establish goals and standards for schools and arrive at directions for change? The approach to values employed in this book is goal-oriented or 'teleological'. It takes as its starting point basic human values such as survival, happiness, friendship, self-respect, fulfilment, a sense of meaning in life and so forth; or, in a phrase, 'human well being' (or 'the good life'). The central claim, which will be elaborated in Chapter 1, is that the purpose of schooling (and indeed of all human enterprises) is to promote human well being (or basic human values, or 'the good life'). The defence of schools, then, is that they already contribute in major ways to the well being of students and other members of society; and the criticism is that they do not promote human well being as much as they could, in general and especially for certain racial, ethnic, gender and other sub-groups.

Such an approach to values, of course, is not the only one that has been advocated, in ethics or in education. However, it is broadly representative of one major tradition in moral philosophy, from at least Aristotle's time to the present. And it has the advantage that even people who disagree with it can gain insights from its application. Whether we are 'teleologists' or 'deontologists', it is important to know which kind of schooling will promote human well being and which will undermine it.

The basic 'manifesto' of this book is as follows:

1. School and society are indeed closely linked: only to a limited degree can the school resist the influences of its wider community (and of the global community). If substantial improvement is to be achieved, school and society must work together.

2. As a basis for reform we need a new vision of the goal of school and society, namely, to promote human well being, and promote it as equitably as possible throughout society and around the world.

3. The school can better play its distinctive part in achieving this goal if it greatly increases its emphasis on 'personal and social education'. While not neglecting traditional 'basics' such as literacy, numeracy and scientific knowledge — indeed, programs in these areas should be enriched in certain respects — the school should give much more attention than at present to fields such as values, culture, religion, politics, economics and ecology.

4. In approaching these areas, schools should not adopt a neutral stance, but rather advocate certain outlooks and attitudes. The teaching method, nevertheless, should be interactive, with teachers and students gaining insights from each other (and from other sources) into what constitutes a sound worldview and way of life.

5. The school should 'practice what it preaches'. Its organization and atmosphere should as far as possible embody the approaches to personal and societal life being advocated, thus setting an example to students and also enabling them to learn by doing as well as by study and discussion.

6. Students should study a largely common curriculum in non-selective schools and heterogeneous classes. This is necessary in order to promote the ideal of equality, build a sense of community, and ensure that there is input from students of different backgrounds. It is also

feasible, because in a school which emphasizes personal and social issues, students of different backgrounds can all contribute and benefit.

A book such as this cannot, of course, be fully comprehensive. In Part 1 — 'Getting Our Bearings' — I have focused on just a selection of key goals and pedagogical issues, and four major interest groups, namely, students, teachers, parents and 'society'. In Part 2, which deals with specific problem areas, I have concentrated on issues of compulsion and indoctrination and questions related to religion, race, ethnicity, gender and class. In Part 3, which suggests new priorities for the school curriculum, I have been able to discuss only moral and values education, religious and spiritual education, political education and (all too briefly) global education. It is my hope, however, that this will be sufficient to illustrate and make plausible the central idea — that the aim of schooling is to promote human well being — and set schooling and educational inquiry off in some new, worthwhile directions.

One final word about how to approach the book. Many of the chapters contain a relatively theoretical part and a more practical part. For example, the chapter on ethnic bias discusses the nature and role of ethnicity before going on to talk about multicultural education. The reason for this is that I believe even the most practical problems in schooling cannot be resolved without dealing with fundamental issues. I have tried to make the theoretical sections as accessible as possible, avoiding unnecessary jargon and providing relevant examples. However, readers may sometimes find it useful to begin toward the end of a chapter and then, having taken note of the practical suggestions, proceed to the earlier sections to consider the rationale behind them. This advice applies to the very first chapter, where the section on 'the nature and source of values' might well be read last, at least on the first run through.

Part One
Getting
Our Bearings

Chapter 1

The Purpose of Schooling

In approaching schooling from a values perspective, our first task is to identify the purpose of schooling. Only then can we evaluate particular aspects of school life and establish directions for improvement.

Some writers have claimed that schooling does not have a purpose: it is simply an end in itself. However, I see this as an over-reaction to attempts to use schools *merely* to serve external ends, ignoring their intrinsic values and everyday quality of life. While the internal values of schools are important, schools which lack broader goals have difficulty discriminating between more and less worthwhile activities, and tend to go on doing the same things simply because they have been done in the past.

As indicated in the Introduction, the position I will take in this book is that the basic values of schooling have their roots in the values of life as a whole. Accordingly, at the outset of our discussion I will outline an approach to values in general.[1]

The nature and source of values

Some people think value questions are impossible to answer because they are too complex, intangible or personal. They say, 'Oh, that's a value issue', implying that to attempt to deal with it rationally would be pointless: at best, values are a matter of opinion or taste. Others believe that the answer to value questions is obvious: we always know what we should do; what we lack is the will to do it. They cannot understand why schools or universities would devote precious time to the study (as distinct from the inculcation) of values.

The view I wish to propose here is an intermediate one. While value questions are indeed complex and subtle, they are not beyond the capacity of ordinary adults and children. In fact, we all solve hundreds — perhaps thousands — of value problems quite successfully every day. For example, we choose sound ways to nourish our bodies, to travel from A to B, to respond to questions, to make people feel at ease, to fulfil our work obligations and to amuse ourselves. In the school setting, we choose at least moderately appropriate teaching and learning content and methods, and relate to other people — students or teachers — in somewhat satisfactory ways.

Making sound value judgments is rarely an all or nothing thing; rather it is a matter of *degree*. There is seldom just one good alternative in a situation. While this feature of value decisions means that usually our successes are unspectacular and so are easily overlooked, it has its comforting aspect. It means that our task is not to find the correct solution but rather to hit upon as good a solution as possible under the circumstances. If we merely succeed in improving the current situation we are to be congratulated.

But how do we *know* that we have found a sound solution to a value problem, in education or in life in general? What is the criterion of soundness? Indeed, what are values and where do they come from? How do we know that even modest success in value matters is possible?

Values, I wish to suggest, are grounded in 'human well being'. Specific activities of everyday life, including teaching and learning, are good and right (if they are) because they promote well being. We are able to make successful value judgments and decisions only because we have at least some sense of what is ultimately important for people, including the children in our schools.

Human well being, in turn, may be defined in terms of basic values such as survival, health, happiness, friendship, helping others (to an extent), insight, awareness, fulfilment, freedom, a sense of meaning in life and so on. This is an interconnected, open-ended set of values which are largely ends in themselves. They arise out of basic human needs and tendencies: they are inherent in human nature and the human condition. They are what ultimately makes life seem good and worthwhile.

There are obviously many different kinds of values apart from these basic ones: there are spiritual values, moral values, social and political values and a host of intermediate-range and specific values. However, all these values together form a comprehensive *value system* which serves human well being. And within this system, values are constantly weighed against one another. There are no *absolute* values in the sense of values which can never in principle be outweighed by other values. Even the basic human values must be weighed against each other, and are only ends in themselves to a relative degree.

Values, then, may be defined as those things (objects, activities, experiences, etc.) which on balance promote human well being. There is another sense of 'values', namely, those things which humans prize and pursue because they *believe* them to be valuable, whether they are or not. Values in this sense are studied by anthropologists and other social scientists who attempt to describe in a detached way the things humans prize, regardless of their actual merits. However, most educators, moral philosophers and others in practical fields — and we in this book — are chiefly interested in values in the former sense, those things which really *are* valuable and hence worth pursuing.

Are values in this sense objective; or are they subjective, simply a matter of opinion? From one point of view, values might be described as subjective since they are grounded in what humans basically desire and seek. They are not written in the heavens somewhere, unrelated to human nature and human needs. However, in very important ways *values are objective.* Even at the level of basic values, it is an objective question what humans desire and seek. And at more specific levels it is an objective fact that some social arrangements and patterns of behaviour promote well being more than others. Accordingly, it is possible to carry out systematic, objective inquiry into what is good and right. This does not mean that the same things are valuable for all people and for all time. But individual variations in what is valuable can also be studied objectively, since they depend on variations in people's actual needs and circumstances. They are not random or capricious.

Educational values, then, are objective in this sense, and may be explored in a systematic, objective fashion. What is good and right in schooling is ultimately a function of what promotes the well being of the people affected, most notably the students but also teachers, parents and other members of society; and this well being can be analyzed in terms of basic human values. Of course, it is not easy to work out exactly what the impact of the school is on various people's lives. Educational inquiry is an extremely demanding task. However, in varying degrees we may gain such knowledge. And we have no alternative but to pursue it. For without it, we have no basis for saying what should go on in schools or for claiming that schooling is worthwhile.

'Education for life'

The approach to the values of schools which I have just outlined is sometimes referred to using the phrase 'education for life'. The idea behind this slogan is that schooling is not an end in itself: its purpose is to serve life, both within the school and beyond it.

The concept of 'education for life' is associated with John Dewey and the 'progressive education' movement. In *Democracy and Education*, Dewey said:

> There is a standing danger that the material of formal instruction will be merely the subject matter of schools, isolated from the subject

> matter of life-experience. Thus we reach the ordinary notion of education: the notion which ignores its social necessity and . . . identifies it with imparting information about remote matters . . . .[2]

For Dewey, education had to be tied to life if it was to be effective. And schooling found its justification in serving all areas of life, not simply the narrowly intellectual and cultural.

People often object to this approach, saying that it 'opens the floodgates'. Once we accept that schooling is for life, it becomes the arena for a multitude of pursuits. Sex education, driver education, business education, film studies, folk dancing, ethnic studies, peace studies: any or all of them and others may become major aspects of a school program. And these, it is thought, either are not important enough to take up precious school time or are simply not the sort of thing that schools should be concerned with.

However, while we might well query such activities we should equally raise questions about more traditional school subjects. The mistake those who are opposed to education for life make is to assume that there is some easy way to work out what should be in the curriculum and what should not. Perhaps traditional subjects *are* more important than sex education or peace studies. But whether they are or not must be found out through detailed inquiry with an eye to the short- and long-term well being of all those affected. We cannot just *see* what is more important or deduce it from the meaning of the word 'education'.

Opening up the school in this way to new activities may certainly pose a problem of shortage of time for existing subjects. But to refuse even to consider reducing the time allotted to traditional subjects is to side-step the question of value and purpose completely. Within whatever time we have, we must achieve the best possible *balance* of elements in the curriculum. We cannot arbitrarily rule out one set of activities to leave room for another.

While the attempt to connect schooling to the needs of life as a whole is essential, we must be aware of its pitfalls. In the present century, the problems of seeking 'relevance' in education were seen, for example, in the early disasters of substituting 'social studies' for history and geography and 'environment studies' for science. This experience showed that there is a danger of throwing out the old before we have something better to put in its place. A curriculum must be developed which forges genuine links between the old and the new and preserves as far as possible the best of the old. Teachers must be involved in and prepared for the changes, and learning materials must be created to support the new program.

Another danger of taking 'life' as our source of direction is that of becoming unduly vague and abstract in describing the tasks of schooling. Educators and school authorities notoriously draw up pompous lists of aims for education without indicating precisely what they mean at the school level. The 'real issues', as Richard Peters puts it, 'are obscured by talk about self-realization, life, happiness, and so on'.[3] While I think it is a mistake to reject the notion of extrinsic aims for schooling, as Peters tends to do, it is clear that a statement of aims alone is not enough and must be accompanied by concrete proposals about content and process.

Yet another danger is that of becoming too preoccupied with external and long-term aims to the neglect of ones close at hand. We may see schooling as *merely* a means to future ends, so that we do not value and enjoy it for its own sake. In literature teaching, for example, the goal of exploring life outlooks for future use may be sought to the neglect of present understanding and enjoyment. This problem was identified early this century by Dewey. In *Democracy and Education* he warned against seeing education as mere *preparation* for life, stating that 'in our search for aims in education, we are not concerned . . . with finding an end outside of the educative process to which education is subordinate.'[4] Peters also comments that the means/end model 'encourages an *instrumental* way of looking at the problem of justification . . . it is assumed that education must be justified by an end which is extrinsic to it.'[5] In similar vein, Alasdair MacIntyre speaks out against society's preoccupation with 'getting on', commenting that 'one goes to primary school in order to get a degree in order to get a job in order to rise in one's profession in order to get a pension.'[6] Our 'utilitarianism', as he calls it, relies on a 'criterion of action, extrinsic to action itself, used to judge effects and consequences'.[7] As a result the activity itself — in this case schooling — is not valued. While I believe these writers have overstated their case, since schooling must *in part* be justified by ends which are extrinsic to it, nevertheless their warning is important. Schooling must also *in part* be valued for its own sake. Many basic human values can be fulfilled in the process of schooling itself; we must try as far as possible to foster *in schools* 'the good life' we would wish for students in later years.

A new social context for schools

The role of the school cannot be derived simply from basic human values. It is also a function of prevailing social conditions. One factor we must take into account today in wealthy industrialized countries is society's greater dependence on schools. More is now expected of schools, and they are central to the way of life of virtually all young people from about age 4 to age 16 to 18.

In previous eras, only a small proportion of the population went to school, or, in the case of working-class children in the early days of mass education, schooling lasted just a few years and was simply to impart basic literacy and numeracy skills. This situation has changed, however, partly because of a demand for universal access to extensive schooling; partly because the economy no longer needs or wants child and youth labour; and partly because of the need for extended day care, due to increased participation of female parents in work outside the home. As well as being desirable from an educational point of view, schools are now necessary to keep young people out of the home, off the streets and off the unemployment or welfare rolls. And this trend is continuing. With the growing desire of women for equal occupational opportunity and the increasing dependence of families on the income of female parents, early full-time day care and 'pre-schooling' are becoming more common. And with continuing youth unemployment and the decline in the status or availability of apprenticeship programs, adolescents are staying at school longer and more frequently going on to college and university (which, in their earlier years, are becoming more school-like).

What implications does this have for the purpose of schooling? In the first place, obviously, it increases the importance of the child care function of the school. But beyond that, it must modify substantially our conception of the nature and role of school activities. With the extended years and hours of schooling, and the broad range of young people attending school, we must ask: What should people in modern industrialized societies do for the first fifth to a quarter of their lives? We cannot simply 'warehouse' them for such a long period of time. And we cannot fill the whole school day and year with traditional school subjects, which were developed for workers' children who could only afford three or four years of schooling, for young eighteenth-century gentlemen whose station in life was already secured, or for sixteenth-century clerics and lawyers in training.

Some writers have argued that we should resist the trend toward an expanded role for schooling and, on the contrary, reduce school years and hours or even do away with schools completely. Carl Bereiter, for example, in a book significantly titled *Must We Educate?*, maintains that the teaching activities of the school should be restricted to skills training, and many teenagers should avoid the 'adolescence' which schooling encourages and go straight into an adult vocation.[8] And Ivan Illich in *Deschooling Society* recommends that schools be abolished, thus freeing young people to pursue learning on an individualized, voluntary basis. Our vast system of compulsory schooling, he argues, discourages active involvement in learning on the part of young people, and leads us all to mistake certification for learning and schooling for education.[9]

However, while there is some plausibility to these positions, the difficulties are several. In the first place, the child care function of the school is so essential in contemporary industrialized societies that it seems idle to talk of abolishing schools or reducing the time spent in them, at least in the foreseeable future. If anything, the time should be increased because of the pressure on parents (especially women) working outside the home. Secondly, the completely self-directed approach advocated by Illich is neither politically nor psychologically feasible. Communities currently want more control than that over the activities and learning of their young; and the young themselves typically want to do things in groups: as social beings, they usually need support in the pursuit of academic learning. The modern school, despite its shortcomings, fulfils many current needs both societal and personal. And thirdly, assuming a continuation of something like the present levels of time and resource allocation to schools, it would be wrong to restrict formal learning activities to skills training, as Bereiter suggests. There is so much more that young people need to learn in order to live life to the full, and the opportunities outside the school, while important, are usually insufficient under present societal arrangements.

Goals for schooling

As the purpose of schooling is to promote human well being, as education is 'for life', and as schooling currently and increasingly takes up such a large part of the young person's life, the goals of the school should cover a wide range of human concerns. They should reflect the priorities of life in general. Because schooling falls in the earlier rather than the later part of life, there will be an emphasis on preparation for the future. But there must also be a stress on the present, both because students should have well being in the present as well as the future, and because present experiences have a large influence on what students can do and be in the future.

We will now look at a number of goals of schooling. The list offered here is not meant to be exhaustive. Rather it includes goals which are especially important or which have been neglected and which must be emphasized if schools are to fulfil the broad mandate we have been discussing.

(a) *Basic skill learning*, and (b) *Academic mastery*. These goals, which have received the lion's share of attention in the past, are obviously important and should continue to be a major preoccupation of the school. We might note, however, that there is an urgent need to extend our understanding of them so that they support other goals of schooling. For example, 'basic skills' should include social and moral abilities as well as 'the three Rs'. And traditional academic subjects such as history and literature should be studied in such a way that they shed light on political, cultural and religious issues and aid aesthetic and spiritual development.

(c) *Aesthetic development*. It might be assumed that this goal is taken care of by present programs in literature, art and music. However, the distinctively aesthetic aspects of literature are commonly disregarded, and the neglect appears to be increasing with the stress on *functional* literacy and 'language arts' conceived in terms of reading and writing skills. Literature study in many jurisdictions is becoming less common; where it occurs, it often takes the form of arid textual analysis rather than reading for aesthetic enjoyment and development. In the case of art and music, these so often are relegated to an optional, almost accidental place in the school, rather than being a major, integral part of the curriculum. We might note also that schools often fail to take advantage of the opportunity to achieve informal aesthetic education through a school environment that is aesthetically interesting and attractive.

(d) *Moral and political mastery.* This should include gaining sufficient understanding of societal and economic phenomena to enable one to make sound moral and political judgments. Further, the focus in this area should be global as well as local and national, so that one's actions take account of wider consequences and responsibilities. It is extraordinary that these key dimensions of life have been given so little room in the school curriculum. Admittedly, they are controversial, and hence difficult to address in the schools of societies which like to shield their young from contentious issues. However, it should be obvious that they are of such crucial importance that they must not be overlooked. Moral education and 'preparation for participation in a democracy' are goals to which schools have traditionally paid much lip service. The time has come for them to receive serious, comprehensive attention.

(e) *Life skills.* These are related to moral and political mastery but go beyond them in certain respects. They include competence in areas such as personal life planning, family living, career choice and change, health care, stress management and even such specific matters as budgeting and household management. There is a tendency in our somewhat romantic and perfectionist culture to downplay education in these 'practical' aspects of life and feel that, at most, competence in them should be 'caught' not 'taught'. It is thought that they are too trivial or practical to be dealt with extensively in the school. However, so long as the school occupies so much of the child's time, it has a responsibility to attend to these essential learning areas. Further, we should not exaggerate the separation between so-called 'practical' matters and the 'more weighty' issues dealt with in literature, history, politics and social studies. Ideas about the goals of life and the nature of society can have significant implications even for career planning, stress management and the like.

(f) *Spiritual development.* This may include religious development, in the popular sense, but it need not. By spiritual development, I mean growth in such qualities as awareness, breadth of outlook, integration, wonder, courage, love and gentleness. This may be achieved in part through religious knowledge and participation, but many people who possess these attributes to a high degree are not religious in the traditional sense. Once again, as with the moral and political domain, this is a controversial area. But once again, also, it is clear that the qualities in question are so important that the school should not neglect them; and we do in fact have a fairly good sense of the nature of these qualities, and some ideas about how they might be fostered.[10]

(g) *Social participation and development.* Schools should be much more active than at present in providing for social experience and learning. Within the classroom, the atmosphere and learning procedures should be as interactive as possible, and in the school generally there should be extended times and excellent facilities for social activity. The social aspect of schooling is already prominent in the minds of students, and for many it is the main feature which reconciles them to school attendance; but it largely manifests itself *despite* the system. The school must be a much more willing and creative supporter of this area of school life. Especially now that young people spend so much of their time at school, we cannot plausibly downplay social life on the ground that students have plenty of opportunity for it elsewhere.

(h) *Equality in school and society.* This is an ideal to which the school can perhaps only contribute to a limited extent, because of the constraints of the larger society. However, it is a crucial goal of schooling which in the past has been neglected, in practice if not in theory. We will discuss it at some length in the section which follows.

In concluding the present section I would like to consider briefly the problem of how we can possibly fit all these different pursuits into the school timetable. In an earlier section, I suggested that the traditional school subjects should not be seen as sacrosanct, and that the central question is not how they can be preserved but rather what is the most appropriate balance of all the important tasks of the school. But having seen how many additional tasks there are, we might wonder whether something more comforting might be said to harassed educators. After all, just as the increasing need for child care is a hard reality with which the school must contend, so is the continuing demand for teaching basic skills and traditional academic content. How can we satisfy this demand while substantially increasing the emphasis on the many other goals just listed?

There are three suggestions I would make at this point. First, we must look for ways of achieving *synergy*: pursuing several goals at the one time. We may find, for example, that the study of literature and sex, or history and global peace, can be combined, to the advantage of both. Buckminster Fuller, who was a strong advocate of synergy, argued that academic specialization in the modern world has resulted in extraordinary inefficiencies, and that in fact one can often discover more in each of several fields studying them together than one could in any one of them studying it alone for the same period of time.[11]

Secondly, we need to integrate more fully the various levels of schooling: pre-school, elementary, and secondary. At present, at lower levels we often underestimate what children are capable of, and at higher levels we often ignore what they have already done. Upper elementary children, in particular, have a voracious appetite for academic learning and could cover a substantial amount of material which is currently dealt with in high school.[12]

Thirdly, we need to clarify more fully what we are aiming at in schooling, and so pursue it more effectively. Bereiter in *Must We Educate?* attributes much of the inefficiency of schools to confusion over goals. And John White in *The Aims of Education Restated* comments that, 'if the 15,000 hours of compulsory schooling were more carefully thought through, there would be *plenty* of time to do all the things I have been pressing for.'[13] While one may not be quite as sanguine for the large program I have proposed, it seems plausible that greater clarity about the goals of schooling will itself place us in a better position to attain these goals in the time available.

Schooling for equality

The ultimate goal of schooling, I have claimed, is human well being. An obvious question, however, is *whose* well being should the school promote? How do we decide between different students and different societal sub-groups? The criterion of well being does not by itself settle this issue. And the goals for schooling reviewed in the previous section (with the exception, of course, of the last one) do not relate directly to the question of the *distribution* of benefits.

I wish to propose that *equality* — both within the school and beyond — be a major goal of schooling. The reasons for this are several. In the first place, there does not appear to be any reason to favour some *types* of people over others on the basis of race, religion, sex, class and the like.[14] Secondly, inequality in a community — large or small — creates friction between people, which undermines *for everyone* the opportunities for well being. Thirdly, and more positively, equality in relationships renders more possible *for everyone* mutual assistance in pursuing the good life. And fourthly, a degree of concern for the well being of others as well as oneself seems to be a part of human nature, so that to reasons of enlightened self-interest may be added innate altruism.[15] Whether or not these arguments justify *complete* equality of well being is perhaps not clear at this stage. But they certainly support a much higher degree of equality than we have at present.

It should be noted that these arguments do not require that we renounce self-interest. Indeed they are to a large extent based on self-interest. An underlying assumption here is that people must look after their own needs and the needs of their 'inner group' if they are to grow as individual and social beings and have the necessary personal resources to help others. If we follow this approach, then, it will be necessary at each stage to show individuals and groups how their own well being will be increased or at least not substantially diminished by a move toward greater equality. This presents a major challenge but one which, in my opinion, we must accept. If teachers, students and others are to have sufficient motivation to pursue equality, they must see its connection to their own well being.

It is sometimes suggested that a world in which everyone was equal would be dull and unattractive. 'Variety is the spice of life', it is said. However, what is being proposed here is not complete uniformity but rather *equality of well being*: people may vary greatly in the manner in which they achieve well being. Admittedly, equality of well being is difficult to assess. Further, one must be careful not to deny people material equality on the ground that 'rich and poor alike can be equally happy.' However, it is essential to recognize that the goal is equality of well being, and that this often allows for − indeed requires − inequality along some other dimensions.

Equality, then, should not be viewed as an absolute. Our basic goal is to promote human well being, and sometimes a particular type of equality may not serve that end. For example, if we gave all students the same grades and the same evaluative comments, regardless of the quality of their work, the teaching-learning process would be undermined and no-one's interests would be served. And if we held the more academic students back in their learning so that the less academic students might catch up to them, we would seriously prejudice the well being of the former and trigger hostility toward the latter, not to mention ourselves. However, despite this caveat, it is apparent that in a great many respects schools at present promote inequality in *inappropriate* ways, ways which unnecessarily and unjustly reduce well being. Notably, students are frequently discriminated against on the basis of religion, race, ethnicity, gender and class. While the precise nature of ideal equality is not entirely clear, and will become clearer only as we approximate it more closely, we already know of many ways in which equality should be increased.

How exactly can the school promote equality in a society and world in which inequality is extreme and widespread? This question will be addressed at many points in the chapters which follow. However, a brief account of the difficulties and opportunities is appropriate here in order to clarify the general role of schooling in this area.

Two myths about schools have been dispelled in the past couple of decades. The first is that schooling *by itself* can lead to extensive economic and occupational advancement for less privileged young people and hence reduce inequality in society; the second is that the school, by influencing the lives of our future citizens, can *single-handedly* change social and moral attitudes (including those that underlie inequality) and transform society.

With respect to economic and occupational advancement, in the prosperous '50s, '60s and early '70s there was so much overall increase in wealth in industrialized countries that it was possible to maintain the illusion that schooling was helping particular classes of people to move toward equality. In fact, however, there was no average upward mobility relative to other social sub-groups; and the improvement which occurred was due not so much to increased schooling as to economic factors. Of course, without schooling lower class children would not have had access to certain jobs, and so the extension of schooling to *all* classes did bring some people of lower class background into occupations in which they had not previously been represented. However, inequality persisted and may indeed have increased.

With respect to the moral and cultural renewal of society, hoped for by such educational theorists as John Dewey and George S. Counts, the limitations of the school in recent decades have also become apparent. Perhaps some small gains have been made as students of different backgrounds have rubbed shoulders in common schools, and as young people have had access to ideas which may not have been current in their family and community circle. But by and large the school has mirrored society rather than changed it. The curriculum, the teachers and the structure and norms of the school have reflected society's values and practices, including those which reinforce inequality.

What then can schools do? I believe that, despite the past history and continuing difficulties, schools have some degrees of freedom. They can be a drag on society, undermining attempted improvements; they can remain precisely in step with the larger society; or they can play a relatively strong role in specific types of advance. In the matter of equality, while they probably cannot achieve major gains by themselves, it is feasible for them to be more at the leading edge than they have been in the past.

Among the things that schools can do both to reduce inequality and to mitigate its effects are the following:

(a) Devise and implement programs of moral, social, political and cultural education — including experiential learning and social action — which assist movements to reduce inequality in the larger society and globally.

(b) Become involved in these larger movements, thus developing a greater awareness of the issues and what needs to be done, and also influencing the society in ways which will in turn have an impact on the school.

(c) Work to establish a school community which is as egalitarian as possible in teaching content and procedures, attitudes, language, relationships and privileges.

(d) Modify the content and methods of teaching so that students of lower socio-economic levels can learn more at school. (This of course will not reduce inequality if there is a corresponding improvement in teaching content and methods for students of higher socio-economic backgrounds; but even where it fails to reduce inequality, it is still a worthwhile measure).

By proceeding as far as possible in these directions, the school can become an instrument not only for furthering human well being but also for promoting it more equitably across different sectors of society. We must now go on to consider what type of school is needed to help achieve these ends.

Notes and References

1 I have elaborated and defended this approach to values more fully elsewhere, e.g. in Beck, C. (1972) *Ethics: An Introduction,* Toronto, McGraw-Hill Ryerson, and Beck, C. (1974) *Educational Philosophy and Theory,* Boston, Little, Brown, Chapters 1 and 10.

2 Dewey, J. (1916), *Democracy and Education,* New York, Macmillan, pp. 9–10.

3 Peters, R.S. (1963) *Authority, Responsibility and Education,* 2nd ed., London, Allen and Unwin, p. 95.

4 Dewey, J., *op. cit.,* p. 117.

5 Peters, R.S., *op. cit.,* pp. 9–10.

6 MacIntyre, A. (1964) 'Against Utilitarianism', in Hollins, T.H.B. (Ed) *Aims in Education: The Philosophic Approach,* Manchester, University of Manchester Press, p. 1.

7 *Ibid.,* pp. 2–3.

8 Bereiter, C. (1973) *Must We Educate?* Englewood Cliffs, NJ, Prentice-Hall, Spectrum, *passim.*

9 Illich, I. (1971) *Deschooling Society,* New York, Harper and Row, *passim.*

10 A fuller discussion of spiritual development, in this sense, and spiritual education will be presented in Chapter 14.

11 Fuller, R.B. (1969) *Operating Manual for Spaceship Earth,* Carbondale, Ill., Southern Illinois University Press, Chapters 2 and 3.

12 Goodlad describes as a 'soft spot' of schooling 'the substantial repetition and slow progression of subject matter in the upper grades of the elementary school and into the junior high years'. He says that 'the years from age 7 or 8 to 11 or 12 are relatively stable ones', well suited to substantial academic accomplishment. Goodlad, J. (1984) *A Place Called School,* New York, McGraw-Hill, p. 327.

13 White, J. (1982) *The Aims of Education Restated,* London, Routledge and Kegan Paul, p. 158.
14 This issue will be taken up in detail in later chapters, especially in Part 2.
15 For an elaboration of some of these points, see for example Brown, A. (1986) *Modern Political Philosophy,* Harmondsworth, Middlesex, Penguin, pp. 166–72.

Chapter 2

What Kind of School?

Looking at schools from a values perspective, we have seen that (a) they should promote the well being of students and other members of society, both now and in the future, and (b) they should play their part in reducing inappropriate forms of inequality in both school and society. What kind of school most effectively accomplishes these objectives?

A comprehensive school

To begin with, schools should be comprehensive; that is, students of different socio-economic backgrounds and scholastic achievement levels should be educated in the same schools and in the same classes. We should have neither academically differentiated schools nor 'streaming' or 'tracking' within schools.

Why, in general, is it preferable to have schools of this kind? A major reason is that having separate and segregated schools exaggerates differences between children, encouraging stereotyping and negative labelling. It implies that children are so different from each other that they have to be educated in different schools or classes.

In fact, as Mortimer Adler maintains in *The Paideia Proposal*, all children are 'educable for the duties of self-governing citizenship and for the enjoyment of things of the mind and spirit that are essential to a good human life', and so should be educated in 'a one-track system of schooling, not a system with two or more tracks'.[1] And as Bernard Barker claims in *Rescuing the Comprehensive Experience*, 'all children not most severely handicapped have sufficient ability to justify schools basing their work upon the prospect of cooperative citizenship for everyone'.[2] Barker argues for unstreamed schools, asking rhetorically: 'if it is agreed that differences between pupils should lead to a diverse teaching programme, why bring them together in the first place?'[3]

There are, it should be acknowledged, differences between children.

But there are also a great many commonalities which segregated schooling encourages us to overlook. Further, those differences which are used to justify academic streaming are not innate in the students but arise largely from socio-economic diversity. As far as we can tell, the incidence of high and low *innate* ability is the same in different social classes.[4] Accordingly, when we separate students on the basis of 'academic ability' (and hence, effectively, social class) we are doing children of lower socio-economic status the twofold disservice of reducing their opportunity to apply their innate ability and reinforcing the popular belief that they are innately less able. As a result, we exacerbate their already substantial problems of image, self-image and academic deprivation. By contrast, placing all students in the one school and stream makes the statement that: (a) all these students are of equal worth as human beings; (b) all have extensive innate ability, with the same range of innate ability within each socio-economic grouping; and (c) all can benefit from a roughly similar education, are capable of living 'the good life' (which does not differ fundamentally from class to class), and are equally entitled to do so.

Another reason for having comprehensive schools is to reduce harmful divisions in society and promote community. Separate schooling helps maintain and even increases the prejudice and antipathy which already exist between sub-groups. Comprehensive schooling provides an opportunity for students of different backgrounds to come to understand each other and learn how to deal as constructively as possible with each other. If we believe that community and democracy are important, and that all children are 'educable for the duties of self-governing citizenship', then we should seek 'progress toward the fulfillment of democracy by means of our educational system.'[5] And this may be achieved in part by bringing children together in the same school and the same classes.

It might be argued that people of different socio-economic backgrounds are so diverse in their life-styles that the school will be unable to achieve joint learning and genuine community. However, as Barker points out, in society today

> . . . there is an underlying coherence and unity created by a shared experience of living. Tens of millions drive their own cars, have telephones, pay mortgages, build extensions or install double glazing and central heating. Broad swathes of the population share in a comfortable existence made possible by electronics and mass production . . . .[6]

This common experience, combined with the widespread literacy which sustains 'the vast circulations of newspapers, magazines and books', means that there is a 'shared, literate, common culture' which offers a 'promising climate for the comprehensive experience'. There is 'a consensus about what is important (which is) only partially distorted by the language of class'.[7] And the people themselves claim community membership, believing that they are 'entitled to enter public controversy', as evidenced by the fact that politicians and journalists feel obliged to 'address themselves to an educated mass audience'.[8] From this perspective, a school system which practices rigid segregation on the basis of academic achievement is lagging behind the wider society.

A final reason for a comprehensive approach to schooling is to give all students — both 'academic' and 'non-academic' — a greater range of educational experiences. As Adler maintains, 'all children are destined for learning, as most are destined for labor by their need to earn a livelihood. To live well in the fullest human sense involves learning as well as earning'.[9] The point here is not only that students from less privileged backgrounds should have access to academic learning, but also that so-called 'academic' students should have an opportunity to learn in more 'practical' areas. The so-called 'higher track' at present is higher 'only in the sense that its aims are more difficult to accomplish. But even it is not now directed to the right objectives.'[10] '(T)welve years of general, nonspecialized schooling' is best for *all* students, both because it is 'the most practical preparation for work' and because 'it prepares our children to be good citizens and to lead good human lives'.[11]

Along similar lines, David Reynolds and Michael Sullivan in *The Comprehensive Experiment* say that the comprehensive school 'must aim for the academic and social development of all its pupils'. It must give to all children 'social development that parts of the system of education have managed to in the past', and also to all children 'the intellectual development that other parts of the education system have delivered.'[12]

Mixed 'ability' grouping

I have said that schools should be comprehensive not only in their student enrolment but also in their internal structure: they should not assign students to distinct academic streams or tracks. The practice of integrating students of different scholastic attainment in the same classes is often called 'mixed ability' grouping. However, this is an unfortunate expression since, as we have seen, most of the so-called difference in 'ability' assumed here is *not* in innate ability but rather in achievement related to socio-economic status. A better term would be 'mixed achievement' or 'mixed attainment' grouping.

But whatever the reasons and the terminology, there *are* at present differences between students in academic interest and attainment; and it has often been queried whether indeed it is a good idea to teach all students together. A common view is that mixed achievement grouping in schools (and universities) has led to a lowering of standards among more academic students, both because of a 'watering down' of the curriculum and because teachers are less able to cope with mixed classes.[13] Further, as Jeannie Oakes points out, many people believe streaming is better even for lower track students, since 'slower students develop more positive attitudes about themselves and school when they are not in day-to-day classroom contact with those who are much brighter', and besides 'students learn better in groups of those who are academically similar'.[14]

The research evidence, however, suggests that these types of argument against integrated schools and classes cannot be sustained. Oakes concludes, on the basis of a vast school study, that there is not a 'levelling down' of standards in mixed classes; on the contrary 'classes in practice are geared to the *highest* level of students, not the lowest'. Students do not learn better when grouped with those who are academically similar; rather, 'heterogeneous classes are considerably more advantaged in terms of classroom content and processes than many average- and nearly all low-track classes', and '*everyone* usually seems to do at least as well (and low and average students usually do better) when placed in mixed groups'.[15] With respect to student morale, Oakes states that far from being an improvement, streaming for low track students results in 'lower self-concepts, school deviance, and dropping out of school altogether'. Among the very large number of heterogeneous classes studied, over 80 per cent had markedly better teacher-student relationships and over 50 per cent had substantially better peer relationships than in a typical low track classroom.[16]

Hurn is less definite than Oakes in claiming that being in a low track disadvantages students at the high school level. But at the elementary level, he suggests the negative effects of being placed in a low track class may be substantial. He says:

> . . . the evidence from observational studies of elementary schools implies that part, and perhaps a large part of (the) differences on objective tests may reflect the results of grouping practices in schools.
>
> . . . What are slight differences in reading readiness at age 5 may become, by age 6 or 7, quite large differences in scores on objective tests.[17]

> . . . students assigned to low-ability groups in the first years of school have fewer opportunities to practice and demonstrate their reading skills. The sheer organizational problems of managing the activities of children who find the student role unfamiliar or difficult to play, may have the unintended consequence that these children fall further behind.[18]

Hurn's analysis is especially interesting in suggesting that, at the lower end, streaming may make the teacher's task more difficult rather than easier.

In Britain, where the widespread incidence of comprehensive schools is a relatively recent phenomenon, it appears on the basis of extensive preliminary research that students perform no worse (and no better) academically in the newly formed comprehensives than they would have if they had remained in either an academic or a non-academic selective school.[19] Focusing specifically on two comprehensive schools involved in an intensive case study, Reynolds and Sullivan note that, initially, the schools were held back from going further in the direction of mixed ability teaching and 'a more relevant curriculum' by 'the fear of adversely affecting the attainments of the able child'. However, in the '70s the schools came to the view 'that changes in these two areas had brought positive benefits and that, as our results confirm, the able child was still having his or her talent developed even after modification of the ability system'. The authors conclude: 'It seems important, then, that schools continue to develop in this way by a further expansion of mixed ability teaching'.[20] Reynolds and Sullivan point to some social benefits of segregated schooling, but feel that these could be attained also in comprehensive schools once new traditions and a degree of stability had been established.

The interesting — and fortunate — fact is that students of widely varying academic attainment can study in the same class without unduly interfering with each other's learning. Goodlad states: 'There will continue to be, I believe, even under highly favorable teaching conditions for all, substantial differences in intellectual orientation, knowledge, and work habits among high school graduates'. But on the basis of a life-time of experience of schooling and extensive recent study, he maintains that it is still possible for students of all types to have mastered 'a balanced curriculum', to have completed 'a common school', largely in heterogeneous classes, by the end of high school.[21]

This approach places considerable demands on teachers to take account of different interests and types of insight in the class. But it does not require studying different topics with different students. Furthermore, even within so-called 'homogeneous' classes there is an enormous diversity of interest and ability which teachers, as far as possible, should come to terms with. Goodlad is very critical of the common assumption that 'the grouping practice itself has largely taken care of pupil variability'. He says that this device 'practiced in the name of individual differences actually may contribute to thwarting attention to students' individual learning problems'.[22]

Having academic diversity in a class often requires adjusting the language used in discussing issues. However, even the most profound issues and concepts can be addressed in simple language; and the excessive use of jargon in academic contexts is today a major impediment to inquiry. Bernard Barker makes a strong plea for the use of simpler language, at least initially, in heterogeneous classes, making the assumption that this will by no means hinder — indeed, it will assist — learning and inquiry:

> The grand strategic error of the comprehensive school is to begin teaching with the abstract language and prose that it is the task of education to create. An effective teaching method will begin with pupils and their relationships, not with textbooks and foreign tongues. The aim must be to develop to the full the natural, local, active language all the children possess . . .; to enrich and extend that form, reaching towards literacy through written exercises arising from an experience to which the child can relate impersonal terms.[23]

Of course, in a class which is mixed both academically and socio-economically, different students will often be coming to the same issues from different directions. In a politics class, for example, some students may belong to the powerful groups of society and others to the relatively powerless. In economics, some may be the 'haves' and others the 'have nots'. In religion, students may come from different religious backgrounds and some from none at all. However, with careful handling, these differences can be an advantage rather than a disadvantage. Students can see the different points of view expressed, argued and validated by the very people who have them; they can learn first hand how to interact with people of other sectors of society; they can begin (or extend) the process of compromise for mutual advantage and, as far as possible, for greater social justice; in short, they can learn how to live as members of a community, even of a 'democracy'. As Charles Bailey and David Bridges say, students can learn how to live in 'fraternity' (sic) with all other people.[24]

There seem to be no good academic reasons, then, against heterogeneous schools and classes. High achievement students perform equally well in both streamed and mixed situations,[25] and low achievement students if anything perform better in mixed classes. Indeed high and low achievement students can help each other in certain ways. In terms of morale and interpersonal relations, too, low achievement students seem to be better off in mixed classes. What is possible, however, is that high achievement students are often more comfortable in a segregated upper stream (though they do not learn more), and able teachers usually enjoy teaching upper stream classes more than mixed or middle and low stream classes (though they are no more effective in upper stream classes).

Given all these considerations, I believe that educators should come out strongly in favour of classes which reflect the full range of academic achievement and, of course, the full range of socio-economic and ethnic characteristics.[26] It seems that the only advantage of streaming is a modest increase in comfort for a minority of teachers and academically oriented students. While this is not to be dismissed lightly — for example, alternative rewards should perhaps be found for senior and particularly able teachers — in my view it is outweighed by the considerable advantages of mixed grouping which benefit not only students of lower socioeconomic status but ultimately all members of the community.

A common curriculum

What has been said so far lends support to the concept of a 'common school', one which has not only mixed classes but also a 'common curriculum'. A major common core of subjects is necessary to avoid segregation of students and also to ensure that students receive a *general* education, one which covers all the main areas of learning important for their present and future way of life.

In the past, subject specialization has been justified on the ground that students differ widely in their needs. However, student needs are much more similar than we have recognized: human beings are fairly similar in their *basic* way of life — the basic pursuits outlined in Chapter 1 — and hence in the studies which are of relevance to them, especially during the years prior to vocational training. They differ more in the *way* they learn than in *what* they need to learn. As Goodlad says: 'the concern over individual differences in learning and interest, on which the appeal of electives primarily depends, is in part a misinterpretation of and an overreaction to these differences. The data on individual differences . . . have more compelling implications for pedagogical than for curricular differentiation.'[27] And Goodlad believes, as we have seen, that even the pedagogical differentiation can be accommodated within mixed classes and a common school experience.

Several educational writers in recent years — notably, Adler, Boyer, Goodlad and Barker — have recommended strongly that a common curriculum be established in schools, with only limited time allowed for electives. Goodlad's proposal is the most detailed, and I will briefly outline its main features.[28] His suggestions focus on the high school, which is where extensive options are usually introduced.

Goodlad proposes a percentage system which, while it seems complicated, helps us to understand the type of schooling he has in mind. During the final four years of schooling the allocation of time would be as follows:[29]

literature and language (English and other)	— 14–18%
mathematics and science	— 14–18%

society and social studies	— 12–15%
the arts	— 12–15%
the vocations	— 12–15%
physical education	— 8–10%
individual interest and talent development	— 10% or more

Within each domain (except the last), a minimum of two-thirds of the curriculum would be common. By providing a range in each case, allowance is made for school and school district initiative in the light of local needs and interests, while preserving the general shape of the program.

The final domain — individual interest and talent development — could have 20 per cent or even more allocated to it, depending on the time allotted to the other domains. The use of time in this category would be a matter of individual student choice within very broad guidelines. The basic notion is that students would develop and refine at least one area of interest and talent — linguistic, artistic, psychomotor or cognitive — 'to the level of excellence required to hold an audience . . . or to be capable, ultimately, of instructing others'. This domain must *not* become a dumping ground either for electives deleted from other domains or for remedial work: any remediation must be accommodated within the maximum time provided for the relevant domain. Students would be given 'vouchers with which to exercise their choice', and might use them to employ a tutor or participate in a college course or work training program. Much of the activity in this domain would occur outside the school, taking advantage of external facilities and instructors.

Goodlad acknowledges that 'not everyone will agree with this prototype: indeed the level of consensus may prove to be quite low'. But he believes that, whatever variations there may be in specifics, the fundamental issues raised by such a proposal must be squarely faced. While we should not stifle local creativity in devising different practical solutions, the basic educational goals must be achieved.

My own view is that Goodlad's proposal has great merit and should, broadly speaking, be implemented. The modifications and specifications I would suggest are as follows. First, a much clearer account of the domain of 'vocations' must be given if it is to be retained. As it stands, it seems to open up the danger of at least a partial return to vocationalism and streaming. Secondly, the various domains must be described in such a way that a *major* personal and social education component — moral and political mastery, life skills, spiritual and social development, etc. — is involved, in accordance with the principles outlined in Chapter 1. And thirdly, the 'common' element in each domain should be increased to at least 80 per cent (rather than two-thirds); otherwise, there is the danger that a one-third component of various domains might be combined with the 20 per cent or so of individual interest time to produce a curriculum which was insufficiently 'common'.

Of course, as Goodlad notes, if the basic principles of a sound curriculum are understood and accepted, the details will tend to fall into place. And, I would add, if they are not understood or accepted, any number of guidelines will not ensure success. However, believing Goodlad's ideal 'prototype' of a 'balanced and relatively common curriculum'[30] to be a very significant contribution, I have responded to it seriously with these modifications.

A non-vocational approach to schooling

From the principles discussed so far, it follows that neither schools nor school programs should be 'vocational' in the traditional sense. There is plenty of important learning to be done by everyone to take up the school time available. It has been recognized for some time that school vocational programs tend to be artificial, and that occupational training is best done 'on the job' or in a training program designed for a specific trade or profession. One suspects that vocational programming in the school has arisen largely out of the perception that 'non-academic' students cannot benefit significantly from standard school subjects and something more concrete and practical must be found to fill in their time. Commenting on the emergence of what he calls 'false vocationalism' in schools, Adler says:

> As the school population rapidly increased in the early decades of this century, educators and teachers turned to something that seemed more appropriate to do with that portion of the school population which they incorrectly and unjustly appraised as being uneducable — only trainable.[31]

If, as I have argued, all students can benefit greatly from a school program with a personal and social education emphasis, the rationale for vocational schooling becomes even weaker.

It is important to exclude not only 'trade' vocationalism but also 'professional' vocationalism, that is, the use of large amounts of school time for training mathematicians, scientists, computer programmers, musicians, artists and academics in general (language and literature specialists, historians, geographers and so on). There should of course be extensive study in these areas, but it should be largely interdisciplinary in nature and constantly related to issues of personal and social significance. It should not be seen by students, teachers or parents as primarily designed to give students a professional 'head-start' in specialized fields. Such an approach undermines the 'common school' experience, often renders subjects remote and uninteresting, and places much of the emphasis in schooling on the external rewards of grades, credits and credentials. Good school programs should in fact produce budding scientists, historians and literary figures; but this should not be — and need not be — at the expense of a general education.

Interestingly, universities seem little more excited about students who have already mastered large quantities of physics or history than industry is about students who have done large amounts of shop. They see many students as having specialized too early, as having reached premature closure. What they look for, rather, is a young person who is thoroughly numerate and widely literate, has good writing, research and study skills, and above all is thoughtful, imaginative and lively. This does not mean that young people should not learn a great deal at school. Indeed, my own view is that schools should cover much more ground — including academic material — than they do at present. However, as mentioned before, the learning should be across a wide spectrum. Unduly specialized training — whether for manual or for professional occupations — should not take place in schools.

Schools should *in a sense* play a part in preparing students for the work world. Adler, while opposed to 'false vocationalism', says that schooling should be 'truly vocational' in that it gives students 'the basic skills that are common to all work in a society such as ours' and enables them 'to understand the demands and workings of a technologically advanced society, and to become acquainted with its main occupations.' Adler in fact believes that traditional 'vocational' education has the opposite consequence from that which is intended.

> That kind of specialized or particularized job training at the level of basic schooling is in fact the reverse of something practical and effective in a society that is always changing and progressing. Anyone so trained will have to be retrained when he or she comes to his or her job . . . .
>
> As compared with narrow, specialized training for particular jobs, general schooling is of the greatest practical value . . . it will provide preparation for earning a living.[32]

In similar vein, Goodlad says:

> the provision of general, not specialized, education is the role of primary and secondary education . . . the answers to deficiencies must arise out of questions pertaining to what constitutes general education for all — not college entrance requirements on one hand, and job entry requirements, on the other. Good general education is the best preparation for both.[33]

We might note in closing that some activities which have traditionally been the concern of lower stream, vocational programs should be retained in the school: learning to type, for example, and various forms of manual training. These, however, are important 'life skills' for *all* students and should neither be restricted to a particular category of students, namely, the 'non-academic', nor emphasized to such a degree for those students that their access to academic studies is reduced.

Notes and References

1 Adler, M. (1982) *The Paideia Proposal: An Educational Manifesto*, New York, Collier Books, pp. 5 and 7.
2 Barker, B. (1986) *Rescuing the Comprehensive Experience*, Milton Keynes, Open University Press, p. 9. Note that one might take exception to Barker's qualifier with respect to handicapped children here while appreciating the general drift of his remarks.
3 Barker, B., *op. cit.*, p. 5.
4 See Bowles, S. and Gintis, H. (1976) *Schooling in Capitalist America*, London, Routledge and Kegan Paul, especially Chapter 4.
5 Adler, M., *op. cit.*, p. 6.
6 Barker, B., *op. cit.*, p. 145.
7 *Ibid.*, pp. 147–8.
8 *Ibid.*, p. 150.
9 Adler, M., *op. cit.*, p. 12.
10 *Ibid.*, p. 16.
11 *Ibid.*, p. 20.
12 Reynolds, D. and Sullivan, M. with Murgatroyd, S. (1987) *The Comprehensive Experiment*, Lewes, The Falmer Press, pp. 129–32.
13 See, for example, Hurn, C. (1978) *The Limits and Possibilities of Schooling*, 2nd ed., Boston, Allyn and Bacon, p. 291.
14 These views are cited *but not held* by Jeannie Oakes. See her (1985) *Keeping Track: How Schools Structure Inequality*, New Haven, Yale University Press, p. 192.
15 *Ibid.*, pp. 194–5.
16 *Ibid.*, pp. 196–7.
17 Hurn, C., *op. cit.*, p. 191.
18 *Ibid.*, p. 291.
19 Reynolds, D. and Sullivan, M., *op. cit.*, pp. 51–4.
20 *Ibid.*, p. 121.
21 Goodlad, J. (1984) *A Place Called School*, New York, McGraw-Hill, p. 166.
22 *Ibid.*, p. 165.
23 Barker, B., *op. cit.*, p. 56.
24 Bailey, C. and Bridges, D. (1983) *Mixed Ability Grouping: A Philosophical Perspective*, London, George Allen and Unwin. Apart from their unfortunate general use of the term 'fraternity' these authors provide a valuable extended discussion of mixed schooling.
25 Oakes, J., *op. cit.*, p. 194: 'The brightest and highest achieving students appear to do well regardless of the configuration of the groups they learn with'.

26 This is a paraphrase of Jeannie Oakes' conclusion, *op. cit.*, p. 206. John Goodlad, similarly, proposes 'the elimination of any arrangement designed to group in separate classrooms on the basis of past performance students presumably enrolled in the same subject.' He goes on: 'Students should be assigned to classes randomly in a way that assures heterogeneity'. Goodlad, J., *op. cit.*, p. 297. And Ernest Boyer says: 'Putting students into boxes can no longer be defended . . . we recommend that the current three-track system . . . be abolished. It should be replaced by a single-track program — one that provides for a core education for all students plus a pattern of electives . . . .' (1983) *High School: A Report on Secondary Education in America*, New York, Harper and Row, pp. 126-7.

27 Goodlad, J., *op. cit.*, p. 289.

28 *Ibid.*, pp. 285-98.

29 Note that to arrive at the 14–18 per cent range for the first two subject domains, it was necessary to round Goodlad's figures very slightly.

30 Goodlad, J., *op. cit.*, p. 163.

31 Adler, M., *op. cit.*, p. 19.

32 *Ibid.*, pp. 18-19.

33 Goodlad, J., op. cit., p. 292.

Chapter 3

Students: Meeting Their Needs

In the preceding chapter, one of the central themes was that of treating students equally (or less unequally), increasing the effectiveness of schooling for disadvantaged students, and attempting through the school to reduce inequality and harmful divisions in society. However, it is not only less advantaged students who suffer from bad schooling or benefit from good schooling. In this chapter, we will look at issues concerning the school experience of *all* students, whatever their background.

'What schools do to kids'

Perhaps the major immoralities of schooling lie in the way in which we treat students, whose well being is supposed to be our central concern; and equally, the main focus of schooling with a values emphasis should be on righting such wrongs and genuinely 'meeting student needs'.

Many of the wrongs done to school students were documented in the '60s and '70s by school critics such as Paul Goodman, John Holt, A.S. Neill, Herbert Kohl, Jonathan Kozol, Ivan Illich, Carl Bereiter and, at the end of the '70s, Michael Apple. We will look briefly at the criticisms of some of these writers. It may be felt that at certain points these accounts are exaggerated; but I believe there is considerable truth in them, and we need to keep returning to them to be challenged again and ponder how these problems might be overcome.

In *The Underachieving School*,[1] John Holt claims that while there is some physical abuse in schools, most of the harm done to children is non-physical. For example, while inquiry — and learning to inquire — should be central to education, in fact the school directs students *away* from the problem and toward finding (or stealing) an answer that will satisfy the system. Students become preoccupied with trying to please, to second-guess the teacher; they do not 'own' their learning, do not identify with it.[2] Gradually they lose their curiosity, resourcefulness and confidence. We teach them that 'learning is separate from living' and that they 'cannot be trusted to learn and (are) no good at it'. (This despite the fact that they have already to their credit the great achievement of learning to talk). We teach them that 'learning is a passive process, something that someone else does *to* you, instead of something you do for yourself'.[3]

Further, we distort children's values. We teach them that 'in real life you don't do anything unless you are bribed, bullied or conned . . . nothing is worth doing for its own sake.' We teach them that only explicit, certain, examinable knowledge is worth having: 'to be wrong, uncertain, confused, is a crime'.[4] We teach them to be indifferent to other people, notably the other children in their class: social interaction is subordinated to scholastic pursuits. And we downgrade their need for 'play, noise, excitement'; their desire 'to be touched, held, jostled, tumbled, picked up, swung about'.[5] The greatest paradox of all, for an educational institution, is that in teaching children to read, we teach them to hate reading; in teaching them to learn, we teach them to regard study as a chore.[6]

In addition, according to Holt, we undermine children's self-respect. We tell them: 'Your experience, your concerns, your curiosities, your needs, what you know . . . counts for nothing'. We do not acknowledge their undoubted current talents: their verbal fluency, expressive ability, intelligence, vivacity, wit.[7] We invade their privacy, and as a result destroy their sense of self-worth.[8] And these things we do to virtually *all* children, not just a disadvantaged sub-group.

Kozol agrees with most of Holt's criticisms of schooling. However, he believes that they omit a whole dimension of what schools do to children, namely, political desensitization and 'domestication'. Holt concentrates on psychological aspects of the school, neglecting the political and ideological. Even if students experienced schools as interesting, free, caring, sociable, aesthetically pleasing places, this would not necessarily be a sign of good schooling. Citing John Kenneth Galbraith, Kozol says: 'In a social order such as ours, people need to think themselves unmanaged, independent, free, if they are to be controlled with maximum success'.[9] Schools are *not* 'underachieving', he maintains, but like 'an ice-cold and superb machine' are doing their job only too well.[10] 'John Holt's views on how our children fail and how they learn, are now being used by corporations . . . in order to develop the most clever methods ever known for teaching children how to phantasize a sense of freedom that does not exist'.[11]

According to Kozol, schools have a major negative impact on children in the ethical domain. The very capacity to conceptualize, let alone combat, social evil is systematically undermined. Words such as 'death' and 'suffering' are made to lose most of their meaning; and insofar as they retain meaning, the presence of death and suffering among the poor and among the people of non-aligned nations is effectively hidden.[12] A similar task is performed with words such as 'force' and 'violence'. One type of violence (that of the victim) is condemned, while another (that of the victimizer) is condoned: 'violence serving US geographical expansion or industrial investment somehow wins an ethical exemption. It does not "count". It does not seem illegal, violent, unjust'.[13] Not only do schools distort the ethical perceptions of children: they also take away their capacity to act ethically. Children are taught to obey, never to 'say no': 'school defines the act of SAYING NO, in general, as unsound and unwholesome'.[14] We must always 'go along with anything that is already set in motion when we get there', and we must never object to anything unless we have a clearly developed, acceptable alternative to propose.[15] Children are made to feel that they are powerless, and 'to look upon historic transformation not as the product of their own intentions, aspirations, dreams'. 'It is tragic enough that millions of young people have no sense of Active Ethics: yet this is not the worst. They have no sense of leverage either. Power is beyond them'.[16]

Ivan Illich and Carl Bereiter, like other school critics, have concerns about the less than pleasant atmosphere and stifling and perverting effects of schools. However, they have added a distinctive analysis of the nature and causes of the ills of schooling. According to Illich, schools do to children what modern institutions in general do to the whole population: they 'institutionalize' and hence largely destroy life processes which should take place in a natural and free manner. Schools teach students 'to confuse process and substance . . . to confuse teaching with learning, grade advancement with education, a diploma with competence', just as, in society generally, 'medical treatment is mistaken for health care, social work for the improvement of community life, police protection for safety, military poise for national security, the rat race for productive work'. Through a process of 'institutionalization of values', people are '"schooled" to accept service in place of value'.[17] School children are alienated from their nature and needs, and led to focus on jumping through hoops which having nothing to do with education. Because schooling is obligatory, something we do not choose for ourselves, we quickly forget its purpose: the institution itself, for rich and poor alike, comes to 'guide (our) lives, form (our) world view, and define . . . what is legitimate and what is not'.[18] Only if society is 'deschooled' and education becomes a matter of free choice will children be able to take control of their own learning for their own purposes and acquire genuine education as distinct from 'schooling'.

Carl Bereiter believes that schools, because of their training and child care functions, probably could not be abolished completely. However, he accepts much of Illich's account of how confusions have arisen over the nature and role of schooling. If students and parents were given greater freedom of choice — over type of school, length of schooling, daily attendance and so on — the goals of schooling would be clearer and there would be greater commitment and effectiveness. At present, because we lump all school tasks together — including training and child care — under the opaque concept of 'education', we end up doing none of them well. What we 'do to kids', then — to all kids, rich and poor — is force them to spend endless hours in institutions where they neither enjoy themselves very much nor learn more than a small proportion of what they might.[19]

Michael Apple in *Ideology and Curriculum* continues the documentation of the profoundly constraining effect of schools on the outlook and behaviour of children. Especially striking is his account of how children are influenced at the kindergarten level, in the first few months of school.[20] While he is concerned elsewhere in the book with 'the differential distribution of classroom knowledge', he focuses here on 'the "deep structure" of school experience' which affects *all* children.[21] The kindergarten classroom observed was not exceptionally repressive: on the contrary, it was in a school system reputed to be 'one of the best . . . in the area, if not the nation', the teacher was perceived as 'competent . . . by administrators, colleagues, and parents',[22] and the classroom 'was considered by many other school people to be a model.'[23] Yet within a few weeks the children had become remarkably passive and conforming. 'The teacher made it clear . . . that good kindergarteners were quiet and cooperative'. At one point, two large stuffed dolls which happened to be in the classroom were mentioned as models of behaviour: 'Raggedy Ann and Raggedy Andy are such good helpers! They haven't said a thing all morning'.[24] A high degree of teacher direction came to be accepted, even when it appeared quite arbitrary. The intrinsic interest and meaning of activities ceased to be important. Children learned to apply the term 'work' to a whole new set of activities: 'colouring, drawing, waiting in line, listening to stories, watching movies, cleaning up, and singing'.[25] Whether something was called 'work' or 'play' depended simply on whether or not it was prescribed; and the point of work activities was to get them done — to fulfil the requirement — rather than to do them well, enjoy them or achieve some end. 'During music, for example, the teacher exhorted the children to sing loudly. Neither tunefulness, rhythm, purity of tone nor mood were mentioned to the children or expected of them'.[26] Thus, children were quickly forced 'to adjust their emotional responses to conform to those considered appropriate by the teacher';[27] and, generally, they became alienated from the very activities with which most of their daily life was concerned.

In concluding this brief survey of 'what schools do to kids', we might note that society does many similar things to adults: so many of us are at least in part alienated from our work, and our behaviour so often reflects what is expected of us rather than what we believe in and have freely chosen. Accordingly, it might be argued that school merely introduces students to outlooks which they must adopt if they are to 'get on' in society generally. However, I believe this is at best a partial justification. The school need not simply mirror society. It can link up with reform movements in the larger society and, through a modified organization, atmosphere and pedagogy, attempt gradually to shift away from those approaches to human activities and relationships which are undesirable in both school and society.

Open, child-centred, interactive schooling

In order to overcome many of the problems identified by school critics, it is necessary for schooling to be more child-centred and democratic. If we are to avoid stifling the curiosity and initiative of students, undermining their confidence, making them passive and conformist, cutting them off from their feelings and desires, fostering in them artificial and inappropriate values, we must allow more room for student input and control. What happens in schools must to a great degree be influenced by student interests, wishes, moods, insights and abilities.

Even when we believe that students are heading in a wrong direction, we must try to avoid simply imposing our objectives or point of view on them. As Dewey emphasized repeatedly, learning is like growing: what is to be must emerge from what is. Learning must proceed from the known to the unknown, from the desired to the desirable. Accordingly, we must discuss and reason with students, presenting relevant information and arguments, so that as far as possible the position they come to is freely chosen.

Within a compulsory and common school experience, individual students are obviously not completely free to go their own way. Further, as we will see in Chapter 6, there is in general a limit to the extent to which individual humans can freely, rationally choose what they believe and value. However, the *degree* of freedom and rationality should be as great as possible and students should be encouraged constantly to pursue those aspects of issues which interest them. Having a common curriculum does not preclude considerable flexibility and individualization in the study of subjects. Indeed, part of the point of heterogeneous classes is to bring together people with different backgrounds and interests so they can share their distinctive insights.

Among the school critics of the '60s and '70s, Herbert Kohl was a particularly eloquent advocate of an 'open' form of schooling which took account of student rhythms and input. He maintained that the teacher must be flexible about what will happen in a given day, week or year. 'Planning in a non-authoritarian classroom must be based on the possibility of abrupt changes. Subjects arise and are dropped or develop in many different ways. There is no predicting who will be interested and active at a given time'.[28] There must be planning; but equally one must be willing to have plans modified or set aside. Kohl concluded, after a remarkable year with a so-called 'disadvantaged' grade six class, that 'any successful classroom has to be based upon a dialogue between students and teachers, both teaching and being taught, and both able to acknowledge that fact'.[29]

The notion of flexible, interactive education has been promoted in recent times by Paulo Freire. While his focus has been mainly on adult learning, his ideas are widely seen as applicable to the school setting. According to Freire, 'education is suffering from narration sickness', the teachers assuming that their task is 'to "fill" the students with the contents of (their) narration — contents which are detached from reality, disconnected from the totality that engendered them and could give them significance'.[30] Such an approach turns students 'into "containers", into "receptacles" to be "filled" by the teacher'. 'This is the "banking" concept of education, in which the scope of action allowed to the students extends only as far as receiving, filing and storing the deposits'.[31]

In contrast with this 'banking' method, Freire advocates an approach of 'dialogue' and 'problem posing'. Among the key elements in his pedagogy are the following: 'teachers' and 'taught' learning together; personal knowledge, learning things oneself, from the inside outward; praxis, learning in the context of life and action; a high degree of trust in the learners' ability and respect for their essential humanity; recognition that learners know a great deal already; recognition that learners must create their world, not just receive ideas from others.[32] In many ways, Freire's position is reminiscent of Dewey's. However, he goes beyond Dewey, notably in his emphasis on the ideological nature of the 'banking' method of education and the need for political action to change it.

An open, interactive approach to schooling must be so in fact and not merely in appearance. So-called 'discovery learning' is often a disguise for an insidious form of schooling in which teachers believe that they already know what the answer is but allow students to 'discover it for themselves' at the best psychological moment. This method should perhaps be called 'timed-release learning' rather than 'discovery learning'. There are two problems with it: first, if teachers *do* already know the answer, they should share it with the students so that time is not wasted and everyone can get on with inquiry into the host of questions to which we do not yet have an answer; and secondly, if teachers keep 'the answer' hidden, there is a danger that it will be largely imposed on the students, in subtle ways, without adequate scrutiny. The main point of student involvement in learning is that often we do *not* know the answer, and in order to discover it we need the very considerable assistance students can provide. If teachers (or students) *think* they know an answer they should put it on the table so that a genuine dialogue can ensue over whether or not it is indeed correct. An undue reluctance to say what one thinks suggests that there is not an open, interactive learning situation in which students can disagree with or modify what the teacher says, or propose alternatives of their own. Of course, teachers should choose appropriate ways and times to say what they think so as not to stifle discussion or upset the natural rhythm of inquiry. But this is necessary so that knowledge may be arrived at more quickly, not so that students may discover for themselves what is already known.

Effective schooling

While stressing the need for open, interactive teaching and learning, however, we must not forget that sheer ineffectiveness has also been identified by critics — notably Holt, Illich and Bereiter — as one of the main scandals of schooling. We do students a grave injustice by wasting much of their time for a fifth of their lives, during their most formative years. Of course, according to writers such as Dewey, Kohl and Freire, as we have seen, there is a close connection between student-centred, dialogical schooling and effective schooling. But how to achieve that connection is not always obvious. We must ensure that approaches to teaching and learning are found which *both* respect and engage students *and* involve optimal learning efficiency.

The difficulty is that so-called 'student-centred' or 'progressive' schooling has often not been described in sufficient detail, and highly ineffective forms of education have been implemented in its name. Dewey, for example, was often vague in his pedagogical proposals and as a result had to fight a constant rearguard action against those who misunderstood him. In *Experience and Education* he expresses regret that people have seen 'the new education' as 'an easy way to follow, so easy that its course may be improvised, if not in an impromptu fashion, at least almost from day to day or from week to week'. He stresses that, in fact, 'the road of the new education is . . . a more strenuous and difficult one', and if it is to succeed teachers must give 'constant attention to development of the intellectual content of experience' and 'obtain ever-increasing organization of facts and ideas'.[33]

Because of such misunderstanding (or lack of clarity), some features of 'traditional' schooling have been rejected which should rather have been incorporated, at least to a degree, into more progressive approaches. And I believe the same danger exists today with Freire's anti-banking, dialogical, problem-posing method. Freire, like Dewey, is often too vague (and perhaps inconsistent) in describing the nature of pedagogical intervention and the relationship between 'oppressed' students and 'liberating' leaders (who, after all, are still called leaders).

Stereotypical 'traditional' schooling is seen as emphasizing structure and traditional content. There is a pre-established syllabus, explicitly outlined. Teaching is largely by means of instruction and didactic learning materials. Students are taught facts which other people have discovered. 'Progressive' schooling, by contrast, is represented as stressing flexibility and skill learning. Insofar as there is content, it is mainly from the contemporary world and from the present experience of students. The teacher is a facilitator for learning which is largely student initiated and follows the students' interests and needs. Students learn by discovering for themselves.

However, whatever one wishes to call it, it seems obvious that *truly* progressive schooling must incorporate — at least to a degree — some features of traditional schooling. Otherwise, despite its claim to liberate students and meet their needs, it will be too ineffective to do either. Schooling must be 'traditional' in at least three ways.

First, it is essential that students learn many facts and skills discovered or developed by others. Students cannot discover for themselves — even with teacher facilitation — everything they need to know in life. It is true that students must integrate material from others into their *own* conceptual and motivational structure if it is to be fully learned and utilized. But such material is nevertheless essential; and often the integration process takes many years: an element of 'banking', of 'storage' for future use *is* often necessary.

Secondly, it is very important for teachers to have an explicit syllabus or plan of study. Without one, most teachers are at a loss and in fact fall back on fragments of course outlines remembered from the past, or become even more wedded to a textbook with a convenient layout than they otherwise would be. Learning should go significantly beyond following a syllabus, and teachers should feel free to modify their plans in appropriate ways, as Kohl emphasizes. However, having a syllabus does not necessarily preclude more adventurous teaching and learning and may indeed facilitate it by providing a secure base from which to experiment. Further, a syllabus need not be the same for all teachers in a region or even in a particular school: it may be the teacher's own creation. But we should recognize that many teachers may benefit from centralized help in developing their syllabuses.

Thirdly, it is important for teachers to have access to prepared teaching/learning materials (preferably many different sets of them so they can pick and choose). While the ablest teachers depart from their materials in many ways, they still usually consider them a significant component in their overall approach. And many teachers rely quite heavily on materials prepared by others, and without them would teach much less well than they do.

These remarks point only to a few elements that are important for effective schooling: many others are required, including the student–oriented, dialogical components associated with 'progressive education'. Further, one may *have* these traditional elements in one's pedagogy and still teach very ineffectively, as we all know only too well. However, their importance remains. Without them, students will not acquire many insights and skills which it is vital they have.

The school as a nice place to be

Apart from their other deficiencies, schools have been judged to be unhappy places: in Holt's words, 'dull, ugly, and inhuman'.[34] I believe this criticism to be exaggerated, since students when asked usually concede that school is 'OK'; and they are often quite glad to go off to school, if mainly to see their friends. However, there is no doubt that schools could, in both their formal and informal aspects, be considerably 'nicer places' than they are at present.

In Chapter 1 I emphasized that school should be more aesthetically interesting and attractive than at present, and that greater attention should be paid to the social life of the school, including providing better facilities for student initiated social activity. In the present chapter I have spoken of a respectful, interactive relationship between teachers and students which would result in a more congenial school atmosphere. The point is that, if we are to respect students' needs, we must strive to make schools 'good' places to be, just as we do, for example, with homes, offices, theatres and shopping centres. There are cost limits here, of course; but as the example of the home suggests, a warm, caring atmosphere can be created even with limited means. Further, I believe that the unattractiveness of schools has often reflected not a shortage of resources but rather an ageist bias against young people, which sees them as not needing or deserving the same provision as adults.

Bereiter discusses at length the matter of the pleasantness or otherwise of the lives of children, and suggests that we must see the issue in historical perspective.[35] He observes that from about the middle of the nineteenth century 'an amazing transformation . . . occurred in which schools became not only tolerable but valued and integral parts of the lives of most children'. Some of the good features of what we now call 'traditional' schools are noted. First, 'the traditional school was — in contrast to earlier schools and some urban schools today — a safe and peaceful place for children to be.' Secondly, 'most children expressed satisfaction with it — about 80 per cent, according to various studies conducted over a span of forty years'.[36] And thirdly, 'in the traditional school children generally felt that what they were doing was important'. Whatever our view of traditional schooling, we must agree that these features — 'peace, enjoyment, and the child's sense that what (one) does is important' — are qualities we must continue to seek, ones which critics find lacking in many present day schools.

However, the difficulty we are now facing, Bereiter points out, is that the foundations on which traditional school life was built, namely, working for marks, ritual and 'good student' morality, are crumbling.[37] Students and teachers alike have lost the high regard for traditional school activities which justified the hard work and accepting outlook. '(T)he perspective of the outer world is penetrating the school'. In a society in which barriers between adult and child worlds are breaking down, it is not possible to sustain the artificial ethos of the traditional school, where the pursuit of marks was an end in itself. 'The word seems to have passed down . . . that a great deal of school work is pointless, that grades don't really tell how good you are, and that the school rituals are a subject for derision'.[38] It is difficult for schools to be enjoyable places under these circumstances.

The solution, according to Bereiter, lies in finding a genuine as opposed to a contrived basis for the meaning and worthwhileness of children's activities, one which can withstand both external scrutiny and the children's own questioning. The activities must *in fact* be worthwhile, and not merely be thought to be so, as was often the case in the traditional school. Training, for example, must be in skills that are genuinely useful and must be conducted efficiently by well prepared teachers using well researched methods and materials. Child care, similarly, must be approached in a much more satisfactory manner; the school must offer 'a safe, pleasant place for children to be with each other, with many more interesting things to do than are available at home'.[39] The opportunities for socializing, recreation and 'free' activity in schools must be increased and not be constantly spoiled by making them into pseudo-educational pursuits.

One of Bereiter's main strategies for improving the quality of life of young people is to restrict the role of the school to skill training and child care, developing *outside* the school more adequate opportunities for meaningful, enjoyable activity. The school he envisages would be 'a useful and an enjoyable place, but not a very important one. Many children could afford to stay away from it most of the time without loss'.[40] Much of the 'better life for children' which Bereiter advocates should, he believes, be found in the wider community rather than in the school.

While, as noted in Chapter 1, I do not believe that the role of the school can be reduced in the way Bereiter recommends, we can learn from his proposals about alternative forms of activities for young people, applying them to the school setting. Schools have become too uniform in their pattern of life: virtually everything takes place with groups of fifteen to thirty-five young people of roughly the same age sitting in rows in a box-like room with a teacher at the front and minimal resources. School, as it is said, is largely 'chalk and talk'. Small wonder students 'misbehave' from time to time: adults placed in a similar situation would probably do the same. We must take very seriously Bereiter's detailed suggestions for increased 'cultural resources for children', including 'intellectual recreation', 'resources that encourage doing', 'quiet places', 'age intermixing' and 'user-programmed facilities'.[41]

There is much of value, then, in Bereiter's various proposals for enabling young people, both in and out of school, to lead meaningful and enjoyable lives. But there is one principle which he applies to the issue which must, I believe, be rejected. He assumes that it is usually a mistake to try to mix activities: training and child care, training and education, child care and education. Such mixing, he suggests, results in inefficiency in the pursuit of goals and a relatively unhappy atmosphere. However, while the mixing of goals *may* have this consequence, especially when accompanied by confusion about the goals, this is by no means necessary. Indeed, in most situations in life we pursue many different objectives at once, and we would have a much lower level of well being if we did otherwise. The principle of *synergy*, noted earlier in connection with the effective study of school subjects, applies equally to pursuit of the broader goals of life.

In the adult world, learning, social life and recreation are often successfully linked. Even employment and social life are often tied together, with many people looking forward to going to work largely because of the human contact they have there. In school, similarly, effective skills training and enjoyable social interaction could occur at the same time, provided we were sufficiently aware of and concerned about *both* goals to look for ways of pursuing them together. Moreover, contrary to Bereiter's claim, it seems feasible for the same *people* to serve in both an effective training role and a creative and humane child care role. Those who train should as far as possible be the kind of warm, caring, interesting people that Bereiter says we need as child care professionals. Such people can learn how to do basic skills training, a capacity which, as Bereiter himself maintains, can be acquired fairly quickly if the goals are clear and the necessary programmes and materials are available. It is difficult to see why a humane, pleasant atmosphere is incompatible with effectiveness in achieving basic tasks. One rarely hears a parallel argument in connection with adult workplaces: on the contrary, it is suggested that if work were made more enjoyable there would be less absenteeism and greater application to the tasks at hand.

Similarly, it is difficult to see why 'education' must be excluded from schools if children are to enjoy themselves and acquire skills effectively. Admittedly, Bereiter works with a rather unusual concept of education: as the 'making over' of children to other people's values. But what is called for, in my view, is a more adequate understanding of education and of its relation to values. Bereiter sees values as the children's (and their parents') own business, something which should remain unaffected by schooling. But this is to imply that one's values cannot be improved through learning, which presupposes an anti-intellectual view of values and of life in general. Moreover, it is simply not *possible* to create a school which does not have a value impact on students. Even the way we train, and the reasons we give for training, are value laden, not to mention how we relate to children in fulfilling our child care role.

To put the point more positively, an *essential* dimension of making school 'a nice place to be' is inquiry into better ways to live, both as individuals and in groups. Schools *must* be educational, because they must be one of the major sites where we find out how to achieve values of humaneness, gentleness, beauty and community that are so often lacking in both school and society. Schools must engage in the kind of systematic study and experimentation that is necessary if these values are to be attained in an appropriate form and on a solid political and motivational base. Niceness in schools and soundness in values are inextricably linked; and accordingly schools must be at the leading edge of value inquiry and values education. This is a tall order, and one which Bereiter seems to think is beyond the capacity of schools. He comments: 'School people are for the most part worthwhile people for children to be around; but they are not people who should be carrying the burden of mankind's destiny'.[42] But who *should* carry this burden: politicians, moral philosophers, priests, educational theorists, parents, individuals working in isolation? The school, I would suggest, is as worthy and capable as other institutions to participate in the communal activity of working out how to make society in general — and the school in particular — a better (and hence nicer) place to be.

Notes and References

1 Holt, J. (1971) *The Underachieving School*, Harmondsworth, Middlesex, Penguin.
2 *Ibid.*, pp. 20–2.
3 *Ibid.*, pp. 23–4.
4 *Ibid.*, pp. 24–5.
5 *Ibid.*, pp. 29–30.
6 *Ibid.*, p. 71 f.
7 *Ibid.*, p. 27.

8 *Ibid.*, pp. 110–13.

9 Kozol, J. (1984) *The Night Is Dark and I Am Far From Home*, 3rd. ed., New York, Continuum, p. 4.

10 *Ibid.*, p. 1.

11 *Ibid.*, p. 5.

12 *Ibid.*, pp. 51–7.

13 *Ibid.*, pp. 11–12.

14 *Ibid.*, p. 20.

15 *Ibid.*, pp. 17–18.

16 *Ibid.*, p. 79.

17 Illich, I. (1971) *Deschooling Society*, New York, Harper and Row, p. 1.

18 *Ibid.*, p. 2.

19 Bereiter, C. (1973) *Must We Educate?*, Englewood Cliffs, NJ, Prentice Hall, Spectrum, *passim*.

20 Apple, M. (1979) *Ideology and Curriculum*, London, Routledge and Kegan Paul, pp. 50–60.

21 *Ibid.*, p. 50.

22 *Ibid.*, p. 58.

23 *Ibid.*, p. 53.

24 *Ibid.*, p. 54.

25 *Ibid.*, p. 55.

26 *Ibid.*, p. 56.

27 *Ibid.*, p. 27.

28 Kohl, H. (1969) *The Open Classroom*, New York, A New York Review Book, Vintage, p. 56.

29 Kohl, H. (1967) *36 Children*, New York, Signet, New American Library, p. 107.

30 Freire, P. (1972) *Pedagogy of the Oppressed*, New York, Herder and Herder, p. 57.

31 *Ibid.*, p. 58.

32 See especially Chapter 2 of Freire, P., *op. cit.*

33 Dewey, J. (1963) *Experience and Education*, New York, Collier Books, pp. 86–91.

34 Holt, J., *op. cit.*, p. 31.

35 Bereiter, C., *op. cit.*, pp. 82–90.

36 Bereiter refers here to Jackson, P.W. (1968) *Life in Classrooms*, New York, Holt, Rinehart and Winston, pp. 41–81.

37 Bereiter, C., *op. cit.*, p. 84.

38 *Ibid.*, p. 87.

39 *Ibid.*, p. 88.

40 *Ibid.*, p. 98.

41 *Ibid.*, pp. 103–8.

42 *Ibid.*, p. 98.

Chapter 4

Teachers: What Can and Cannot be Expected of Them

The purpose of schooling, I have said, is to promote the well being of students and, less directly, of parents and other adults who are affected by the way our young people are educated. A key group of 'other adults' are teachers, both as ones whose well being must be provided for and as front-line agents of schooling who influence the outcome of the enterprise.

The public is in two minds about the value of what teachers do. As Dan Lortie says in *Schoolteacher*: 'Teaching . . . is honoured and disdained, praised as "dedicated service" and lampooned as "easy work" . . . (T)he real regard shown those who (teach) has never matched the professed regard.'[1] This ambivalence is unfortunate in at least two ways. It often deprives teachers of the respect and sense of meaning they need for personal well being and energetic application to their work. And it undermines efforts to achieve school reform, since people are not sure where to lay the blame or where to look for improvement.

In this chapter we will begin by looking at the phenomenon of teacher blame and then go on to attempt a more precise determination of the nature and limits of the teacher's role.

Blaming teachers

Teachers must be held accountable, academically, morally and in other ways. Even where they are not fully conscious of the influence they have on students, they cannot be completely absolved of responsibility since ignorance in such matters is at most a partial excuse. However, we have often witnessed an *excess* of blame of teachers for the ills of schooling. The influence of schools and the power of teachers to control what goes on in schools have been overstated (or misstated) and accordingly, in cases where schooling has gone wrong, too much of the fault has been ascribed to teachers.

Many school critics in the '60s and '70s, for example, poured scorn on traditional ways of maintaining order, teaching basic facts and skills, evaluating achievement and relating to students. The teacher–student relationship should, they asserted, be characterized by much greater gentleness, respect, trust and warmth than at present. Since these comments were largely addressed to teachers, it was widely believed, even by teachers themselves, that they were to blame for this state of affairs. If only they cared more, tried harder, had better interpersonal skills, were better people, things would be different. Great teachers such as Herbert Kohl and James Herndon were held up as examples of how one should perform in and out of the classroom; and it was assumed that more dedicated application to the task could take one a long way toward scaling these heights.

Kozol in particular provided a strongly negative assessment of the current efforts of teachers. While he placed more emphasis than others of his contemporaries on evils endemic in the social system, he certainly did not spare individuals. In *The Night Is Dark and I Am Far From Home* he calls upon his fellow educators to 'disown and disavow' their privileged middle–class position, saying that if we cannot do so 'we are not ethical men and women, and do not lead lives worth living'.[2] He expresses the hope that his book will 'compel transformed behavior' by provoking 'pain and anguish . . . within the conscience'.[3] At times he shows awareness of societal constraints on the individual: for example, he says: 'I live . . . with multiple contradictions . . . . There is no way I know by which to lead a totally just life within an unjust land'.[4] And he asks poignantly with respect to himself: 'Will (I) not be tempted also to obtain a fine home with a stretch of meadow and a nice, attractive, innovative school nearby for our own children . . . ?'[5] However, his general message is that we must engage in 'fevered confrontation' with the evils which beset our schools, and insofar as we fail to do so we are morally reprehensible.

Over the past decade or so, school critics have not been as hard on teachers. While Rachel Sharp, Anthony Green, Samuel Bowles, Herbert Gintis, Michael Apple and others would agree with Kozol that teachers are implicated in the ills of the school, they emphasize more the 'systemic' nature of the problem and the limited power (and hence responsibility) of individual teachers. Sharp and Green, for example, say that educators are 'unwilling victims of a structure that undermines the moral concerns they profess . . . . What is needed is to go beyond the perspectives of individual actors and to explore the tensions which occur in social structures'.[6] And Apple says that 'the knowledge that now gets into schools is already a choice . . . (and) often reflects the perspectives and beliefs of powerful segments of our social collectivity . . . . (T)hese values now work *through* us, often unconsciously . . . .'[7]

Madan Sarup, dealing specifically with racism and education, takes a middle position on teacher responsibility. He advances the structuralist view that 'the fundamental reasons for the disabilities of black people are the racist attitudes and practices in the larger society itself'.[8] And he is critical of the 'individualist psychological approach' to racism which 'deflects attention from the larger social system as a determinant of social inequality'.[9] He notes that, in some cases, 'racism can be the result of the conscious acts of individuals'; but he comments that among teachers who contribute to the problem some have no awareness of racism at all, and others try hard to combat racism but fail because they see it only in individual terms. Sarup argues for a two-pronged approach: 'racism must be tackled not only at the level of attitudes but also of actions, institutions and ideology'. Individual teacher consciousness and conscience are important, but one must also work to change the structure of society.

A position such as Sarup's on teacher culpability seems an appropriate one to take. If we go too far in absolving teachers of blame we are in danger of undermining their status, crediting them with little power to do either harm *or* good in the current school situation, or to work toward educational reform in the future. However, if we exaggerate their power and responsibility we place them under too heavy a burden of guilt, with a resultant tendency toward low morale and a defensive posture which resists change; and we present a distorted picture of what is wrong with schooling and how improvement can be achieved.

Self-sacrifice, care and burnout

In talking about limits to teacher responsibility, I have (following current literature) referred especially to social and political forces which so strongly influence what goes on in schools. However, there is another type of limitation which must be emphasized, namely, that of the teachers' personal energy and resources to help students. Even when they know what is needed and could in a sense provide it, there is only so much that can reasonably be expected of teachers in terms of self-sacrifice and care. Proposals to improve schooling often assume an increased sensitivity and commitment on the part of teachers beyond what is (in the present ethos) humanly possible or ethically required and accordingly are doomed to failure before their implementation begins.

The approach to values outlined in Chapter 1 acknowledged the need for individuals to look after their own welfare to a considerable extent; and we must now apply this principle to teachers. As we saw, this approach can be justified, even within an egalitarian framework, in terms of the need for people to be strong so they can help others. In the case of teachers, if they are to be in a position to provide substantial and continuing assistance to students, they must attend to their own fulfilment, growth and physical and mental health: there is a limit to the care an exhausted, disintegrated teacher can offer to students. Meeting student needs in the way outlined in preceding chapters must not be a demanding 'add-on' requiring extraordinary powers.

This is not intended to minimize the changes in teacher behaviour which can take place. Rather my concern is to specify prior conditions that must be met. Teachers could, I believe provide much more assistance to students than they do at present. However, in order for them to do so, the content, processes and rewards of teaching must be enhanced so that giving appropriate care to students is a 'natural' and feasible part of the everyday life of teachers.

Carol Gilligan in *In a Different Voice*[10] has shown with reference to the situation of women how extreme self-sacrifice has not, all things considered, worked in favour of social justice. By being prepared to put their interests after those of men, children and other people in general, women have often experienced a reduction in respect, power and morale which has undermined their general well being and effectiveness. Gilligan suggests that while it may be necessary for women to go through a self-sacrificial phase, the ideal is a state of *interdependence* in which women give due attention to their own rights as well as the rights and needs of others. She sees this state as providing a solid basis for the ethic of care which she advocates for women and indeed for all human beings. Since teaching is one of the caring or helping professions (and also a major profession for women), it is especially appropriate to consider Gilligan's ideas in this context.

Another line of inquiry which has bearing on the issue of teacher self-sacrifice is that dealing with the phenomenon of 'burnout'. Teacher burnout in particular has received increasing attention in recent years, whole books being written on the subject.[11] Burnout as defined by Herbert Freudenberger[12] is an extremely disabling ailment in which a person who began with high ideals for achievement is reduced to a state of exhaustion, joylessness, frustration, anger and cynicism. According to Freudenberger, people in the helping professions are especially prone to this condition since they are commonly motivated at least in part by ideals of service to others in choosing their profession. When they find that they can achieve less than they expected, they are inclined to take on yet further tasks in order to approximate more closely their original ideal; but with increasing pressure and exhaustion they become even less effective and hence more disappointed. Freudenberger and others have given primarily a psychological analysis of this condition, with emphasis on expectations and compulsions established in early childhood and blocks to self-knowledge which make therapy difficult. However, I believe that in many cases the problem is one of an inadequate *value* system, which leads one to expectations of oneself which are either beyond the human capacity to bear or contradictory and self-defeating. The resulting exhaustion and debilitating disintegration are precisely what we have been discussing in relation to an ethic of self-sacrifice and care which neglects the needs of the moral agent, in the present instance, the teacher.

The necessity of emphasizing support for teachers — rather than undue self-sacrifice — has been noted in recent writing on schools. Boyer in *High School*,[13] Goodlad in *A Place Called School*[14] and Theodore Sizer in *Horace's Compromise*[15] document the difficult circumstances under which teachers currently must work. They refer to long teaching hours with minimal time for preparation; contact with huge numbers of children in the course of a week; lack of teaching materials; threat of physical violence; many additional tasks beyond teaching such as grading, filling in a multitude of forms, monitoring attendance, lunchroom and hallway supervision; having to teach in areas for which they are not prepared either academically or pedagogically; isolation from fellow teachers and other adults; inadequate and often unpleasant physical space for preparation and relaxation; lack of status and recognition both inside and outside the school; lack of opportunity for further study and other forms of professional development; and, perhaps above all, having to work under the constant gaze of a classful of students. As Sizer says: 'Teaching has its share of malingerers and incompetents . . . . However, if one were to select a profession in which malingering was easy, one would not pick teaching. While the classroom is a very private place as far as other adults are concerned . . . it is very much a public activity for the students'.[16]

All of these conditions of teaching take their toll. Says Boyer: 'The result for many teachers is a sense of alienation, apathy, and . . . "teacher burnout".'[17] And Goodlad concludes: 'Merely holding teachers accountable for improved student learning without addressing these circumstances is not likely to improve the quality of their professional lives and the schools in which they teach'.[18] It seems, then, that teachers are already in a position of considerable self-sacrifice, offering care in a situation which is draining and often unfulfilling. Any major advance in achievement of the goals of schooling will require improvement in the lot of teachers *as well as* the students.

The role of teachers in school reform

Educational writings sometimes enthusiastically proclaim that teachers are *the* crucial component in educational reform. For example, in *A Nation Prepared*, the 1986 Carnegie report on the teaching profession, it is asserted that 'in this new pursuit of excellence (in education) . . . *the key to success* lies in creating a profession equal to the task — a profession of well-educated teachers'.[19] Similarly, Sizer states that who the teachers are 'is *the crucial element*. An imaginative, appropriate curriculum placed in an attractive setting can be unwittingly smothered by journeymen instructors . . . . On the other hand, good teachers can inspire powerful learning in adolescents, even under the most difficult circumstances . . . .'[20]

However, the fact of the matter is that, in addition to the teachers, the curriculum and a range of other elements are also important. Potentially able teachers may have their effectiveness limited by an unimaginative, inappropriate curriculum and discouraging conditions of the kind reviewed in the previous section. As Goodlad observes, 'the notion that "everything depends on the teacher" is simplistic and exaggerated'. There are many factors at work, including 'a school's sense of mission, the principal, policies and directions of the central office, parental interest and collaboration, traditions, (and) the stability of the faculty and student population'.[21] Recent research on school effectiveness, notably the *Fifteen Thousand Hours* study,[22] has shown that there are 'marked' variations from school to school in the production of 'good behaviour and good scholastic attainments', beyond what may be attributed to the distinctiveness of the teaching staff or the student intake.

A major new work on educational reform has recently appeared which focuses especially on the contribution of teachers. In *Education Under Siege*, Stanley Aronowitz and Henry Giroux argue that the dependence of the school on external societal forces has been exaggerated. They find fault with 'radical critics' such as Bowles and Gintis, Willis, Whitty and Apple, saying that they have become 'mired in the language of critique', underestimating the capacity of educators — including school teachers — to play a strong, positive role in society.[23] While I believe that Aronowitz and Giroux in turn have somewhat exaggerated the role of teachers in school reform, they have provided a valuable perspective on the issues we are concerned with here.

Resisting the pessimism of recent school critics, these authors wish to restore 'the language of possibility' to discussion of schools. They say we must 'move to the terrain of hope and agency . . . one steeped in a vision which chooses life and offers constructive alternatives'.[24] Their message is that schools *can* break out of the cycle of cultural and political oppression, chiefly through the efforts of teachers. The crucial step is this: 'educators at all levels of schooling have to be seen as intellectuals, who as mediators, legitimators, and producers of ideas and social practices, perform a pedagogical function that is eminently political in nature'.[25]

Other educational reformers, according to Aronowitz and Giroux, 'either ignore the roles of teachers in preparing learners to be active and critical citizens, or they suggest reforms that ignore the intelligence, judgment, and experience that teachers might bring to bear on such issues'.[26] We must rather see teachers as 'transformative intellectuals' through whom 'critical reflection and action become part of a fundamental social project to help students develop a deep and abiding faith in the struggle to overcome injustices and to change themselves'.[27] Teachers must 'develop forms of knowledge and classroom practices that *validate* the experiences that students bring to school'; then they must '*critically engage* the experiences that students bring to the school'; in this way, they will be able to 'provide students with the skills and courage they will need in order to *transform the world* according to their own vision.'.[28] Thus, 'teachers must be seen as . . . critical theorists who provide the moral and intellectual leadership necessary for developing active forms of community life engaged in the struggle for equality and democracy'. To achieve this end, teachers must be 'both scholars and activists, whose sphere of intervention is not just the school but the community at large'.[29]

Teachers can have such a powerful influence, according to Aronowitz and Giroux, because of the key *political* function of knowledge in a society. Knowledge is crucial in 'producing and legitimating existing social relations'; hence educators, who develop knowledge, play a 'critical role' in determining the nature of society.[30] Educators must recognize 'the partisan nature of human learning' and, in line with this insight, work to provide 'a theoretical foundation for linking knowledge to power and commitment to the development of forms of community life that take seriously the principles of fraternity (sic), liberty, and equality'. The educational enterprise, then, will be 'steeped in the ethical and political imperative of educating students to provide the moral and intellectual leadership necessary to struggle for a qualitatively better life for all'. Thus, 'it is at this *nexus between school reform and societal reconstruction* that the languages of critique and possibility both meet and inform each other.'[31]

In order to be able to fulfil their role of leading society to a better future, educators must fight for 'ideological and material conditions within the schools that will allow them to function as intellectuals. That is, conditions which will allow them to reflect, read, share their work with others, produce curriculum materials, publish their achievements for teachers and others outside of their local schools, etc. At the present time, teachers labour in the public school under organizational constraints and ideological conditions that leave them little room for collective work and critical pursuits'.[32] These constraints can and must be overcome. Education must be restored to 'an honourable and autonomous place in our culture'.[33]

Now, in my view, the approach to schooling (and education generally) proposed by Aronowitz and Giroux is basically sound. As I argued in Chapter 1, education is integral to the general pursuit of well being for humans, and so it is tied to the furthering of human interests which we associate with politics and economics. The way we learn to view the world is inseparable from how we live and how we rank and treat each other. Knowledge production and transmission, then, is a fundamentally political function; and teachers accordingly have a key role to play in creating a just political, economic and social order.

However, we must see the contribution of educators in perspective. They play an important *part* in a society-wide effort. They are *a* key but not *the* key. It is not possible — nor desirable — for them to be as autonomous as Aronowitz and Giroux suggest. The outlook of educators is constantly influenced, often unconsciously, by views developed in other sectors of society; and to some extent this is how it should be, since educators cannot know everything that is needed for the sound development of a community. To a degree, *all* members of a society should be 'intellectuals', working on their own life problems and making input into shared perspectives. Aronowitz and Giroux in a sense acknowledge this by talking of students — and everyone is a student at some stage — as co-workers in this enterprise. However, I feel they do not stress sufficiently the extent to which educators must be co-workers with others in society in an ongoing way if major reform is to be achieved, both within schools and beyond.

I do not wish in any way to belittle the role of the teacher. Educators are a crucial factor in school and society reform. However, it does not do teachers a service to ascribe to them powers they do not have in order to enhance their reputation. This leads eventually to disillusionment and low self-esteem among teachers and disappointment and recriminations at the public level. It also gives a distorted picture of what needs to be done to achieve reform.

What *can* we expect of teachers?

So far, my main emphasis has been on what *cannot* be expected of teachers. I have said that we should blame teachers less, recognize the limits of their role and, insofar as we want them to contribute more, provide them with better conditions and more moral support.

But if schools are to achieve their goals more fully and become 'better places for kids', they will have to change in certain respects, and this will involve an increase in the contribution of teachers. What improvements in teacher performance should we look for? In considering the following selection of possibilities, we should keep constantly in mind that other groups and institutions in society will have to play their part if teachers are to move in these directions: beyond a certain modest level, they cannot be expected to 'go it alone'.

(a) In accordance with the recommendations of Aronowitz and Giroux, teachers must become 'intellectuals' to a greater extent than they typically are at present. This does not mean that they should be 'egg-heads' or 'academics', in the pejorative sense of these terms. Rather, they should have greater awareness of the interconnected theory that bears on both the content and method of their teaching. And this awareness should not be merely as a result of receiving more ideas from others (although that is important); teachers should not, any more than students, be the objects of a pure 'banking' education. Teachers must be intellectuals in the sense that they are engaged in constant cooperative inquiry into the content and method of schooling, an inquiry in which their own experiences and thoughts provide major input. It is only in this way that teachers will be able to have the broad educational impact on students, in all areas including the personal and social, that I have suggested is essential for worthwhile schooling.

(b) Again as suggested by Aronowitz and Giroux, teachers must become more politically aware and involved, both inside and outside the school. They need not all become radical egalitarians, of course; and given their largely middle class status this would be unlikely. But they should recognize that very often they are being used by power élites to promote values to which they have no commitment; and that even as members of the middle class they have an interest in fostering certain learnings, social structures and types of human relationships which will be of benefit to less privileged people as well as themselves. Teachers must see that what they do is inescapably political in nature and become more adept at having the kind of political impact they believe is appropriate. And they should involve themselves increasingly in movements outside the school, both to increase their political sophistication and to help promote broad societal changes which will in turn support their political work within the school.

(c) Teachers must become more respectful toward students than is common at present. I do not wish to imply that we are currently *unusually* disrespectful toward students. However, we do participate to a degree in the ageist, discriminatory stance toward young people that is current in society. And in *some* ways our record *is* worse than that of other adults since tradition dictates that, as teachers, we should adopt an authoritarian role in relation to students. As outlined in the previous chapter, a more democratic, interactive approach to students is needed *both* in order to draw more fully on student initiative and insight and thus make schooling more effective *and* in order to make schools 'nicer places' for students (and teachers) to be.

Some may see the partial lowering of barriers between teachers and students as a threat to order in the school. However, I believe that the potential loss of control in this way can be more than compensated for by increased teacher respect resulting from a clearer grasp of school goals and greater command over the content and methodology of teaching. The main source of disorder in schools is the students' sense that teachers do not know what they are doing or why.

(d) Teachers must be growing in social, moral and spiritual characteristics. This is implicit in the intellectual and political development mentioned earlier; but it needs to be made explicit. As I suggested in Chapter 1, and will argue at greater length in later chapters, especially in Part 3, it is impossible to separate the intellectual, social, political, moral and spiritual domains. And progress in all of them, on the part of teachers and others, is crucial for the enterprise of schooling. If students are to develop in these areas — a central objective of schooling — it is essential that teachers be progressing in similar ways, so that they can address the relevant issues well in their teaching and also establish a type of school which informally promotes personal and social growth.

In closing, I wish to stress yet again that these elements of teacher growth — in intellectual depth, political sophistication, respectful interaction with students, and social, moral and spiritual traits — cannot be produced forcibly. Teachers must be impelled toward them not out of fear or guilt but because of positive desire to build a better life for students, themselves and other members of society. To a large extent they must come 'naturally'. They are things we *can* expect of teachers, but only as reforms in school and society render them humanly possible, indeed an accepted part of everyday life. It is time for all of us — including teachers — to work toward such reforms in the way we live.

Notes and References

1 Lortie, D. (1985) *Schoolteacher: A Sociological Study*, Chicago, University of Chicago Press, p. 10.
2 Kozol, J. (1984) *The Night Is Dark and I Am Far From Home*, 3rd ed., New York, Continuum, p. 6.
3 *Ibid.*, p. 7.
4 *Ibid.*, p. 185.
5 *Ibid.*, p. 55.
6 Sharp, R. and Green, A. (1975) *Education and Social Control: A Study in Progressive Primary Education*, London, Routledge and Kegan Paul, p. 227.
7 Apple, M. (1979) *Ideology and Curriculum*, London, Routledge and Kegan Paul, p. 9.

8 Sarup, M. (1986) *The Politics of Multiracial Education*, London, Routledge and Kegan Paul, p. 26.

9 *Ibid.*, p. 11.

10 Gilligan, C. (1982) *In a Different Voice*, Cambridge, Massachusetts, Harvard University Press, *passim*.

11 See, for example, Cedoline, A. (1982) *Job Burnout in Public Education*, New York, Teachers College Press.

12 Freudenberger, H. (1980) *Burnout*, New York, Bantam.

13 Boyer, E. (1983) *High School: A Report on Secondary Education in America*, New York, Harper and Row, pp. 154–71.

14 Goodlad, J. (1984) *A Place Called School*, New York, McGraw-Hill, pp. 167–96.

15 Sizer, T. (1985) *Horace's Compromise: The Dilemma of the American High School*, Boston, Houghton Mifflin, pp. 180–7.

16 *Ibid.*, pp. 180–1.

17 Boyer, E., *op. cit.*, p. 159.

18 Goodlad, J., *op. cit.*, p. 196.

19 *A Nation Prepared: Teachers for the 21st Century*, (1986) Report of the Task Force on Teaching as a Profession, Carnegie Forum on Education and the Economy, Carnegie Corporation of New York, p. 2. Italics added.

20 Sizer, T., *op. cit.*, p. 180. Italics added.

21 Goodlad, J., *op. cit.*, p. 168.

22 Rutter, M., et al. (1979) *Fifteen Thousand Hours: Secondary Schools and Their Effects on Children*, Cambridge, Massachusetts: Harvard University Press; see especially pp. 177–9.

23 Aronowitz, S. and Giroux, H. (1985) *Education Under Siege*, Massachusetts, Bergin and Garvey, p. 5.

24 *Ibid.*, p. 19.

25 *Ibid.*, pp. 19–20.

26 *Ibid.*, p. 23.

27 *Ibid.*, p. 36.

28 *Ibid.*, pp. 156–7. Italics added.

29 *Ibid.*, p. 160.

30 *Ibid.*, p. 41.

31 *Ibid.*, p. 141. Italics added.

32 *Ibid.*, p. 42.

33 *Ibid.*, p. 20.

Chapter 5

Parental and Societal Rights

While parents especially, and other societal members as well, play a major role in the *education* of young people, they are often largely excluded from their *schooling*. This is problematic in the minds of many parents, who believe that schools should respect their wishes to a greater degree. And other adults also sense that, as 'taxpayers' and people whose interests are affected by the type of citizens the schools 'produce', they should have more control over schooling. To what extent should the school be influenced by the needs and expressed wishes of parents and other adults? What *rights* do they have in this respect?

Parents' rights versus the rights of their children

Parents have substantial rights in the matter of the schooling of their own children, since they have special concern for the well being of their children, and special interest in the kind of people their children will become: they have to 'live with' the results of schooling in a way that others do not. If children gain new beliefs and values at school, their parents are affected by the pleasing or troublesome consequences. If children do not learn enough at school to prepare them for employment or give them access to an appropriate occupational training program, their parents must pick up the pieces.

Parents are also directly affected by the attitudes and practices of the school toward them. The school can support or undermine the self-respect of parents through its approach to racial, ethnic, religious, class and related matters, or simply through the importance it attaches (or does not attach) to the parental role. It can also cause parents untold frustration and expenditure of time, whether by effectively requiring them to coach their children at home because the school's teaching is inadequate, or by forcing them to conduct extensive lobbying to try to get satisfaction from the school.

Sharp and Green have documented the kind of self-effacement and subtle diplomacy that parents often must exercise to have the influence that is needed.[1]

Parents, then, have a major and legitimate interest in how their children's schooling is conducted, and educators should take full account of this fact. The rights of parents, however, must be weighed against those of their children, whose most appropriate way of life may not be precisely the same as that of their parents. Sometimes parents demand 'for their children's good' a type of schooling which is based largely on their own preferences. In the short term at least, many children need to try on new attitudes and behaviour patterns in order to establish their own identity and also be able to assess more objectively their parents' way of life. And even in the long term a somewhat different way of life from that of their parents often appears necessary. What 'works' for parents may not be satisfactory for their children, who have different personality characteristics and have to compete and cooperate within a different generation and make their mark in a culturally and technologically changed world. Parents must have something of the detachment described in Kahlil Gibran's well known lines:

> Your children are not your children.
> They are the sons and daughters of Life's
>   longing for itself.
> ......
> You may strive to be like them, but seek not
>   to make them like you.
> For life goes not backward nor tarries with
>   yesterday.
> You are the bows from which your children
>   as living arrows are sent forth.[2]

One must be careful, of course, not to exaggerate (as perhaps Gibran does) the need for separation between one generation and the next. Family life and extended family life have been neglected in the present century, and growing mobility has led to what Vance Packard, speaking of the United States, has called 'a nation of strangers'. There are signs today of an increasing return of children to the family circle (often quite literally). Nevertheless it must be recognized that there will always be a 'generation gap' of sorts, with differences in needs between parents and children which the school must respect.

It has sometimes been assumed that, while the *interests* of parents and children may differ somewhat, parents have *knowledge* of what is best for their children. And certainly parents have a intimate knowledge both of their children and of the family, social and cultural setting from which they come:

they are in a good position to assess many aspects of what will threaten and what will enhance the well being of their children and the life of their family and community. But the notion that parents know what is best for their children and therefore should *completely* control their schooling must be rejected. Apart from the danger alluded to earlier of parents misusing their authority, consciously or unconsciously, in the service of their own interests, there is the obvious fact that students too have great insight into their present and likely future needs and should have a major say in their education. Furthermore, teachers also have essential input to make since they, over the years, have had an opportunity to watch the development of many hundreds of young people of the same age, rather than just the handful that most parents have been able to observe closely.

Where the interests of parents and children not only differ but actually conflict, it should be recognized that parents have a right to protect their own interests to some extent. Here again the position Gibran takes is perhaps too extreme. Parents have a life to lead, and just as children legitimately press for their needs in the family, so too may parents. It is a romantic and mistaken view of the family which sees everyone's interests coinciding. And it is an unsound approach to the ethics of parenting which requires parents always to sacrifice their needs to those of their children. Most parents try to discourage their children from becoming too different from themselves, through schooling or by other means, for fear that this will loosen ties within the family. Children are usually less concerned about this because, although a close family life offers advantages to them as well, as they grow older and move toward establishing a new family or inner group of their own they are not as greatly affected as their parents by reduction in the cohesiveness of the original family. But the parents' concern is a legitimate one, and must be supported by the school at least to a degree.

Parents' and children's rights versus those of society

Parents and students are not the only ones who have rights with respect to schooling. Others in the wider community must also 'live with' and depend on the emerging new generation and so should have a major say in what goes on in schools. And like parents, they have a right to promote their interests to a degree even when these do not coincide completely with the interests of students (or parents).

While its benefits have sometimes been exaggerated, schooling is undoubtedly an important factor in maintaining a good society and building a better one. Schools can *help*, for example, to keep inquiry alive in a society, promote aesthetic creativity and enjoyment, ensure that democratic decision making is informed, increase economic productivity and promote social justice and harmony. It seems legitimate, then, for society members in general to seek some control over schooling so that they can influence it in these directions. If, on the other hand, we deny that schooling can have consequences which benefit society in this way, it is difficult to see why the general public should be expected to pay such large sums to maintain the school system.

Of course, in many ways the interests of parents, children and other society members coincide, and the issue is what is best for *humans* rather than for any one of these three categories. For example, a general societal need for ecological awareness and responsibility is paralleled by a similar need in particular children and families, who will benefit from sounder ecological policies and practices. However, in other cases interests will conflict, and what is important for society in some general sense may undermine the distinctive individual needs of students and/or parents. For example, an attempt to use the schools to make up for a national deficit in scientific and technological capacity may deprive students and families oriented toward the humanities of what (for them) would be an ideal form of schooling. Such conflicts must be worked through, giving significant weight to the interests of each of the parties involved.

It seems to me that Bereiter, in his discussion of the ends to be served by schooling, unduly discounts the importance of general societal considerations. He says that while 'society, parents, and children all have a legitimate interest in how children are raised' nevertheless 'society's *legitimate* interest in child-rearing is ... a very limited one'.[3] He compares it with the concern people have about the character of their neighbours and fellow townsfolk. Such concern is natural enough, but 'the idea of the residents of a city forcing would-be residents to pass entrance examinations is repugnant .... A city has to make do with the people who want to live there'.[4] And the same should be true of children as they are born into a society. He sees it as a plain abuse of power for a society 'to determine what the incoming generation should be like in order to be satisfactory as citizens, and to force education upon them to make them become that way'.[5] He gives the example of trying to reduce violence in a nation through education, presenting what he regards as a *reductio ad absurdum* argument against such an attempt:

> Imagine what a successful program of education would involve ....
> (It) would attempt to extinguish violence in every form ... for
> policemen, for sportsmen, for everyone ...; the elimination of
> violent sports ...; the censoring of movies and television ...; the
> lowering of automobile horsepower; making shoving and harsh
> language minor crimes; outlawing the spanking of children;

rewarding gentleness and politeness in all areas of behaviour; encouraging alternatives such as nudism, sex, and free spending. This is not an appealing prospect.[6]

Interestingly, this supposedly 'horrendous' prospect is not as unappealing as Bereiter suggests. He has stacked the case in his favour by making the goal an extreme one — the extinction of violence in *every* form — and by including non-educational measures, such as criminalizing harsh language. Part of the point of an *educational* approach is to try to avoid pure force of this kind and appeal rather to reason. But even so, the example is not particularly convincing. There is much support today for measures such as persuading police, sports people and others to be less violent; censoring violence (and not only sex) in films; reducing the speed of automobiles; outlawing child abuse; promoting gentleness and politeness in behaviour; encouraging alternatives to violence as a source of excitement; and in general trying to foster a more peaceful approach to life at individual, societal and global levels. And justifiably so. Why should one be opposed to nudging a whole society in this direction? It would seem to be in everyone's interests. And the same is true of many other societal reforms which citizens might wish to achieve, at least in part through the schools.

Bereiter's basic argument seems to be that 'the infringement of individual liberties is horrendous'.[7] Elsewhere he says: 'Underlying my whole position on education is the belief that individual freedom should be maximized. I am opposed to public education because I see it as invading the most central area of individual freedom, the freedom to *be* the kind of person one is'.[8] But why place such a high premium on freedom? It is just one among many basic values that humans pursue. Furthermore, such a position ignores the fact that 'the kind of person one is' has *already* been influenced in significant ways by society. 'Individual freedom', to the degree envisaged by Bereiter, simply does not exist. There does not appear to be any solid basis here, then, for denying the considerable claim of society to a say in what form schooling should take.

While insisting on a largely 'hands off' approach on the part of society, Bereiter is remarkably strong in his emphasis on the rights of parents to control their children's schooling. He says that '(t)he interest that parents have in the rearing of their own children is of a wholly different kind, going much deeper'.[9] He rejects the conception of compulsory education as a means whereby society protects children's rights, saying that 'as soon as the state goes beyond dealing with the most obvious mistreatments of children it encroaches gravely upon the civil liberties of parents'.[10] But if the freedom of the child is so important, as he has insisted, how can it be so easily set aside in the interests of the civil liberties of parents? What are some of the *less* obvious mistreatments of children by parents which society should ignore? Once again it seems that the argument is not compelling, and we are left with the more plausible position that the rights of all three parties — children, parents and society — must be respected to a very substantial degree by the school.

The rights of sub-groups: the need for pluralism

We have been speaking so far of the rights of 'society' in general. Society, however, is made up of many sub-groups, each of which may wish to influence schooling. We noted in previous chapters the control that social and economic power elites have over the school. In addition, religious and ethnic sub-groups have traditionally promoted their values, traditions and interests through schooling. Such groups are not necessarily privileged — they may be minority groups which in many respects are underprivileged — but they have some distinctive goals (along with the common goals they share with the rest of society).

When we talk of parents seeking to control schooling, it is often in fact the sub-groups to which they belong which are the main initiators of demands. Within sub-groups, people vary in what they want and in the intensity with which they want it. Some parents may in fact be placed in a serious dilemma by the package of demands made by the leaders of their religious or ethnic group. They may agree with some of its components and not with others. They may be glad to see their group given due respect in the community and have their children gain some familiarity with its traditions; but they may only reluctantly accept the exposure of their children to the more doctrinaire and exclusivist teachings of their group, for lack of an alternative type of schooling.

What right do sub-groups have to control schools? It seems obvious that they should have some influence over schooling so that they may develop in ways that are important for them, their members and the rest of society. As I will argue in later chapters, religious and ethnic sub-groups can be valuable, not only to their own people but also to society as a whole. And as Andrew Greeley maintains,[11] such groups are unlikely to disappear, whether we like them or not, and so long as they persist the rights of their members must be respected, including the right to have a say in what form schooling will take.

But how much say should sub-groups have? One strategy they often employ to maintain their distinctiveness is to run separate schools for their children. But this solution is not without its dangers. While the existence of such schools may suggest that pluralism is alive and well, one might argue that the opposite is the case: the splitting up of the school system of a nation may mark the breakdown of pluralism. As Madhu Suri Prakash points out, allowing each group to set up its own schools (using a voucher system of funding) may 'serve to emphasize incompatibilities, clouding over the moral consensus of which we need to remind ourselves as well as the young'. It may 'rob us of an extremely valuable symbol of our commonness by essentially wiping out the common school'.[12]

The paradox of pluralism is that, in order for a society to be pluralistic and yet still hold together and prosper, its differences must be matched by considerable commonalities in values, goals and procedures. Most notably, there must be shared commitment to those very values such as tolerance, kindness, understanding and dialogue which make a pluralistic society possible. According to Mary Ann Raywid, attacks on the state schools are often indicative of an *abuse* of pluralism which she calls 'obtrusive pluralism'. By 'obtrusive pluralists' she means those who exaggerate their differences from the rest of society in order to get their way in matters of schooling. (Once again, it is often the leaders of a sub-group and not typical members who employ this strategy.) She sees the approach as dangerous since it involves an undue emphasis on 'particularist values not shared by other identity groups' and 'a heightened unwillingness to "go along" quietly with the rest' which may make it difficult for 'common' schools to exist at all.[13] Prakash notes the irony here that 'many of the minorities and interest groups, announcing the independence of their moral outlook from that of "the mainstream" fail to discern that the guarantee of their "freedom to be different" is best safeguarded by the existence of shared pluralist values that they implicitly disregard by denying a consensus'.[14]

The crucial question perhaps is not whether all the schools of a society should be brought under one educational system. After all, there are some independent schools which do not serve a particular interest group and provide a very good education; and many private religious and ethnic schools are quite tolerant ideologically and have a better record than many public schools in serving students of different religious, racial, ethnic and socio-economic backgrounds. Rather, the issue is how do the schools of a society — whether private or public — go about their business. If a private school emphasizes unduly — 'obtrusively' — the differences between the special population (if any) it represents and the rest of society, it may do damage to the students in its care (and their parents), who must learn to live in a pluralistic society, and to the society as a whole. But equally, if a public school system in fact serves the establishment culture (while, ironically, educating few of the children of the establishment, who are sent off to private schools) and fails to provide for cultural sub-groups in the society, thus forcing them to set up their own schools whether they want to or not, it is just as anti-pluralistic and potentially damaging as many of the private schools whose right to exist it questions. As Prakash comments, we must avoid the mistakes of the past where the 'consensus has conveniently been manipulated by groups in power to ignore interests they have had a moral obligation to respect'; we must find 'a solution which does not involve imposing exclusively the moral and religious values of one cultural or religious group while forcefully ignoring competing others'.[15]

Sub-groups do not always set up their own schools. Another strategy for promoting their concerns is to try to influence the public school system. This is one approach of the so called 'Moral Majority' in North America. While seeking public funding (or tax exemption) for private Protestant schools, this movement also monitors the curriculum, textbooks and library holdings of state schools. Where material is found which appears to run counter to conservative Protestant thought and practice, some form of public protest (including perhaps legal action) is mounted, appealing to supposedly established moral and legal principles and religious truths and, in some cases, to minority rights.

This approach is in many ways quite promising, since it involves dialogue, due process and appeal to principle and avoids the radical separation often implied by private schooling. Difficulties arise, however, when the spirit of pluralism is absent, and the objective becomes that of imposing on everyone a form of schooling that is desired only by a sub-group (or certain elements within it). Pluralism, as we have seen, requires a respect for the needs and choices of others and a willingness to engage in the delicate art of compromise whereby the different needs of different people are met as far as possible. A movement which rejects compromise or 'give and take' as an appropriate means of resolving differences is striking at the heart of pluralism and endangering the continued existence of the pluralistic society from which everyone — including the movement itself — benefits.

Notes and References

1 Sharp, R. and Green, A. (1975) *Education and Social Control: A Study in Progressive Primary Education,* London, Routledge and Kegan Paul, pp. 198 ff.
2 Kahlil Gibran (1965) *The Prophet,* New York, Alfred A. Knoff, Pocket Edition, pp. 18–19.
3 Bereiter, C. (1973) *Must We Educate?,* Englewood Cliffs, NJ, Prentice-Hall, Spectrum p. 46.
4 *Ibid.,* p. 46
5 *Ibid.,* p. 47.
6 *Ibid.,* p. 130.
7 *Ibid.,* p. 130.
8 *Ibid.,* p. 18.
9 *Ibid.,* p. 47.

10 *Ibid.*, p. 48.
11 Greeley, A. (1971) *Why Can't They Be Like Us?*, New York, Dutton, pp. 51–2.
12 Prakash, M.S. (1987) 'Partners in Moral Education: Communities and Their Public Schools', in Ryan, K., and McLean, G. (Eds) *Character Development in Schools and Beyond,* New York, Praeger, p. 139.
13 Raywid, M.A. (1977) 'The Blurring of the Fringes: From "Dangerous Organizations" to "Obtrusive Pluralists"', *Educational Leadership,* 34, 7, pp. 498–500.
14 Prakash, M.S., *op. cit.*, p. 138.
15 *Ibid.*, pp. 138–9.

Part Two
Specific
Value Issues

So far, I have outlined the broad goals of schooling and the type of school that is required to attain them. I have also suggested appropriate general orientations toward students, teachers, parents and other members of society.

In Part 2, we turn to several key problem areas in schooling where specific value issues arise and specific solutions are needed. This section of the book, which must be selective, is intended not only to tackle some important and thorny questions in contemporary schooling, but also to illustrate the fruitfulness of bringing a values perspective to bear on education.

Chapter 6

Compulsion

The use of compulsion in schooling — both making children go to school and controlling their activities while they are there — is often regarded as suspect, ethically. After all, freedom is a value celebrated in our literary and philosophical traditions, and freedom of movement, thought, expression, choice and so on are seen as basic rights in society at large. Why should school-aged children be denied freedom? In the previous chapter I pointed out that freedom is just one of the basic values humans pursue, and accordingly the emphasis placed on it must be limited by other considerations. But if there are to be limits to freedom — if there is to be a measure of compulsion — how exactly can this be justified and how is the nature and degree of compulsion to be determined?

Compulsion as a part of human life

To begin with, one should not exaggerate the freedom that even adults have or should have. I am free to board a plane and go to another country but only if I can afford a ticket, am not legally tied by responsibilities at home, am not on bail, have a valid passport and visa and so on. When we *feel* free, it is in part because the various forms of compulsion we are subjected to happen to be in line with our wishes or with what we think is right. It does not mean that our lives are without compulsion. If our wishes or our conception of what people should be allowed to do changed, we might suddenly feel very constrained, even without any change in circumstances.

Some of the constraints on human beings are 'natural'. From the earliest times, humans were *forced* to find shelter from the elements, build defences against wild animals and gather, cultivate or hunt for food simply to stay alive and achieve minimum comfort. Other constraints are cultural and traditional in nature. We are *compelled* to fit in at least to a degree with the established way of life of our community if we wish to have the economic, cultural, social and other benefits it affords. As Thomas Hobbes argued in *Leviathan,* if we did not submit ourselves to *some* form of societal order and authority, our lives would be 'solitary, poor, nasty, brutish and short'.[1] Many of the instruments of compulsion which we so often resent and disparage — parliaments, laws, bureaucracies, police forces and the like — are there in part to regularize and make *somewhat* equitable an imposition and self-imposition which is necessary. If people did not at least partly recognize this, no legal system or police force remotely like the ones we have could achieve compliance.

Nor do we accept compulsion simply for self-interested reasons. In the moral domain as well (which goes in part beyond self-interest) we embrace principles which directly influence us toward actions which are altruistic and which we may not otherwise be inclined to perform. Isa Aron has pointed out that moral principles have a 'coercive power' which is necessary in situations 'where the (pure) ethic of caring does not, for whatever reason, operate'. She notes that we do not always find ourselves in an individual, caring relationship with those whom we should help, and so we need a set of moral principles which serve as 'a standard and a template for the requirements of living in society' and which (to a degree) psychologically constrain our behaviour.[2]

Turning from the adult realm to the world of the young child, we find further examples of the need for constraint in human life. Francis Schrag, in an article concerned primarily with arguing for increased freedom for young people, acknowledges that there must be considerable adult control over 'the very young', defined for convenience as 'children below four'. He points out that the very young 'remain unaware of the significance of activity in a fundamental way'. For example, they 'cannot realize that in pushing a button, or touching a wire, or in refusing to go to a doctor when it hurts, they are risking their very lives . . . . Nor can they realize that by pronouncing certain words or scratching their names to a piece of paper they thereby commit themselves to obligations extending over months and years'. Accordingly, 'they need to be protected both from others who would exploit them and from the consequences of their own behavior. The restraint the law imposes on them therefore does them no injury in depriving them of their freedom. On the contrary, it protects their own interest'.[3]

In the realm of ideas, educational writers today are increasingly accepting the inevitability of some direct influence from the society around us. Kozol, for example, says: 'I am not opposed to the idea of adult "imposition" on the minds of children. Indeed, I am convinced there is no way by which to overcome such imposition'.[4] Apple, as we have seen, takes a similar position. He maintains that schooling 'is not a neutral enterprise'; we inevitably transmit certain values to students because they are 'already embedded in the design of the institutions we work in'. And, he goes on, even this way of putting it is misleading; for we ourselves (the educators) have these values 'not at the top but at the very "bottom" of our heads'. Even for adults, complete freedom of thought is impossible to achieve. Indeed, in Apple's view, the very notion of a 'free individual' promotes ideological ends: it serves to 'maintain a rather manipulative ethic of consumption and further the withering of political and economic sensitivity'.[5] It obscures the fundamentally systemic and communal nature of human life.

It is often suggested that one should not be constrained or compelled by *other people*: one should be allowed to decide what to do with one's own life. Control may sometimes be necessary; but it should be either *self*-control or control by 'natural' conditions or consequences. This, for example, was the view developed by Rousseau in *Emile*, where he depicted social influence as the very source of evil. Leonard Krimerman in 'Compulsory Education: A Moral Critique' bases part of his argument against compulsory education on Godwin's principle that 'self-determination has intrinsic moral value'.[6] However, in my view, this implies an unduly individualistic approach to life. It overlooks the extent to which we are influenced in positive ways by others; and it suggests that one should never be 'looked after' by other people in any degree. In fact, we need to be in relationships of direct impact and mutual caring with others. As David Nyberg says in discussing the 'freedom' of free schools, 'it does not take an unusual imagination to conceive of the circumstance in which caring, or loving, means taking away certain freedom'.[7] He cites the example of reducing people's ignorance without their being able to give fully informed consent to what one 'does' to them. He maintains that 'forcibly' reducing people's ignorance in this way may be viewed as freeing them from the constraints their lack of knowledge had previously imposed on them. Nyberg concludes with the nicely ironic suggestion that we need to find a way of 'freeing schools from an unnecessarily constraining sense of freedom'.[8]

One cannot, then, reject all constraint. What one can object to, however, is *arbitrary* constraint, where an individual or agency in a society attempts to compel people in ways that are not necessary for their well being and not justifiable from the point of view of other people's well being. Constraint by humans on humans must be *legitimate*: it must be for the good of the constrained person and/or the good of others in morally acceptable ways. And it is clear that people often exercise power over others which is arbitrary and illegitimate. In particular, adults often compel children in ways that are not justifiable in terms of either the children's good or legitimate benefit to others. We must now address the issue of freedom and compulsion in schooling, bearing in mind that, as we have discussed in this section, the ideal cannot be one where there is complete absence of constraint.

Compulsory school attendance

The directive that all children must go to school was initially addressed as much to parents as to their offspring. Much of the resistance to compulsory attendance in the early days of universal schooling came from people who resented the loss of child labour, not from those who felt that education should take place in the home or some other setting. The justification given by governments then was in part that children must be protected from parental (and other societal) exploitation.

Today, however, parents and the state are largely collaborators in insisting that children go to school. As we noted in Chapter 1, life in wealthy industrialized societies has developed in such a way that the great majority of parents want their children in school so that they are off the streets and out of trouble, quite apart from the concern that they should be educated and gain credentials for employment or further study. The issue now is not so much whether the state should force parents to send their children to school (although this sometimes still arises) as whether *adult society* — government, parents and other adults — is justified in making school attendance compulsory.

Until about age 12, in societies such as ours, the case for compulsory school attendance is in my opinion rather strong (assuming a fairly satisfactory form of schooling). Parents need a safe, pleasant environment for their children coupled with basic education, and the children also need these things. The great majority of parents will insist that their children attend a school-type institution, and would be rightly concerned if the government and other public agencies did not cooperate in ensuring that their children in fact stay at school when sent. In the rare cases where parents do not see any need for their pre-teenage children to be in a safe, pleasant setting or receive a basic schooling, the state is usually justified in forcibly making such provision for the sake of the children, perhaps for the sake of the parents, and also (as discussed in Chapter 5) in the interests of the rest of society.

But what about the period from age 12 to age 15 or 16? Some would claim that for this age-group schooling should not be compulsory since if it is good for children, they will naturally seek it; and if it is not good for them, they obviously should not be forced to participate in it. A parallel might be drawn with university and community college attendance, which is not compulsory but which large numbers of young people accept voluntarily because they value that kind of experience and/or because they wish to have the qualifications it affords. To force children to attend school 'for their own good' implies a kind of paternalism which we do not apply — and apparently do not need to apply — at the university and college level. Also, compulsion carries with it some of the dangers noted in Chapter 3, namely, of reducing students' initiative, interest and sense of direction.[9]

Why is compulsory attendance justified (as I think it is, by and large) in our society for children up to age 15 or 16 and not for college and university students? Partly because at this age children in our type of society are still not usually ready to defend themselves against the abuse, exploitation and deprivation they might be subjected to if left on their own; and partly because (again in our type of society) they have not developed the ability to take their education into their own hands. In other eras and other societies even young children have shown great capacity for self-defence and self-direction, as documented for example by Philippe Ariès in *Centuries of Childhood*[10] and Robert Coles in *The Moral Life of Children*.[11] But we have simply not given that type of opportunity to our children. Some would argue that this is a good thing, others that it is bad. But until there is a major shift in the age at which children are given responsibilities of this type, it is necessary to make schooling largely compulsory for this age group. Indeed, because of the way they are reared and treated, children expect such direction and refuse to take overall control themselves. They frankly disbelieve anyone who suggests that they are free to take such matters completely into their own hands; and they know that if they attempted to do so, adults would see them as precocious and presumptuous and their peers would think their behaviour strange.

However, while I think that in general schooling should be compulsory to age 15 or 16, there are *exceptions* which must be considered (but which also 'prove the rule'). Exceptions need to be taken more seriously and dealt with more sensitively and imaginatively than at present. For example, even in our society, some children clearly do have the capacity and motivation by age 10, 11 or 12 to direct their own education. There have been cases of children of this age going to university to study in a field of their choice and apparently thriving on it. Similarly, one can imagine children beginning an important life career at this age (already we have many examples of this in the case of musicians, dancers, actors and athletes). Parents and the educational establishment should be prepared to make major adjustments of their standard procedures to accommodate these children (while still making available to them a solid common and general education).

Again, on a particular day or in a particular week or even year, school attendance may not be good for a child, and parents and teachers need to be sensitive to this fact. There may be special circumstances in the home or in the life of the child which suggest that a break is needed, to do something else or nothing at all. Schools often understand this to a degree and allow for absence for rather unconventional reasons or without probing the reasons too closely. Parents, too, aided by their children, are often able to think of ingenious excuses. My suggestion is simply that this kind of exemption be seen in a more positive light and made more broadly available to children. We certainly do not wish to produce people who, in later life, find themselves incapable of taking a day (or a week) off from their regular tasks without being overcome with anxiety.

Perhaps the group which most obviously requires exceptional attention are those adolescents who are not doing well academically and who genuinely believe that they would be better off outside the school, particularly if others like them were able to join them and keep them company. However, the special treatment of this category of students is fraught with problems. There is a temptation for a school to let a 'trouble maker' leave the system for the school's convenience even when it is not in the student's best interests. Sarup in discussing racism in schools maintains that the system often resorts too easily to special 'disruptive units' (which effectively take young people out of the school), 'long-term exclusion' from classes and 'teacher condoned truancy'.[12] Also, we often conveniently overlook the fact that the 'trouble' such students make in school may be no greater than they will make for society outside the school. Further, the easy exclusion of students from school can reduce the pressure to modify those features of the school experience which make it intolerable for some students in the first place. As I claimed in Chapter 2, the academic program of the school could be modified in such a way that it would be more accessible and interesting to less 'academically oriented' students (indeed to all students). This does not mean that we should dismiss entirely the possibility of exempting some students in this age-range from school attendance. However, we should be aware of the pitfalls of this option and explore more fully possible modifications of the school experience that would render it unnecessary. Unless a school is particularly unsatisfactory, dropping out is usually not a beneficial move for young adolescents, *especially* for those from disadvantaged backgrounds and with lower levels of academic attainment. They often have fewer resources than advantaged students to enable them to make up for lack of schooling.

Pure, brute force is rarely if ever appropriate; and while I have spoken of (normally) compelling children and younger adolescents to participate in school, this would not be justifiable (or indeed possible) if the young people in question were violently opposed to what we require of them. The fact is (as we saw in Chapter 3) that many children enjoy and approve of school, and most of the rest find it 'OK'. Those who dislike it intensely in a given form usually have to be accommodated, either by changing the form or in some way exempting them from school. It is essential that the interactive approach to schooling advocated in Chapter 3 be followed even with respect to school attendance itself. Much more attention should be given to children's objections to schooling and their ideas about positive alternatives; and children and adults should work together in establishing better alternatives both within and beyond 'school' as such. We must avoid an absolutism with respect to compulsory attendance which sees it as right regardless of the objections raised. After all, the whole point of making it compulsory in the first place is for the good of the children, the parents and society, in that order. We must be constantly on the lookout for cases where schooling is not of value for any of the parties concerned; and be prepared either to change the experience accordingly or exempt children from compulsory participation.

Required school content

The compulsion associated with schooling goes beyond having to attend. Once there, children must engage in study and other activities, conducted in a certain manner, over which they have only limited control. As we saw with respect to school attendance, if children object *very* strongly something is usually done, either to the activity or to the child: the content of schooling has perhaps been influenced more than we realize by children's expressions of preference over the years. Nevertheless, a major element of compulsion is involved, and it raises important questions in a so-called 'free' and humane society.

We saw in Chapter 3 that for schooling to be effective — as it must be if students' needs are to be met — it must have a degree of structure. The teacher must enable students to gain access to material in a somewhat ordered way, while always remaining open to suggestions from them as to better ways of locating, presenting and exploring material. It would seem to follow from this that *some* degree of compulsion is necessary. The teacher must serve at least as a coordinator or chairperson, with power to direct students' attention to certain information, ideas and procedures, keep them working away at the problems under review, and by and large prevent them from behaving in a disruptive way toward each other. Sometimes, with certain activities, leadership of this kind may come from one or more students rather than the teacher. But because of our 'ageist' society this will not happen very often, and even when it does there will still exist a situation of compulsion: the role of coordinator or 'chair' of the group will simply have passed to another individual or group.

In an 'interactively' run classroom decisions about what to do and when will to a degree be decided by the class, as a group or as individuals. However, in the collective situation of the classroom, there is a limit to the opportunities for individualization and student choice even for the most talented and flexible of teachers. And as we have seen, there are limits to the extent to which students in our society have the ability — or the motivation — to control their own learning. Accordingly, much of the content of schooling is determined by the teacher, by the learning material and by traditions of what is done in schools.

While a degree of imposition is thus unavoidable within the school, this does not mean it should be exercised in a cavalier fashion. As far as possible, the school should listen to and take account of what students (and parents and others) have to say about the content of schooling. We should never adopt the attitude: 'What right have they got to question what we do?'; for, as we have noted often, schooling is ultimately *for* students (and parents and others) and so they have *every* right to raise questions. We must try to ensure that we only impose school content in ways that are genuinely justifiable in terms of the well being of the students and others involved; and in attempting to ensure this, we must seek constant input both from students and from external sources.

Notes and References

1 Hobbes, T. (1914) *Leviathan*, London, J.M. Dent, Everyman's Library, p. 65.
2 Aron, I. (1988) 'Caring and Principles: Opponents or Partners?', *Philosophy of Education 1988*, Philosophy of Education Society, pp. 130–1. Parentheses added.
3 Schrag, F. (1978) 'From childhood to adulthood: assigning rights and responsibilities', in Strike, K. and Egan, K. (Eds) *Ethics and Educational Policy*, London, Routledge and Kegan Paul, pp. 62–3.
4 Kozol, J. (1984) *The Night Is Dark and I Am Far From Home*, 3rd ed., New York, Continuum, p. 2.
5 Apple, M. (1979) *Ideology and Curriculum*, London, Routledge and Kegan Paul, pp. 8–10.
6 Krimerman, L., in Strike and Egan, *op. cit.*, pp. 86–7.
7 Nyberg, D., 'Ambiguity and constraint in the "freedom" of free schools', in Strike and Egan, *op. cit.*, p. 139.
8 *Ibid.*, p. 143.
9 On the problem of 'overjustification' resulting from compulsory schooling see L. Krimerman's article 'Compulsory Education: A Moral Critique', *op. cit.*, pp. 85–6.
10 Ariès, P. (1962) *Centuries of Childhood: A Social History of Family Life*, New York, Random House, Vintage Books.
11 Coles, R. (1986) *The Moral Life of Children*, Boston, Atlantic Monthly Press.
12 Sarup, M. (1986) *The Politics of Multiracial Education*, London, Routledge and Kegan Paul, p. 26.

Chapter 7

Indoctrination

Some parents claim, in private at least, that school has had a bad influence on their children, leading them to abandon home values in personal, social and political matters. Religious groups sometimes condemn the school for encouraging children to adopt a sceptical, materialistic outlook. Some educational writers accuse the school of supporting a competitive, exploitative ideology which perpetuates inequality in the world and undermines the cause of peace. In each case, the charge is at least in part that the school is engaging in indoctrination: it is influencing children to hold certain unfortunate 'doctrines.' Even where it is recognized that the values in question came largely from the wider society, the school is blamed for going along with these values and participating in their inculcation.

An intriguing feature of these criticisms is that it is not always clear whether they are directed at indoctrination in the sense of a method of inculcation or at the content being transmitted. Often one suspects that if values, beliefs and behaviour patterns acceptable to the critics were being inculcated, the charge of 'indoctrination' would quickly be dropped. But writers on the subject claim that method and aim are at least as important aspects of indoctrination as content. In attempting, then, to come to terms with this area and the school's responsibility with respect to it, we must begin by trying to understand more precisely what indoctrination is and what grounds there are for objecting to its presence in schools.

What is indoctrination?

Educational writers have discussed at length the nature of indoctrination but have had great difficulty reaching agreement.[1] Some maintain that we indoctrinate when we teach questionable *content*; others say that indoctrination is a function of the *manner* in which we teach; others see the *aim* or *intention* of the teacher as crucial; and yet others say that what is really significant is the *result* of our activities: we produce an indoctrinated person.

My own view is that all of these elements are important, but one's aim or intention is not as crucial as some writers have suggested. It is true, as I.A. Snook says, that we can hardly be described as doing *anything* if we are not acting with intention. But this applies to all activity: it is not peculiar to indoctrination. Further, it seems clear that we can indoctrinate without intending to: probably by far the largest part of the indoctrination that goes on in schools is of this type. We may even indoctrinate when our intention is precisely to avoid indoctrination, as some of the studies of so-called 'open' and 'progressive' schools have shown.

I believe that the *content* aspect of indoctrination is of major importance. One of the chief ways of indoctrinating is to teach beliefs and values which are objectionable in some respects. John Wilson emphasizes this type of indoctrination, focusing particularly on the teaching of untruths as if they were truths and uncertainties as if they were certainties.[2] As I will argue later, I do not think that teaching false beliefs is always wrong and hence indoctrinative. But Wilson's stress on content as a criterion of indoctrination is justified; and certainly we should see the school as having a fundamental responsibility to help students arrive at true — or at least well founded — beliefs.

However, teaching objectionable content is not the only criterion of indoctrination. Another key way of indoctrinating is to teach even supposedly sound beliefs and values in such a *manner* that students are incapable of reconsidering them, whether at school or in later life. Richard Hare emphasizes this aspect of indoctrination when he argues that some inculcation of moral ideas in young children is necessary if they are to have a sufficiently broad range of beliefs by which to live. The crucial point, he maintains, is that these early beliefs should not be taught so forcefully that when children are ready to think for themselves they are psychologically incapable of questioning them.[3] There is a technology of teaching which we recognize as indoctrinative: where reasons are not discussed, questioning is discouraged and an unduly strong emotional attachment to beliefs is created. This is seen as inappropriate even when we are certain that the content we are teaching is true and of vital importance to children.

The two characteristics of indoctrination which I have highlighted so far — inappropriate content and overly forceful method — may occur either separately or together. As we have just noted, it is possible for the teaching content to be entirely appropriate and yet for indoctrination to take place because of the manner in which the content is taught. Equally, if the content is inappropriate, indoctrination may still take place even with the most gentle and tentative of teaching styles. Indeed the 'soft sell' is often just as effective as the 'hard sell' in indoctrination. Obviously, however, teaching which combines both aspects — a strong technology which induces an unshakeable acceptance of inappropriate beliefs — constitutes the clearest (if not the most common) case of indoctrination.[4]

Another characteristic of indoctrination which I wish to emphasize has already been assumed in the foregoing discussion, namely, that it is always wrong. Indoctrination involves *inappropriate* content and/or method which is likely to have an *unfortunate* outcome (although with luck it may not). 'Indoctrination' is a value word with a pejorative connotation.

It is sometimes suggested that the term 'indoctrination' does not (or should not) always have a negative meaning. For example, some people who feel that we have gone too far in allowing children to arrive at their own beliefs and values are inclined to say that a measure of indoctrination — especially in early childhood — is a good thing and should be reinstated in the school and elsewhere. However, it seems to me that the interests of people who hold this view are not well served by using the word 'indoctrination'. Although there was a time when it simply meant 'instruction in doctrine',[5] today it has such negative connotations (in English) among all ideological groups, from left to right, that we must regard indoctrination as bad by definition.[6] Accordingly, people who wish to argue for a more forceful teaching of beliefs and values to young children would be well advised to use a word such as 'instruction' or, possibly, 'inculcation' in attempting to make their case. In this book I will use the term in its generally accepted pejorative sense.[7]

What is wrong with indoctrination?

I have said that indoctrination is, by definition, always wrong; but what exactly is wrong with it? In the first place, where it involves transmitting false or unfounded beliefs, indoctrination is usually harmful because students are left with beliefs which are not a reliable basis for judgment and action in the real world. They are likely to make mistakes in their interaction with other people and the environment generally, and be hindered in their pursuit of 'the good life' for themselves and others. And to the extent that they pass on the same beliefs to other people, the circle of harm spreads.

False or unfounded beliefs are not always harmful. I cannot accept Wilson's claim that 'the concept of indoctrination concerns the truth and evidence of beliefs, and our objection to it is basically that in the realm of belief we must put truth, evidence and reality first, and other considerations second'.[8] Wilson maintains that we should never teach false or unfounded beliefs because we think they are 'good' for children, or because they are traditional, or because we think they will 'help to keep society together'.[9] But in my view, these are sometimes legitimate grounds for teaching beliefs the 'truth' of which is questionable. Some dubious myths, for example, are tied in with a total religious way of life — fundamentalist, orthodox, liberal or whatever — which is *good* for the people who embrace that way of life. There is always danger when false or unfounded beliefs are taught, and certainly such teaching should be avoided other things being equal. But indoctrination is by definition concerned with the teaching of *harmful* beliefs; and it *sometimes* happens (although often it does not) that the teaching of false or unfounded beliefs does more good than harm. Where this clearly is the case, such teaching should be described as a 'nurture', 'initiation into communal myths' or the like rather than indoctrination.

But the harm done by inappropriate content (whether false or otherwise) is not the only basis for objecting to indoctrination. Indoctrination which fulfils the second criterion — use of unduly forceful teaching methods — can also do considerable harm. Teaching which neglects appeal to experience and reason and induces excessively strong psychological attachment to ideas inhibits the later dropping of beliefs which further learning suggests are mistaken. Also, it prevents the development of a more imaginative, reasoned and complex approach to life. Indoctrination (in this sense) tends to short-circuit a natural, free response to phenomena and our experience of them. We do not come to 'own' beliefs for ourselves but rather continue to be dependent on our early learning experiences and the teachers who engineered them. In more extreme cases, indoctrinative methods may result in emotional problems such as phobias and excessive guilt feelings. This may happen even where the content of our early learning was in fact sound, since our commitment, though correct in a sense, is compulsive. (This is why it is often important for teenagers to rebel even against eminently sensible parental rules.) And in cases where the content was unsound, our normal attempts at re-educating our conscience may be frustrated by fear and guilt arising from the manner in which the content was originally taught.

Emotional attachment to beliefs, of course, is not always harmful: in many ways it is essential. Some psychologists believe that in order to achieve a state of maturity we must pass through somewhat extreme stages — of morality, faith, ego development and so forth — during which we place 'undue' emphasis on a particular dimension of life so that it becomes thoroughly ingrained in us. And in everyday living unless we are strongly committed to certain ideas about what is important we may not have the motivation to do what is needed. Educators are faced with a dilemma: commitment to ideas is necessary for action, but it can also render people disinclined to question and revise their ideas. Obviously some middle course is needed between too much and too little attachment to beliefs. If we are to avoid indoctrination in schooling we must find (or help our students find) that middle course.

Legitimate direct influence in schools

Indoctrination, we have seen, is in part a *method* of teaching which influences students to adopt certain beliefs without engaging their reason and free choice and induces an overly strong attachment to beliefs. It should be recognized, however, that *some* 'direct influence' on students is necessary and indeed desirable in schooling; and being desirable it cannot strictly speaking be called 'indoctrination'. We must examine this phenomenon in order to become still clearer about what indoctrination is and what schools can and cannot legitimately do.

Richard Peters has pointed out that education involves being 'initiated' into language, concepts, assumptions and methods of inquiry, all the implications of which one cannot possibly grasp or give rational assent to at the time. One can modify the forms of thought and life to which one is introduced but only from within, so to speak: 'individual inventiveness can only emerge against a background of a public tradition which has provided both the milieu for problems and the procedures for tackling them'.[10] Accordingly, while a student may resist some elements of such a package at the point of initiation, much of it is absorbed uncritically. Although in order to count as 'education' the initiation process must meet certain 'minimum requirements of wittingness and voluntariness',[11] students cannot evaluate fully what they are learning.

Peters' account of education, here, is not an unduly hierarchical one, positing the teacher as an unquestioned authority qualified to form the thinking of students singlehandedly. In many ways teachers are in the same boat as students, having themselves experienced a similar initiation. The teacher has a clear superiority only at the beginning of the process.

> The cardinal function of the teacher, in the early stages, is to get the pupil on the inside of the form of thought or awareness with which (he/she) is concerned. At a later stage, when the pupil has built into (his/her) mind both the concepts and mode of exploration involved, the difference between teacher and taught is obviously only one of degree. For both are participating in the shared experience of exploring a common world.[12]

Both student and teacher, then, have been and continue to be subject to the direct influence of cultural traditions which were in process of formation long before they were a glint in their parents' eyes and against which, for the time being, they have only limited protection.

While one may wish to quarrel with some aspects of Peters' analysis — for example, his assumption that there is a single, unified public culture, and that existing forms of thought are largely appropriate — one must, I believe, accept his claim that education involves a major non-rational, non-voluntary component. Teachers necessarily set forth various concepts, principles and methods in the course of introducing students to a subject area — whether it be physics, history or ethics — and students inevitably adopt much of this framework, at least initially, without questioning it to any great extent or realizing all that it implies. Even where several alternative views are presented the range is limited and certain positions are favoured for working purposes. No matter that teachers say — and I think we should say it often — that students must assess these ideas and their implications for themselves, students often largely accept them in the beginning. And frequently they do not go beyond this 'beginning stage' because they do not study the topics long enough or deeply enough to arrive at a position that is 'their own'.

Another writer who has stressed the role of direct influence in schooling is Emile Durkheim. Focusing particularly on moral education, he attempted to achieve a balance between social learning and autonomous choice. He talks of the importance of affective learning, saying that 'since we are and always will be sensate as well as rational human beings', complete autonomy is an impossible ideal.[13] He describes the task of moral education as that of fostering respect for rules ('discipline'), a positive regard for social groups ('attachment') and 'enlightened allegiance' or 'informed consent' to societal authority ('autonomy'). But as the term 'informed consent' suggests, this respect for and allegiance to the society's morality must be based at least in part on individual understanding and judgment; the school must foster insight into the positive ends served by rules so that as far as possible they are accepted rationally. Durkheim criticizes Kant's exclusive emphasis on following rules out of a sense of duty, stating that 'we never act completely out of duty, nor ever completely through love of the ideal'.[14] He regards Kant's concept of moral freedom and autonomy as entirely fanciful: 'to conceive of a purely autonomous will, Kant is obliged to acknowledge that the will, insofar as it is purely rational, is not subject to the law of nature. He has to make of it a faculty set aside from the world'. Such an autonomy 'has not and never will have anything to do with reality'.[15] However, Durkheim develops an alternative concept of moral autonomy which is far from being a merely token gesture in the direction of freedom and rationality. 'To teach morality', he says, 'is neither to preach nor to indoctrinate; it is to explain'. We must 'help (the child) understand the reasons for the rules (she/he) should abide by'; otherwise 'we would be condemning (her/him) to an incomplete and inferior morality.'[16] Further, Durkheim does not see inculcation for societal maintenance riding roughshod over the needs, any more than the thoughts of the individual: 'if (an institution) does violence to human nature, however socially useful it may be, it will never be born, much less persist since it cannot take root in the conscience'.[17]

Durkheim's attempt to emphasize *both* the importance of autonomy and rationality *and* the direct impact of society on the individual is perhaps brought out best in the following quotation:

> Society is a product of innumerable forces of which we are only an infinitesimal fraction . . . . It is necessarily thus with morality, an expression of social nature. So it is a dangerous illusion to imagine that morality is a personal artifact; and that consequently we have it completely and from the beginning under our control . . . . We can only conquer the moral world in the same fashion that we conquer the physical world: by building a science of moral matters.[18]

Thus for Durkheim in all fields of human endeavour — physical, moral, social, or whatever — the answer lies not in individual action but in building a communal 'science' whereby people work together rather than in isolation on the complex, dialectical task of transforming both their consciousness and their society. Being educated involves being directly influenced by ideas which, nevertheless, we have a hand in developing and which we continue to subject to critical assessment.

The social nature of learning — with its inevitable consequence of direct influence — is not, in my opinion, something to be resisted or regretted *in general*. As we saw in Chapter 6, the direct impact which our family, friends and others have on us is often for our own good; and it is also often for the good of society as a whole. As Richard Hare says, taking an example from moral learning, children have to realize that what is wrong for others to do to them is wrong for them to do to others. And 'unless *some* non-rational methods are used, it is unlikely that all our children will come to absorb this principle as deeply as we could wish; and to that extent less of their thinking about action will be moral thinking, and their actions will show this'.[19] Such a state of affairs would be to the clear disadvantage of everyone, including the children themselves.

This does not mean, however, that we should indulge in any and every form of direct influence on the ideas of students. It should only be exercised if it is clearly necessary, either directly or indirectly, for the well being of the interested parties (most notably the students). Such influence should be kept to a minimum, both because we need students to be actively and consciously involved in working to improve our intellectual and cultural traditions, and because as Durkheim argued, the more consent is 'informed' and allegiance 'enlightened' the more effective our social and moral arrangements will be. But if we shy away from *every* situation in which students might conceivably be directly influenced, for fear that we might 'indoctrinate' them, we will be incapable of making available to them the education they need, and will leave them at the mercy of those forces in society which already so strongly influence their beliefs and values.

The fact of indoctrination in schools

Indoctrination occurs in schools to a much greater extent than most people realize. To begin with, there is the practice of teaching as simple certainties the 'facts' and principles of school subjects. While, as I have argued, it is not possible to have a fully explicit and rational presentation of everything that is taught in schools, there should be a *more* reasoned treatment of topics than at present. In science, for example, students are given very little background on the complex lines of experimentation and theory from which accepted 'truths' have emerged. As Apple says, 'in our schools, scientific work . . . is seen (and taught) as always subject to empirical verification with no outside influences, either personal of political'. Such teaching 'critically misrepresents the nature of the conflicts so often found between proponents of alternative solutions, interpretations, or modes of procedure in scientific communities'.[20]

When we move from science to the humanities and social sciences, there is even greater diversity of belief and interpretation, and yet students are again so often kept in ignorance of this disagreement: they are indoctrinated into particular conceptions of social reality and encouraged to hold to them more firmly than is justified by current knowledge. With respect to the teaching of social studies, for example, Apple notes two related problems: first, society is depicted as 'basically a cooperative system' with few internal conflicts; and secondly, this is represented as the way things *should* be: 'internal dissension and conflict in society are viewed as inherently antithetical to the smooth functioning of the social order'.[21] Apple argues not only that this is a false account of the nature of society, but also that it prevents students from arriving at a sound approach to social reform. Students come to see themselves (and humans in general) as 'value-transmitting and value-receiving persons rather than value-creating persons'; they are unaware that conflict 'performs the considerable task of pointing to areas of needed redress' and is 'a basic and often beneficial dimension of the dialectic of activity we label society'. As a result of this systematic ideological bias, schools come to distort not only controversial issues but also straightforward 'factual' information. Even in so-called 'inquiry-oriented' social studies curricula there is 'a signal neglect of the efficacy of conflict and the rather long and deep-seated history it has held in social relationships'. As a result, 'children are confronted with a tacit emphasis . . . on a stable set of structures and on the maintenance of order'[22]

Kozol makes similar observations about the teaching of social sciences, although in characteristically stronger language. He claims that a deep and largely deliberate distortion of social concepts and facts takes place in schools in order to cover up the violent exploitation and extreme inequality in the US and abroad. Such misrepresentation, he maintains, 'is not a mindless or an unexpected outcome . . . . Just children are a formidable danger to an unjust nation unless they can be etherized successfully when they are still young. It is the major function of the public schools to offer us that ether'.[23] He cites the biased interpretation of historical events, and the hopelessly lopsided representation of historical figures of 'strong radical intent'. It is not mentioned, for example, that Martin Luther King urged his disciples to defy unjust laws; that Henry David Thoreau at one point refused to pay his taxes, and often spoke scathingly of 'the cautious philanthropic people of his day'; or that Helen Keller fought 'with passion to expose the unfair labour practices' of the time.[24] Despite Kozol's perhaps overly moralistic tone, it is difficult to deny that history is taught largely as he says, that such teaching has most of the results he describes, and that advantaged people in wealthy countries breathe more easily as a consequence.

Commentary on the indoctrination which takes place in schools has gone beyond the explicit curriculum (important though this is) to the 'structural' features of schools (and of society) which reinforce biased points of view. Theorists have often spoken of the 'hidden curriculum' which fosters acceptance of such values as punctuality, reliability, neatness, hard work, competitiveness, individualism, aggressiveness, militarism and so on. The objection to the hidden curriculum is not always to the values taught — obviously punctuality and hard work, for example, have a place — but rather to the unreflective (that is, indoctrinative) manner in which they are taught. Allegiance to these values becomes an automatic reflex, without due consideration of reasons, qualifications, exceptions, individual differences and alternative values. Much of the hidden curriculum is important and without it society would be worse off than it is at present. However, its indoctrinative qualities must be overcome, as far as possible, by *supplementing* it with extensive consideration of relevant facts and arguments and competing moral, social and political theories.

In recent years, the study of structural influences on and in schools has focused on the way in which *inequalities* in society are perpetuated through schooling. There are many elements in this process of structural 'reproduction', but indoctrination is one of the more important. Discrimination against non-whites, ethnics, females, lower class children and so on is built into the organization, language and practices of the school so that the advantages certain types of people have in the larger society are maintained or even strengthened. This requires that most of the members of the school accept certain 'truisms' about who is more capable, likeable, deserving. The existing inequalities must be seen as justified and 'natural'. Such understandings and perceptions are found in the explicit curriculum of the school, as we have seen, but are also taught indirectly through the way different children are assessed, streamed, referred to, listened to and related to. Indoctrination here is structural not only because it is an aspect of the way the school is run, but also in that it reflects corresponding structures in the larger society. Teachers and students alike slip very easily into concepts, attitudes and evaluations which have been with them since the day they were born; and attempts to break out of these structures are usually quickly counteracted by external sanctions of many different kinds.

Despite what I have said about the necessity and desirability of *some* direct influence, then, it is clear that there are many forms of influence in schools at present which are indoctrinative and must be opposed. Moreover, I believe that there is much the school can do. The foregoing analysis was intended not to reduce us to gloomy inaction but rather to show that the task before us is a complex one which will require a concerted effort across both school and society. We will now consider, in the five chapters which follow, five specific areas in which value issues arise for the school and in which, among other things, there is a problem of indoctrination to be tackled.

Notes and References

1 See especially Kilpatrick, W.H. (1951) *Philosophy of Education*, New York, Macmillan, pp. 123–4; Green, T. (1964–65) 'A Topology of the Teaching Concept', *Studies in Philosophy and Education*, 3, Winter, p. 299; Wilson, J. (1964) 'Education and Indoctrination' in Hollins T.H.B. (Ed), *Aims in Education*, Manchester, University of Manchester Press, Chapter II; Hare, R.M. (1964) 'Adolescents into Adults', in Hollins, *op. cit.*, Chapter III; White, J.P. (1967) 'Indoctrination', in Peters, R.S. (Ed), *The Concept of Education*, London, Routledge and Kegan Paul, pp. 177–91; Snook, I.A. (1972) *Indoctrination and Education*, London, Routledge and Kegan Paul; and Snook, I.A. (Ed), (1972) *Concepts of Indoctrination*, London, Routledge and Kegan Paul.
2 Wilson, J., *op. cit.*, especially pp. 26–9.
3 Hare, R.M. *op. cit.*, especially pp. 59–62.
4 It should be noted that some theorists would not use the word 'teaching' to refer to indoctrination. They might then describe what we are discussing here as 'so-called teaching' or perhaps 'inculcation'.
5 See Snook, I.A., *Indoctrination and Education, op. cit.*, pp. 16 and 17.
6 This is the position taken, for example, by Snook, *ibid.*, pp. 1, 4 and 66. He says: '"Indoctrination" implies a pejorative judgment on a teaching situation'.
7 Some people feel so strongly about this point that they wish to use the word

'indoctrination' and attempt to restore it to its former respectability. I believe this is a mistake strategically, but one cannot object to it on etymological grounds. We might note in passing that 'inculcation' is of dubious value as an alterantive word. It, too, has rather negative connotations, as confirmed by the Shorter Oxford English Dictionary which defines it in terms of grinding something in with one's heel.

8 Wilson, J., *op. cit.*, p. 28.
9 *Ibid.*, p. 28.
10 Peters, R.S. (1966) *Ethics and Education*, London, Allen and Unwin, p. 57.
11 *Ibid.*, p. 54.
12 *Ibid.*, p. 53. Parentheses added.
13 Durkheim, E. (1961) *Moral Education*, New York, The Free Press, pp. 113–14.
14 *Ibid.*, p. 88.
15 *Ibid.*, p. 113.
16 *Ibid.*, pp. 120–1.
17 *Ibid.*, p. 38.
18 *Ibid.*, pp. 119–20.
19 Hare, R.M., 'Adolescents into Adults', *op. cit.*, pp. 63–4.
20 Apple, M. (1979) *Ideology and Curriculum*, London, Routledge and Kegan Paul, pp. 88–9.
21 *Ibid.*, pp. 92–3.
22 *Ibid.*, pp. 93–8.
23 Kozol, J. (1984) *The Night Is Dark and I Am Far From Home*, 3rd ed., New York, Continuum, pp. 13–14.
24 *Ibid.*, pp. 63–9.

Chapter 8

Religious Bias[1]

We have been discussing the nature of indoctrination and the harm it does in schools. We turn now to a particular area of indoctrination and discrimination, namely, religious bias. Religious bias in and through schooling is an important value concern because of the harmful effects it has in the lives of students and in society generally.

It might be thought that religious bias is a religious rather than a value issue, and should be left to theologians and other experts on religion. However, this rationale has for too long been used to exempt religion from moral scrutiny. While religion may in some degree be an end in itself, many things have been done in the name of religion which general value analysis would show to be unacceptable. How can educators campaign, as we commonly do, against discrimination on the basis of race, gender and class and yet calmly sit by while people discriminate on the basis of religion? We must not make an absolute out of religious values any more than other categories of value: all should be weighed in terms of their contribution to human well being.

This is not an anti–religious position. Religion often serves to reduce discrimination rather than promote it. As Gregory Baum says, religion is 'ambiguous' on this matter: it can foster prejudice but it also had the potential 'to overcome prejudice and enable (people) to appreciate outsiders for what they are.'[2] Besides, much of the prejudicial treatment of humans in modern times (and earlier) has been meted out in the name of non–religious ideologies such as nationalism, socialism and capitalism.[3] However, we must be aware of the tendency, often strengthened by schools, to regard one's own religion as superior and to discriminate against other people on the basis of their religion (or lack of religion).

The nature and effects of religious bias

Religious bias typically involves both the *belief* that a particular religion is superior to other religions (or non-religious ways of life), and the prejudicial *treatment* of people who do not belong to that religion. Sometimes religious bias takes the form of favouring a whole category of religions over others, for example, monotheisms over polytheisms, or 'great religions' over lesser known paths. Our main focus here, however, will be on the case where just one religion is favoured.

Religious bias arises partly out of the human tendency to distinguish between the 'we-group' (in this case, the members of one's own religion) and the 'they-group' (all non-members) and to look down on and discriminate against the latter. Now, as we saw in Chapter 1, favouring one's own group to some extent is legitimate: it is essential to friendship, community and various other human goods, and is necessary for personal and social growth. By religious 'bias', then, I mean (in part) favouritism and discrimination of a degree and type which goes beyond legitimate group solidarity. How do we determine what is illegitimate 'we-group' behaviour? This is a complex task. But a clear type of case is where the 'they-group' is signficantly harmed and there is minimal or no benefit to the 'we-group'; another instance is where discrimination against the 'they-group' results in inter-group conflict of such intensity that everyone is worse off. Where the 'we-group' benefits substantially from discriminating against the 'they-group' a definitive judgment is more difficult to make, but it is possible to establish at least *broad* limits to the extent to which one group may legitimately pursue its well being at the expense of others.

Apart from a simple 'we-group' orientation, the other main source of religious bias is indoctrination into the belief that one's own religion is *superior* to other religions (and to non-religious ways of life). This may involve the belief that one's religion is the one true way: the *only* way to a good, holy life, to salvation, union with the divine, enlightenment, nirvana, heaven or whatever is considered the essence of human perfection and well being, now and in the future. Or one may simply believe that one's religion is the better way: the one most able to lead to a good life and glorious future.

Interestingly, the belief that one's religion is superior often persists long after one has 'given it up'. For example, people of Christian background who have ceased to practice their religion often continue to look upon people of Asian, African and native American religions as 'pagans' and 'idol worshippers' and regard their beliefs and practices as more bizarre and harmful than those of Christianity. Accordingly, even so-called 'unbelievers' often must experience a profound re-education in order to reduce religion-related prejudice in society.

Religious bias causes problems for people on several levels. It results in low self-esteem among member of minority or non-favoured groups, who tend to internalize dominant societal views even about themselves. It leads to discrimination against certain groups in terms of their access to education, professional training, employment, political power and so on. At local, regional and national levels it creates friction between different religious and non-religious sub-groups. And globally, it contributes to hostility and acts of military and economic aggression between nations, and undermines efforts at cultural, educational and economic cooperation.

The belief that one's religion is superior does not typically do as much harm in good times. People of a dominant religion are then inclined to be tolerant toward people of other religions, acknowledging that 'they are humans too'. But the very word 'tolerant' suggests that we are looking down on them and showing gracious restraint. When a crisis comes, a major conflict of interest, our restraint so easily evaporates. After all, we are holier than they, 'God is on our side', and while they are human, they are not as fully human as we: should not the right and good survive, prevail and be rewarded? And so we have purges, holy wars, inquisitions, pogroms and holocausts, not to mention countless less dramatic acts of prejudice.

Religious bias is not the only factor leading to persecution. In part, the notion of religious superiority is used as an excuse to do things we want to do anyway out of self-interest, hatred or whim. However, the idea that we are in the right is a major contributing factor. Further, so long as we have this belief it is difficult to work on and get rid of other negative attitudes. We cannot see them in perspective and recognize how inappropriate they are. For example, so long as Christians believe that Christianity is a better religion than Judaism, it will be impossible to overcome anti-Semitism in the West (which, by subtle processes, will continue to be transmitted to the East as well). And so long as people of European origin see native Americans as being (or having been) *mere* 'animists' and spirit worshippers, in some perjorative sense, it will be impossible to overcome racism towards native Indians in the Americas.

The inappropriateness of religious bias

As we have noted, a degree of inner-group orientation is important and acceptable. What must be ruled out, however, are unjust and dysfunctional forms of discrimination arising (at least in part) out of a belief in religious superiority.

Increasingly, as we learn more about other cultures and religions, it becomes implausible to think that there is one correct or superior religious (or non-religious) path. Observation of the lives of people throughout the world suggests that a great many religious (and non-religious systems) are able, if well developed and interpreted, to help lead people to a good, spiritual way of life and to 'salvation', in a broad sense of the term. It seems that there is not 'one true way' but rather 'many ways'.

Perhaps not *all* religions are capable of sustaining a good, spiritual way of life. The Jonestown religion, for example, which led to the massacre/suicide of so many of its members, including its young children, would seem to be beyond rehabilitation. However, in my view, all the religions which, century after century, have allowed and indeed helped communities to live at least moderately well should be accepted on an equal footing: as being potentially as good as each other. Among them are the so-called 'great religions': Hinduism, Jainism, Buddhism, Taoism, Confucianism, Judaism, Christianity, Islam and so on. To these should be added innumerable other religions, some of them 'polytheistic' and/or 'animistic', which have usually been left off the list of 'great religions'. They include the ancient and contemporary American Indian religions of North, Central and South America, the ancient religions of Mesopotamia, the Middle East and Greece, the ancient and so-called pagan religions of Europe, and the indigenous religions of Central Asia, the Far East, the South Pacific and Australasia.

It is likely that in some matters at a particular time one religion will be stronger than others. For example, it seems to me that Islam today is strong in the extent to which it takes political and economic issues seriously; Judaism is strong in its family and community orientation; and Hinduism and Buddhism show strength in the emphasis they place on connections between body, mind and spirit. However, other religions are likely to have strengths in areas in which these religions are (at present) somewhat weaker. And besides, individuals and groups within other religions can modify and reinterpret their religion so that it becomes strong in similar ways. All religions, because of their history, have unfortunate gaps; but these gaps can be filled, as they so often have been in the past. And the fact that different religions have different gaps at a particular time is no basis for saying *in general* that one is better than another.

Members of the so-called 'great religions', especially in the West, often seem to think that monotheistic religions are in general better than polytheistic religions. Insofar as some of the 'great religions', such as Hinduism and Christianity, appear to have polytheistic tendencies, scholars often go to considerable lengths to show that they are *really* monotheistic (or monistic) despite appearances. However, once again I think we should reject the idea of the general superiority of one set of religions over another. Either a polytheistic or a monotheistic viewpoint may be put to good (or bad) use. The universe contains both unity and diversity, and one purpose of a belief system is to help draw attention to this. Polytheism carries with it the danger of overemphasizing diversity, but equally monotheism (or monism) may overemphasize unity. Whichever position we adopt, we need to be careful to avoid its dangers.

Are all forms of religion acceptable then? Obviously not. Perhaps some religions are to be rejected completely (for example, the Jonestown case); and *all* religions must be open to continual criticism and reform. For example, a major weakness in most living religions today is their support of discrimination against women. Religions should, in my opinion, be quickly changed in substantial ways to overcome this fault. The point, however, is that there is no one religion (or non-religion) that is always and in general freer of faults or more open to reform than the others, so that members of that religion should feel superior and members of other religions should feel compelled to switch to that religion.[4] The Christian invaders of the Yucatan peninsula in the sixteenth century felt superior to the local practitioners of human sacrifice. However, while human sacrifice would appear to be unjustified, the Mayan religion which practised it had displayed many admirable characteristics over the centuries. And the European Christians came fresh from their inquisitions and Jewish, Muslim and Protestant persecutions and killings at home, and proceeded to carry out genocide in the New World. Which is better, a religion that sacrifices people to 'the gods', or one that tortures and kills people in the name of 'God'? Neither religion had reason to feel superior to the other, and both had a great many weaknesses to overcome. And if non-religious critics are inclined to rush in and say that the solution lies in doing away with religion, let them first examine the human rights record of non-religious regimes. Some have been rather satisfactory while others have not: in general their record has been neither better nor worse than that of regimes with official religious connections.

Some might argue that belief in the 'divine', the 'absolute', the 'infinite' or the 'supernatural' which characterizes many religions, is essential to enable us to maintain high spiritual and moral ideals. Without it we sink into an easy 'cosmological religion' or a 'secular humanism' which accepts the present world as defining what it right and sees humans as 'the measure of all things'.[5] However, as we have already noted, the facts of everyday and historical experience contradict such a view. Indeed, the view seems patently absurd in the modern West, where 'otherworldly' religion has participated in a rape of the earth which so many so-called cosmological religions would have seen as evil.

In fact people who do not believe in the absolute or the supernatural, or even in the perfectability of human nature, typically achieve as high a level of spirituality and moral goodness as those who have such beliefs. And it is not difficult to understand why this is so. While extreme ideals have their place (and even 'secular humanists' often make use of them), the important point is that both groups are proceeding in the same direction. Whether perfection is ultimately possible (in this life or the next) is a matter of speculation. What matters in practice is that both supernaturalists and non-supernaturalists see the value of moving *as far as possible* towards ideals of spirituality and morality. Supernaturalists, to be practical, are forced to develop intermediate goals similar to those of non-supernaturalists and adopt feasible means of achieving them. In fact, then, the specific goals and methods of the two groups are much the same, as are the results.

People who lack the motivation provided by belief in the supernatural can nevertheless be inspired by acceptance of what I would call the 'transcendent': that is, those aspects of reality which go beyond but remain connected to our present experience and way of life. Transcendentalism, in this sense, involves being constantly open to the novel, the unusual, the wonderful and the ideal; but unlike supernaturalism it does not envisage a *separate* divine realm, and it does not require that we believe in some ultimate, infinite end–point of our enquiries and strivings. 'Transcendentalists' are just as critical as supernaturalists of reductionist, materialistic, short-sighted approaches to life, but have a different set of concepts and symbols to use in rising above them.

It is often assumed that we have to believe that our religion (or way of life) is *the* true one if we are to be committed to it. Such an assumption underlies much of the fervent advocacy that characterizes religious instruction in sectarian settings. But this view is simply mistaken. We may draw an analogy here with patriotism. I may love my country, cherish its traditions, be loyal to it and even regard it as the best country in the world for *me* (because of my upbringing, distinctive needs and personal ties); but none of this requires that I believe it to be the most lovable, the most worthy of loyalty, the best country in the world for *everyone*. (It is very unlikely that it is, as patterns of migration and re-migration suggest.) Similarly, strong commitment to a religion does not require a belief that it is the one true way or that those who belong to it are superior to those who do not. Indeed, paradoxically, the effort to believe that one's religion is *the* true one often gets in the way of a firm commitment to it, since doubt keeps breaking through. One may support a *good* religion (like a *good* marriage) the more unswervingly and energetically if one does not feel the need to keep convincing oneself that it is the *best*.

It is true, however, that once we accept the notion of 'many ways', our commitment to our own religion will take a somewhat different *form*. We will be prepared to endorse overarching goals that are pursued by members of other religions and 'non-religious' paths as well as by ourselves. We will view the distinctive myths, symbols and practices of our religion as our means of achieving goals which people of other paths are achieving, equally successfully on the whole, by other means.[6] We will not look down on people of other religions, but rather have a sense of fellow-feeling with them and be prepared to learn from their achievements and work collaboratively with them in attempting to answer the large questions of life. Where we recognize gaps in the worldview and way of life offered by our religion we will be prepared to go without prejudice to other traditions — both religious and non-religious — to look for satisfactory ways of filling the gaps. We will be glad when we encounter a high degree of spirituality and religiousness in people of other traditions, no longer viewing it as a threat to the status of our own. We will be committed to our own religion, but without denigrating the religions of others.

Religious bias in and through the schools

In order to grasp the extent of the problem of religious bias in schools, we must keep in mind a point made repeatedly in the preceding chapters, namely that schools are strongly influenced by the surrounding society and have a comprehensive cultural impact on students. They are not narrowly task-oriented institutions with a neutral instructional and child care role to fulfil, even if those in authority might wish to create that impression. Rather they tend to reflect and reproduce society's deepest beliefs, values and attitudes.

Accordingly, when widespread manifestations of religious bias are found in the larger society, even among 'liberal' thinkers, the school should be aware that it has a problem. When someone of the eminence of Alfred North Whitehead dismisses 'tribal religions' as representing a 'primitive phase of religion, dominated by ritual and emotion'[7]; when sociologist Robert Bellah criticizes the traditional religions of China and Japan for failing to grasp 'the radical transcendence of God' and hence for lacking the insight of Judaism, Christianity and Islam into the need for 'a new kind of universalism and individualism'[8]; when liberal theologian Harvey Cox argues that the ideals of the Greek polis left something to be desired because 'the universality and radical openness of Christianity were not yet present to dispel the remnants of tribalism'[9]; and when *very* liberal theologian and sociologist Gregory Baum states that non-Christians have access to salvation but that 'the divine self-communication which takes place in Jesus in an exhaustive and definitive way' is only available to others 'in a hidden tentative, and provisional way'[10]; then the school should recognize that it has a major task of re-education to perform, insofar as it is able.

Religious bias in the wider society enters the school in part through the beliefs, attitudes, language and concepts of teachers and students. Even where religion is not formally taught or discussed, comments are made and attitudes expressed which place certain religions in a better light than others. And negative assumptions about various religions are transmitted through value laden terms such as 'pagan', 'infidel', 'priest', 'animist', 'heretic', 'fanatic', 'unbeliever', 'polytheist', 'witch doctor'.

Religious bias also comes into the school through textbooks, works of literature, reference books, films and other learning materials. The prejudices of authors, editors and producers are added to those of teachers and students. Often these are subtly expressed through the choice of words and phrases or merely through the relative time alloted to the exploits (good or bad) of representatives of respective religions; but such subtlety if anything increases the damage done. Religiously biased works of literature present special difficulties since attempts to censor them are strenuously resisted. While on balance the school is often justified in having students study them, rarely are adequate steps taken to counteract their biasing influence; a fact which in part betrays the bias of the teachers, librarians and administrators who insist that students be exposed to these works.

Preference is often given to a particular religion or set of religions in prayers, songs, ceremonies and formal speeches. As in the case of literature, this may be difficult to avoid (although we must keep up the effort) since it is an integral part of the life of the dominant culture. However, once again, seldom is there a systematic attempt to overcome the prejudicial consequences of these practices through discussion and the provision of relevant information.

The staffing of schools frequently favours one religion over others. It is likely that the majority of teachers, and especially those in more senior positions, will be of the dominant religion. In most Western countries they will largely be Christian, even in areas where the majority of students are not. In countries such as the US and the UK, Protestants will be over-represented; and in France and Italy, an undue proportion will be Catholics. The disproportionate staffing influences the type of curriculum chosen and the patterns of thought and behaviour that are approved in the school. It also makes those students who belong to less dominant religions feel significantly less secure, and deprives them of an array of role models with whom they may identify.

It is not only the staff at the local school who may present a problem; at the school board and government levels they are usually supported by an army of elected and lay people, educational officials and consultants who, in keeping with their status and seniority, are largely of the dominant religion. It is quite common in jurisdictions where adherents of two major religions are equally numerous in the general population to find an overwhelming majority of members of one of those religions in senior educational posts. This means that insofar as what happens locally is affected by the general regulations, curriculum guidelines, learning materials and pedagogical approaches which emanate from central authorities, the already heavy bias in favour of the dominant religion is accentuated.

Another potential source of religious bias, of course, is formal religious instruction, in cases where schools offer it. Until recent times, teachers of religion in schools almost invariably presented their religion as the correct or superior one. Today, many religion teachers are trying to encourage a more tolerant outlook toward other religions and some follow a comparative or 'world religions' or 'multi-faith' approach. However, an even-handed approach is very difficult to attain, especially if teachers believe — as most still do — that their own religion *is* superior. The superiority of the dominant religion is so easily suggested through the very categories of analysis that are employed, and in many other subtle ways.

Obviously, having special religious schools associated with a particular religion can help in the entrenchment of religious bias. This *need* not be so, since a religious school could adopt a pluralist approach to religion. And one should not assume that religious schools will necessarily be more religiously biased than schools with no official religious affiliation. For example, in many Western countries in which Protestant Christianity is dominant, Catholics have had to form their own school network in 'self-defence' against a state system which has a strong though often subtle Protestant bias in terms of staffing, curriculum content, point of view and general ethos. However, the pressures on religious schools to take a biased position are great. Very often such schools are looked upon by parents and especially the professional religious community as one of the chief means whereby the superiority of their religion is to be brought home to their children. Even where the teachers disagree with this perspective they are often effectively required to promote it while in school.

Combating religious bias

As I have suggested, a major cause (and ingredient) of religious bias is the belief that a particular religion or path is superior to others. In order to overcome religious bias, then, a substantial activity of re-examining religion must take place with a view to eliminating this type of assumption from our thinking. Such a re-examination should be conducted in many forums — universities, seminaries and the popular media, for example — but the school as an educational institution has a significant role to play. The details of how this role might be fulfilled will be explored at greater length in Chapter 14 when we consider religious education in general. However, we might note that both the formal and the informal curriculum of the school offer many opportunities to question traditional religious bias and move toward a pluralistic outlook.

In schools with a religion program, a large proportion of the time available should be devoted to the study of religions other than the dominant one(s) of the school's community. This is important symbolically, to show through time allocation the respect due to other religions, and it is necessary to enable students to develop an understanding and appreciation of other religions. There should also be extensive consideration of the nature and role of religion in general, as a universal phenomenon, including a review of the many similarities (as well as the differences) between religions. In particular, there should be explicit treatment of the issue of religious bias. A sustained effort should be made to help students see that their religion (if they have one) is not superior or *the* true way; but that they can, nevertheless, be proud of it and strongly committed to it.

Where a school does not have a religious studies program, every effort should be made to establish one. Apart from the fact that religious (or religion-like) phenomena are of crucial importance to human beings — we all need a worldview, a way of life, a sense of meaning in life and so forth — religious studies are essential to enable students to understand religious individuals and cultures and deal successfully with conflicts between religious sub-groups and between religious and non-religious people. Meanwhile, until a formal program has been set up, issues of religion and religious bias can be dealt with in the context of existing subjects such as literature, history, geography, social studies, family studies and science.

At a less formal level, care should be taken to ensure that religious bias is avoided in the language used and the attitudes expressed both inside and outside the classroom. Students of different religions must be given equal privileges and respect, and an equitable policy must be developed with regard to religious holidays and observances. Strong policies and procedures should be established for dealing with religion-related abusive language and behaviour.[11] More positively, the school should help to arrange activities such as fairs, celebrations, concerts, art shows and lecture series which promote understanding, respect and self-respect in relation to religion.

A central question, of course, for any attempt to reduce religious bias in schools is how teachers are to be selected and trained. The selection of people for teaching is to a considerable degree governed by economic and social factors beyond the immediate control of the education community; but attempts should nevertheless be made to achieve a broader religious representation in the teaching profession (and at 'higher' echelons as well). When we turn to teacher education, the possibilities for improving the present situation appear to be greater. To a large extent people are religiously prejudiced because it has never occurred to them to be otherwise: they know very little about other religions, have been taught from early childhood that their religion is the correct one, and have simply assumed that they could not be committed to their religion unless they saw it as superior. The religious prejudice of teachers, then, could be significantly reduced through more adequate religious education at the pre- and in-service levels, including experiential programs in the community and, if possible, in other countries. And as the treatment of religion in schools becomes more satisfactory, partly as a result of these measures, candidates for teaching will already have a less biased approach to religion by the time they begin their university studies and professional training. A cycle of combating religious prejudice may be set in motion which will steadily become more effective.

Notes and References

1 Some of the material in this chapter is taken, with permission and modification, from Beck, C. (1985) 'Religion and Education', *Teachers College Record*, 87, 2, pp. 259–70.
2 Baum, G. (1972) *New Horizon: Theological Essays*, New York, Paulist Press, p. 129.
3 Many, of course, would see those also as 'religions' in a broad sense of the term. Here, however, I will use the words 'religion' and 'religious' largely in their popular sense. A distinction betweeen popular and broad senses of these terms will be developed in Chapter 14.
4 The attitude being proposed here is captured well by Wilfred Cantwell Smith in discussing the notion of converting to Hinduism. He says: 'Any outsider who wishes to become a Hindu has misunderstood a fundamental Hindu outlook. A sophisticated Hindu might well say: "What: adopt *these* means? These symbols? Haven't you some of your own? The people in the next village have different ones . . ." '. In 'Philosophia, as One of the Religious Traditions of Humankind,' in Jean-Claude Galey (Ed) (1984) *Différences, Valeurs, Hiérarchie: Textes Offerts à Louis Dumont*, Paris, Editions de l'Ecole des Hautes Etudes, pp. 253–79.
5 Robert Bellah uses the term 'cosmological religion' to refer to religions in which 'nature, society, and self are seen as fused in a more or less compact unity'. Bellah, R. (1970) *Beyond Belief*, New York, Harper and Row, p. 101. He is concerned that such a religion does not provide an adequate basis for high ideals.
6 As Paul Tillich says, 'the criterion of every faith is the ultimacy of the ultimate which it tries to express. The self-criticism of every faith is the insight into the *relative* validity of the concrete symbols in which it appears.' Tillich, P. (1957) *Dynamics of Faith*, New York, Harper and Row, p. 123. Italics added.
7 Whitehead, A.N. (1974) *Religion in the Making*, New York, New American Library, Meridian, pp. 22–7, 41–2.
8 Bellah, R., *op. cit.*, p. 101.
9 Cox, H. (1966) *The Secular City*, rev. ed., New York, Macmillan, pp. 9 and 10.
10 Baum, G., *op. cit.*, p. 95.
11 Some of the suggestions made by Madan Sarup for handling racial incidents are relevant here. See Sarup, M. (1986) *The Politics of Multiracial Education*, London, Routledge and Kegan Paul, especially pp. 4–8.

Chapter 9

Racism

Racism, like religious bias, is transmitted to the school from the larger society. And the school in turn contributes to racism through biased teaching about race and discriminatory treatment of students of various races. Many of the principles discussed in relation to religious bias in the preceding chapter apply equally to racism, and some similar corrective measures are in order. However, the area presents many distinctive issues and problems.

The question of how to deal with racial differences is likely to be a persistent one in the wealthy countries of the world. While many are attempting to avoid immigration which would increase their racial mix, as the world becomes 'smaller' and more interconnected there will be compelling reasons for admitting certain people of other races, whether because they are experiencing extreme hardship (e.g. poverty, persecution, displacement, family separation) or because of the contribution they can make (e.g. through their expertise or wealth). And even without new immigration, recognizable differences of race would continue in most cases because of the presence of 'visible minorities' and also racial minorities which are not as noticeable physically but which maintain distinctiveness through religion, culture, family names and the like.

In countries and regions where there are virtually no differences of race, it will still be important to deal with issues of race and racism in schools. With improved communications, increased travel and growth in international and multinational enterprises, it will be necessary for people to interact with members of other races. And in these interactions, racist beliefs and attitudes will carry the potential for considerable harm to all parties.

What is a race?

I will use the term 'race' here to refer to a group of humans who have a *somewhat* common biological history and, as a result, some *relatively* distinctive physical characteristics. The qualifications 'somewhat' and 'relatively' are important. Many races are in fact rather loose biological groupings, with considerable racial mixture in their distant past and some interbreeding with other races more recently; and particular members of a race are often indistinguishable in appearance from members of one or more other races. Racial characteristics, then, are typical rather than essential to every case. An individual who is West African or Nordic or Semitic, for example, may in fact look like a typical member of another race.

Sometimes the expression 'the human race' is used. But the concept of race implied by this usage, if it is legitimate at all, has nothing to do with what we are talking about in the present context. The differences between people of different (human) races are minimal when compared with differences between human and non-human species.

Racial distinctions are made at many different levels. Within a given race there are usually sub-races, each of which could itself be described as a race. When different sub-races are lumped together into a general classification, there is great danger of stereotyping. For example, expressions such as 'the Black race', 'the White race', and 'the Oriental race' are potentially very misleading and perhaps should not be used at all. They often betray a very limited awareness on the part of the speaker of differences within the category in question. Even terms such as 'Anglo-Saxons', 'Blacks of African origin', 'Semites', and 'East Indians' are of dubious legitimacy because they ignore differences which are noticeable to the members of these 'races', if not to outsiders.

Race, as I have defined it, is to be distinguished from culture and ethnicity. Racial differences are genetically transferred, whereas cultural and ethnic ones are not. Children reared from birth in a particular cultural or ethnic group take on the typical values, outlooks, skills and behaviour of that group, regardless of their race. Sometimes the members of an ethnic group are all from the same race: for example East Indians in Kenya or Anglo-Saxon Protestants in New Zealand. But on the one hand, the races involved here clearly extend beyond the particular ethnic groups; and on the other hand, the ethnic groups have many distinctive features which are not racial. Even if one uses a racial label to refer to an ethnic group, this should be seen as a matter of convenience and not as a sign that race and ethnicity are the same thing.

Definitions of race are seldom neutral. For example, those who believe that some races are superior to others in intelligence, industriousness, self-control and so forth, tend to include intellectual, moral and other characteristics in their concept of race. By tying race simply to physical characteristics, I have given expression to my belief that values, abilities and behaviours are *not* race related: that every race has, genetically, the same range of potential in these areas and any systematic differences that occur are the result of socio-economic, cultural and other accidental factors. Such a position does not preclude studies which look for a genetically based correlation between race and non-physical traits. But it assumes that the evidence to date does not justify building such a connection into the concept of race.[1]

If we define race in terms of physical characteristics, as I have suggested, it becomes apparent that a strong case could be made for doing away with talk of race completely. While there are certainly differences of skin colour, physical structure and so forth, these might reasonably be regarded as too unimportant to warrant attention. They have nothing to do with human well being, and are entirely trivial when compared with non-racial traits such as temperament, attitudes, feelings and behaviour patterns. Perhaps we can look forward to the day when interest in racial features will virtually disappear, and references to race will be considered irrelevant except in rare instances. The present discussion of race, then, should be viewed not as implying the long-term importance of racial distinctions, but rather as an attempt to clarify and resolve problems which we are currently experiencing in this area.

Racial prejudice and discrimination

Noting a person's race as such is not necessarily a problem (although, as I have suggested, it should not be taken too seriously, and may one day be viewed as irrelevant). Racism occurs when people are seen as *inferior* because of their race and are *discriminated against* either because of their supposed inferiority or simply because they are of a particular race. Terms such as 'racism', 'racial prejudice' and 'racial discrimination' refer to *illegitimate* attitudes and behaviour related to race. 'Racism', obviously, is a pejorative term.

The main argument against racial prejudice and discrimination is that, since race is merely a matter of inherited physical characteristics, it is simply not an appropriate basis on which to make judgments or decisions. It is irrelevant, for example, to the selection of people as workers, students, parliamentarians, friends, spouses or fellow citizens. As we saw in Chapter 1, the ultimate goal in decision-making is to promote human well being or 'the good life' for ourselves and others; and race has nothing whatever to do with the attainment of this goal.

Sometimes, as we saw in the previous section, *ethnic* groups within a country or region have a racial character. And in these cases, a degree of 'inner group' favouritism may be appropriate: friendship and communal life, as we have observed before, presuppose a relationship of special regard and mutual assistance. However, with respect to cases of this kind it should be noted that (a) the favouritism is on the basis not of race but of ethnicity which happens to run along racial lines; (b) people of the same race who do not belong to the ethnic group will not receive the same special treatment; and (c) the favouritism must be kept within strict limits if it is not to disrupt wider communal, national and global life and illegitimately affect other people's welfare.

Sometimes, to extend this point further, a race may constitute a kind of 'global ethnic group' which must defend its own interests to a degree. Some races in the world today experience almost universal discrimination, whether directly as minority groups within countries dominated by other races, or indirectly in their 'own' countries through global economic, cultural and military action. It may be appropriate, then, for such a race (or group of races) to develop a global sense of solidarity and peoplehood and work internationally to further the well being of its members. However, once again, the decision to adopt such an approach is not 'racist' in that it assumes that the race in question is superior or of special importance. Rather the race has been forced into a concerted defensive posture by the actions of others who have shown prejudice and discrimination toward it. The members of the race will almost certainly look forward to the day when they can return to relating to other people simply on an individual level and on the basis of the various communities they belong to, without reference to race.

One of the biggest hindrances to overcoming racism lies in the notion that there is virtue in racial purity: that it is in some sense a pity to mix races. Historically, this view has often derived from a race supremacist outlook: since our race is superior, we must not dilute it through mixture with inferior races. But some people seem to have a dislike for racial mixture *as such*, even between races which they respect equally. However, this does not make sense biologically: mixture of races does not threaten health and survival, indeed it may promote it. Also, it is not a reasonable position from an aesthetic point of view: people of mixed race appear to be at least as attractive as people who are racially 'pure' (whatever that means, given the mixed origins of so many races). And sheer uniformity is hardly a solid principle on which to base aesthetic judgment. It is true that we appreciate the familiar; but we also appreciate that which is novel and surprising.

Some people seem to be concerned not so much about the biological mixing of races as the juxtaposition of races within a nation: they assert, in particular, that it is important that *their* nation remain racially homogeneous. The reasons for this may again be partly race supremacist (the dominant race in my country is the best one, so let's not add others); or partly aesthetic (it offends my sense of beauty to see too many people of other races or mixed race around). But sometimes people seem to believe that the coexistence of races will somehow, in itself, weaken the nation: economically, culturally, militarily and so forth. Once again, we must simply reject this assumption. Racial characteristics as such do not affect the economy, the culture or the security of a country, and so the juxtaposition of different races within a nation will not by itself affect them either. If the different races form into groups hostile to each other, that is a different matter. However, this is the result not of race but of attitudes toward race, or the linking of race with other conflicts which in principle can be kept separate. Racially related conflict is certainly a problem in many countries. But we must be careful not to *attribute* the conflict to differences in race, so that we see it as inevitable. It is notions such as that of racial superiority and purity, along with vested interests and discrimination, which give rise to the conflict, not the mingling of races.

Perhaps the ultimate sign of a non-racist outlook is the acceptance of mixed-race families. I believe that the time has come in our global village to remove all objections to a shift in this direction. As young people (and older people) meet members of other races and find among them 'kindred spirits', they should be encouraged to form lasting friendships and marriage relationships with whoever is most suitable, regardless of race. Apart from the advantages to the couples in question, such a practice will be of great symbolic value, signalling the irrelevance of race in even the most intimate spheres of life. Of course, often the most suitable marriage partner will be of one's own race because of ethnic ties and historical links between race and way of life. But this is a matter of cultural and not racial compatibility, and there will be many exceptions. And as the incidence of mixed-race families increases, these traditional cultural patterns will change at an accelerating pace.

Many people may experience a sense of loss, at least initially, with the passing of distinct races. However, we should recognize that this feeling is in part based on misinformation about the purity of races in the past, and misconceptions of a racist type about the importance of racial divisions. Further, we should realize that the dropping of race-centred outlooks and behaviour is essential for building the kind of global community that will be needed for human well being in the future. Any loss of the familiar will be more than compensated for by a reduction in inter-group conflict and the creation of rich and exciting new communities and institutions.

Dealing with racism in schools

Given the pervasiveness of racism in virtually all existing societies, there will be no quick solutions. However, as with other societal and global problems, the school can play a part. And because of the extent to which racism derives from misinformation and misunderstanding, the school as an educational institution has a particularly significant role.

To begin with, in the general structure and life of the school there are many measures that can be taken. For example, attention should be given to increasing the racial mix in the teaching and administrative staff and the student body, both to set an example of non-discrimination and to ensure that students have an opportunity to get to know people of other races under favourable circumstances. Streaming or tracking procedures which isolate and disadvantage students of certain races should be replaced by a comprehensive, mixed achievement approach as outlined in Chapter 2, above. Teachers in their speech and behaviour should show equal respect to students of different races and should encourage students to do the same: name calling and the telling of racist jokes should be treated with the same seriousness as other major infractions of school rules. Teachers should attempt to establish a close relationship with students of minority races and offer them moral support and special assistance, where necessary, to help overcome the effects of discrimination. And racist attacks within the school grounds should be strictly forbidden, and procedures worked out for dealing with conflict situations quickly and effectively, preferably without seeking assistance from agencies external to the school.[2]

At the level of formal instruction, there is a great deal of work to be done.[3] Simply by ignoring the culture and history of certain races one conveys the message that people of that race have little to contribute. And by giving information about the deprivation of various Third World countries without mentioning earlier more glorious eras or explaining the causes of the current state of affairs (colonial domination and economic exploitation, for example) one may give the impression that the races in these countries are by nature passive and inept. In order to help overcome misconceptions of this kind, students must be shown 'that the disparities in wealth and development are not "natural" but are "social", that they are *created*.' The school has a responsibility to explain to students 'the *processes* by which inequality came into being and by which it is perpetuated'.[4]

Racism is often embedded in the textbooks we use. As Sarup comments, 'schools can covertly make racism seem reasonable through their teaching materials.'[5] Clearly, a major task is gradually to eliminate racially biased textbooks from the schools and replace them with non-racist materials. However, in the meantime teachers can use existing textbooks to provide illustrations of the pervasiveness of racism in society. Sarup suggests that to censor biased material 'may be less useful than to give children the concepts and skills which would enable them to recognize *the underlying assumptions in a text*'.[6] This may be a feasible way of approaching works of literature which it is important for students to be exposed to but which include racist elements.

In general, it should be stressed that modifying the curriculum to overcome racial bias need not be a negative activity. As Alma Craft has noted, teachers 'are finding that the process of permeating the curriculum (and its assessment) with a multicultural and anti-racist perspective is providing an opportunity to improve the quality and integrity of their subject courses and materials'. She describes, for example, how social science and social studies can be enriched by 'discussion of the causes and effects of intercultural tension' and 'critical analysis of the "facts" of racism and discrimination'; and how the study of biology can be expanded to play 'a key role in challenging pseudoscientific theories of "race", through careful investigation of the role of inheritance and environment in "racial" characteristics.'[7]

The central teaching task of the school in this area, I believe, is to challenge systematically the notion that racial distinctions are important and that some races are superior to others. It is often suggested that the school's role is to foster 'racial understanding and tolerance'. However, as Robin Richardson observes, expressions such as 'sympathetic understanding of different cultures and races' are extremely vague and their meaning must be specified in detail before they can give direction to teachers.[8] Indeed, we might understand, sympathize with and tolerate members of another race while still regarding them as inferior. *Full* acceptance, as distinct from mere tolerance, of other races is impossible to attain so long as students sincerely believe — as many do — that certain races are above others in moral, intellectual and other capacities.

In dealing with racism, it is important not to adopt an unduly moralistic, 'holier than thou' approach. As one commentator has said:

> Everything in our society conspires to make us feel bad about ourselves, hence to project our badness onto scapegoats. Making racists feel bad about themselves fuels racism in the long run . . . . We need to acknowledge with them our own racism, give examples of our own hang-ups, say what enabled us to change . . . .[9]

Most of us have racist beliefs, attitudes and behaviour patterns in varying degrees, and it is easy to slip into racism even if we are opposed to it in the abstract.[10] At an intellectual level, racism has not been studied closely enough in modern times for the ordinary person to be armed against it; and at an attitudinal and behavioural level (as well as the intellectual), we are so easily influenced by the society around us. Accordingly, while engaging in a thorough-going attempt to root out racism, we should approach the area with humility.

Notes and References

1 Reference to research on this issue will be made in Chapter 12, when discussing genetic theories of socio-economic success.
2 On several of these points, see Sarup, M. (1986) *The Politics of Multiracial Education*, Routledge and Kegan Paul, London, especially pp. 4–9; Craft, A. (1986) 'Multicultural teaching', in Wellington, J. (Ed) *Controversial Issues in the Curriculum*, Oxford, Blackwell, pp. 77–8; and Kendall, F. (1983) *Diversity in the Classroom*, New York, Teachers College Press, pp. 1–5 and 32–5.
3 See Sarup, M., *op. cit.*, especially pp. 9–10 and 49–55; and Craft, A., *op. cit.*, pp. 78–80.
4 Sarup, M., *op. cit.*, p. 51.
5 *Ibid.*, p. 9. On racism in learning materials, see also Saracho, O. and Spodek, B. (Eds), (1983) *Understanding the Multicultural Experience in Early Childhood Education*, Washington, DC, National Association for the Education of Young Children, Chs. 6 and 7.
6 Sarup, M., *op. cit.*, p. 52.
7 Craft, A., *op. cit.*, pp. 78–9.
8 Richardson, R. (1982) 'Culture and justice: Key concepts in World Studies and multicultural education', in Hicks, D. and Townley, C. (Eds) *Teaching World Studies*, London, Longman, pp. 20 and 24.
9 Paton, K. 'Talking with (other) racists', quoted in Richardson, R., *op. cit.*, p. 27.
10 On unconscious racism, see Kendall, F., *op. cit.*, pp. 4–5.

Chapter 10

Ethnic Bias

We have been discussing religious and racial bias in general terms. Frequently, however, an 'ethnic' sub-group of people of a given religion, race, national background or the like will experience prejudice and discrimination in a particular national or regional setting. Bias against such groups requires special attention both because ethnicity is a distinctive phenomenon and because it is in relation to specific ethnic groups that religious, racial and other types of prejudice are most often expressed.

The nature of ethnicity

Ethnic groups are usually identified by reference to one or more of the following: a country or region of origin, a religion, a race, a language. However, it is important to recognize that these are in part just convenient labels. An ethnic group has in addition a somewhat distinctive *culture* or *way of life*, deriving in part from the common background of its members but also from more recent individual and group life in their present home. (In the case of indigenous peoples, of course, their 'place of origin' and 'present home' are the same). This local distinctiveness of culture is crucial, since people of the same language, religion, race or (previous) nationality vary enormously around the globe in characteristics and mode of life.

We might note that the importance of culture to ethnicity explains why in many countries multi-ethnic government policies and education programs are appropriately (though somewhat euphemistically) referred to as 'multicultural'. I say euphemistically, because many people would rather talk of — and face up to — cultural diversity than other more 'unpleasant' matters such as religious bigotry, racism and economic inequality. But the usage is also appropriate since it is important to stress the cultural diversity present in a multi-ethnic situation. We must remember, however, whatever terminology we use, that there is more to ethnicity and ethnic conflict than culture. We will address this issue again more fully at the end of the present chapter.

Because of the cultural component in ethnicity, it may seem strange to refer to a racial group as a type of ethnic group. As I argued in the previous chapter, race is simply a matter of physical characteristics and has nothing to do with values, outlooks, way of life and the like. However, it often happens that in a particular country the members of a given race *also* have a somewhat distinctive culture, in part because they have a common country or region of origin and in part because of similar experiences and treatment (perhaps precisely because of their race) in their present country. Accordingly, it is legitimate to refer to them as an ethnic group. But one must constantly bear in mind that their common culture is a historical phenomenon, not in any sense biological in origin, and that members of the same race in other parts of the world often have a quite different culture.

Ethnic groups are typically specific to a particular country, region or city: for example, Palestinian Arabs on the West Bank, French Canadians, Irish Catholics in the US (or, more specifically, in New York or Boston), Tamil Indians in Malaysia, Toronto WASPS, Hungarian Jews in Australia (or Sydney) and West Indians of African descent in Britain. The term 'ethnic group' is sometimes used more broadly to refer to, for example, all Anglo-Saxons, all Blacks of African descent, all American Indians or all Jews; and as we saw when discussing race, this global perspective is sometimes appropriate, especially if the group in question have been subjected to almost universal discrimination and need to pull together to establish their rights around the globe. However, such a usage should normally be avoided. The more geographically scattered the members of the group are, the greater the likelihood that seeing them as a single group will lead to serious distortion because they are in fact very diverse.

It should be noted that many ethnic groups are composed of immigrants who are counted as 'ethnic' because of their migrant status. For example, East Indians in Britain are referred to as an ethnic group even though they would not have been so described in India. In a similar manner, people talk of 'the Italian community' in New York and 'the Greek community' in Melbourne. While the members of these groups may have things in common because they have all migrated to the same country and have shared many similar experiences since they arrived, they in fact have come from very diverse geographic, religious, racial and linguistic backgrounds in their country of origin.

There is a further complexity arising out of the immigrant status of many ethnic groups. The characteristics and way of life of the members of these groups vary greatly depending on the amount of time that has elapsed since they (or their forebears) migrated. Students of ethnicity have found it essential to distinguish between different generations of immigrants of a given group. This underscores still further the diversity that exists in so-called 'ethnic groups' and which often goes unnoticed. The diversity is overlooked especially in the case of 'visible minorities', where outsiders tend to assume uniformity among group members even though many of them have been in the country for several generations.

In most countries today the diversity of religions, races, national origins and so forth is such that it is best to see *everyone* as a member of one or more ethnic groups. Each sub-group, large or small, takes on an ethnic character simply through contrast with other sub-groups. While to established majority or dominant groups this approach may initially seem strange, there is much to be said for it. To begin with, the word 'ethnic' derives from the Greek *ethnikos* meaning 'heathen', obviously a pejorative term: if everyone is seen as ethnic, the etymology of the word (insofar as it is known) will not cause difficulties. Further, and more importantly, for established groups to see themselves as ethnic in nature may lead to greater self-knowledge, and in particular help them to see themselves simply as different from other groups rather than as superior. And finally, such a usage may make people less inclined to assume that there is a stable, 'natural' culture to which newcomers and other minorities — 'the ethnics' — must eventually conform, and encourage rather the concept of a constantly developing common culture to which all sub-groups contribute (while retaining their own identity).

The role of ethnicity

Andrew Greeley, one of the most important contemporary writers on ethnicity, has commented that:

> Ethnic groups are something like the Rocky Mountains or the Atlantic Ocean — whether we like them or not really doesn't matter very much; they are concrete realities with which we must cope, and condemning or praising them is a waste of time.[1]

Despite this, however, Greeley spends some time minimizing the harm that ethnic groups do and drawing attention to their virtues. For example, in *Why Can't They Be Like Us*, he says:

> They keep cultural traditions alive, provide us with preferred associates, help organize the social structure, offer opportunities for mobility and success and enable (people) to identify themselves in the face of the threatening chaos of a large and impersonal society.[2]

Greeley is opposed to the attitude 'Why can't they be like us?' and to placing undue pressure on ethnic groups to assimilate. He presents what he calls a 'stewpot' (as opposed to a 'melting pot') theory of society, and defends the right of ethnic groups to continue as identifiable 'lumps' in the 'stew' and resist being 'melted down' into a unified social order. He observes, however, that ethnic groups will and must engage in 'dynamic innovation'. Speaking specifically of the situation in the US, he says that 'it is in the nature of the stewpot model that in some ways members of American ethnic groups may be becoming more like one another, and in other ways more different.'[3]

While I believe Greeley's rather positive view is justified, we should note also that it is possible to go too far in stressing the importance of ethnicity in general and of particular ethnic groups. It is true that most cultural traditions should be kept alive, both for the sake of the 'adherents' of those traditions and so that they can feed into the general fund of ideas and ways of life of a society; but we should realize that this can often be done without large scale ethnic group *membership* in the traditional sense. Rather, there can be a small group of 'priests' or devotees who constantly ensure that certain ideas and practices are disseminated throughout the society, in much the way that Zen Buddhism permeates Japanese society today. Very few people *are* Zen Buddhists, but the general impact of the tradition cannot be denied. Similarly, one might say, the values and outlook on life of Aristotle are constantly injected into Western culture by a relatively small group of devoted scholars and popularizers; and we all benefit from this without having to become 'Aristotelians'.

Greeley's other arguments for ethnicity may be seen as general arguments for having sub-groups or smaller communities within a society. Once again, we must agree that he is correct: a society *does* need sub-groups which provide a division of labour and 'help organize the social structure'; and individuals *do* need small-group identity within 'a large and impersonal society', congenial 'associates' to live and work with and a familiar and manageable communal context within which they can achieve 'mobility and success.' But this does not necessarily require *ethnic* group membership. Often the same ends can be achieved just as well by other forms of association such as public service clubs, school and university alumni associations, local chapters of political parties, housing cooperatives, neighbourhood clubs, ecological societies, peace groups and so on. Community life is enormously important and has been most unfortunately neglected in the modern West, as writers such as Robert Paul Wolff in *The Poverty of Liberalism* and Robert Bellah in *Habits of the Heart* have established. But community life need not always be ethnic in nature.

One reason for not attaching *too* much significance to ethnicity is that ethnic labelling tends to overemphasize place of origin, religion, race and language. As I argued in the previous chapter, race as such is among the most trivial of human attributes and the less it is noticed and talked about the better. To *define* people in terms of their race is a practice we should try to eliminate as quickly as social conditions allow. Place of origin, while of somewhat more importance, is just one of a great many things we might want to know about a person; and to emphasize it strongly with reference to people who have deliberately left their previous home and are attempting to establish a new life in a new country or region seems perverse. The role of religion in one's life varies from individual to individual, but it is clear that a very large proportion of people who have a religion only wish to apply it from time to time and do not normally wish to be *thought of* in terms of their religion. And language, too, is only of limited significance in defining a person's culture and way of life. French Canadians, insofar as one can generalize at all, are rather different from Belgian French, who in turn differ from French people from France. And among English speaking people there is enormous diversity in culture and way of life, both from one country to another and within various countries.

We must remember that ethnic identification is very often imposed on people by others, and is frequently used for harm rather than good. It was the non-Jews in Berlin, Vienna and Budapest in the '30s and '40s who ferreted out information on who was Jewish and who was not; it is the white people in South Africa who have drawn attention to the blacks and the 'coloureds' and deliberated at length on whether or not East Indians and South East Asians are 'coloured' and if so to what effect. People who stress their *own* ethnicity often do so largely in self-defence, either to try to boost their morale — 'I am an X, and proud of it!' — or to rally fellow ethnic group members together to protect themselves and defend their rights. Most of the time they feel that it makes them less different from other people than others assume, and certainly does not justify their being deprived of jobs and property, separated from spouse and children or exterminated.

There are usually some members of an ethnic group who see it as their special role to maintain and strengthen the life of the group: the leaders, the ethnic 'professionals', people who have made nurturing the group part of their vocation in life. But while such people play a critical and highly valuable role, they sometimes in their zeal forget the perspective of ordinary group members: one must resist pressure on their part to place *undue* emphasis on ethnicity. For the majority of members a more casual participation in the group's life — or no active involvement at all — is more appropriate, given their other interests and affiliations.

Clearly, then, my proposal earlier that *everyone* in a society should be seen as ethnic was not intended to increase the emphasis on ethnicity but rather to show that we are all in it together: we are all ethnics. There is no room for invidious contrasts between those who are and those who are not.

My suggestion, in fact, is that while we should all explore and in certain respects foster our ethnicity — our 'roots' — in general we should recognize that there are limits to the significance of ethnic group membership and ethnic characteristics. We should bear in mind how many other important sub-groups people belong to (or would belong to if they were allowed) and how many other personal characteristics people have which do not run along ethnic lines.

Having said all this, I wish to assert the right of people to maintain their ethnicity. Many people who oppose ethnic expression — religious life, ethnic neighbourhoods, heritage language study, continuing to speak one's mother tongue, maintaining ties with one's country of origin and so forth — do so out of a prejudiced belief that everyone should conform to the 'majority' culture. This is the outlook 'why can't they be like us?' to which Greeley so rightly objects. My point is not that people should be forced or even encouraged to 'assimilate', but rather that their ethnicity should not be over-emphasized — by themselves or anyone else — so that *undue* significance is attached to place of origin, religion, race or language, or to other differences between sub-groups. Pressuring people to give up their ethnicity is one of many ways of unduly emphasizing ethnicity.

Ethnic bias

Two phenomena which might be loosely brought together under the term 'ethnic bias' are ethnic stereotyping and ethnic prejudice. *Ethnic stereotyping* we have already considered indirectly in discussing the nature and role of ethnicity. We saw, for example, how immigrants from the same country are usually quite diverse in terms of both their background and the length of time since they (or their forebears) migrated, and hence how mistaken it would be to assume that all members of a particular immigrant group have the same characteristics. We saw also that ethnic characteristics constitute only a small part of one's personality and way of life, so that even if such characteristics *were* uniform, it would be a mistake to define particular individuals or groups in terms of their ethnicity. The saying 'An Indian is an Indian is an Indian' represented the full flowering of British imperial ethnocentricism. The implication was that if one knows that people are Indians, one knows virtually everything about them, and is justified in viewing them and treating them accordingly. Even if one does not regard an ethnic group as inferior, simply to lump them all together on the basis of ethnic identity is bound to lead to mistaken judgments and inappropriate behaviour. Indeed, even to say 'I like all X's' or 'I am an X-ophile' suggests that one has a stereotyped view of X's to which they might well take exception and which may have unfortunate consequences, despite one's positive feelings.

Ethnic prejudice we might define as the belief — often sincerely held — that one or more ethnic sub-cultures are better than others. It involves not only stereotyping members of certain ethnic groups but also regarding them as inferior.

The approach I would recommend here is in certain respects the same as the approach to religion proposed in Chapter 8. It seems very unlikely that the respective ways of life of various national, racial, religious and other ethnic sub-groups are *in general* better or worse than each other. On certain matters, at a particular time, different ethnic groups may have different strengths and weaknesses. But it is best to assume that, on balance, different ethnic groups are of equal worth and equally deserving of education, jobs, food, civil liberties and so on.

Often an immigrant ethnic group will fall initially into a low socio-economic bracket, especially if they have come from a disadvantaged class or region in their country of origin. And most of the members of a less favoured religious or racial group may continue in a low socio-economic category indefinitely. Associated with this socio-economic status, there may be a relatively low level of scholastic and occupational attainment. However, it is singularly illogical to attribute this status and level of attainment (as people frequently do) to inherent weaknesses in the ethnic group in question: the phenomenon is fully explicable in terms of intractable circumstances and ethnic discrimination itself.

Some ethnic groups present difficulties for the more privileged and established ethnic group(s) in a country, and for this reason are the object of negative comment. They may press for land claims, political autonomy, language rights, separate schools, improved economic conditions; and they may engage in certain kinds of civil disorder in attempting to further their cause. However, once again one must understand this behaviour not in terms of deficiencies in an ethnic culture but rather as a function of the circumstances of the group. People in the dominant group(s) would be likely to respond in much the same way — and with equally good reason — if they found themselves in a similar position. Indeed, their forebears may have done so in the past, and may now be honoured as revolutionaries, liberators or nation builders.

But if all ethnic groups are of equal worth, does this not imply that all cultures or ways of life are of equal worth? And if so, what room is there for criticizing cultures and trying to improve them? I certainly do not wish to rule out culture criticism or reform. As I said earlier, different ethnic groups have different strengths and weaknesses, and as a result they have much to learn from each other. However, the assumption that a particular ethnic group is *in general* inferior should be a last — rather than a first — resort, adopted only after all other explanations have proved inadequate. And the history of the world to date would suggest that other explanations are always available; indeed, even the notion that certain ethnic groups are inferior has ample explanation, in terms of the need for scapegoats for national problems and the search for excuses to do things (such as centralizing power) which dominant groups wish to do anyway.[4] We should, then, accept all ethnic groups (including our own) as of equal worth, seriously and courageously working to live well, with a modest degree of success relative to the circumstances, and confine our critical comment to *specific* areas where we believe there is room for improvement.

We might note in closing this section that people often object not to other ethnic groups as such but rather to having a diversity of ethnic groups within a nation or region. This parallels the preference for single-race nations discussed in the previous chapter. As with race, so with ethnicity, it is argued that the presence of 'foreign' cultural elements can in various ways 'spoil' the dominant culture. One hears the protest: 'This is an X country, and these Y's are destroying our way of life.' For example, David Kirp cites Margaret Thatcher's 1970's vow to bring a 'clear end to immigration' in order to keep 'the British character' from being 'swamped by people with a different culture'.[5]

Such a position, however, is difficult to justify. So-called 'great' cultures have in the past been formed (in part) through the injection of foreign elements into existing societies: for example, Assyrian culture in 'early' Egypt, the Aryan culture in 'early' India, the Buddhist religion in China and Japan, Greek thought in classical Rome, Hebrew thought in Rome and Arabia, Roman culture in 'early' Spain, Muslim culture in medieval Spain and early modern India, and so on. It would seem that the presence of other ethnic groups within a nation is at least as likely to result in enrichment as harm. Apart from strengthening the common culture in various respects, the formation of a multi-ethnic society has a valuable educational impact, bringing people into contact in everyday life with people whose culture embodies different ideas and outlooks. Such an education is especially important in a world where interaction with people of other cultures from outside one's country is becoming increasingly frequent. Yet another advantage of a multi-ethnic society is that it provides a wider range of possible modes of life from which individuals — whatever their ethnic background — may choose, according to their distinctive temperament and needs. Some people, it is true, are temperamentally less able to cope with cultural diversity and change than others, and their right to be left undisturbed should be respected as far as possible. But there appears to be no basis for objecting *in general* to the co-existence and mixture of different ethnic cultures; on the contrary, there is much to be said for it. The only qualification I would make is that one should not place *too* much emphasis on ethnicity, for the reasons given in the previous section. People wish not only to keep their ethnic roots but also to participate freely in developing and maintaining the common culture of their country or region.

Multi-ethnic, 'multicultural' education

To combat ethnic bias in and through the school, there is need for extensive 'multicultural' education (as ethnic studies is commonly called). This can be done partly through the general organization and life of the school. As we saw when considering religion and race specifically, increasing the ethnic diversity of the teaching and administrative staff and the student body can have an important educational impact. Also, the handling of ethnic issues and relationships in the school can serve both to correct immediate inequities and to model appropriate approaches. However, as an educational institution, the school has a significant *formal* teaching role to perform in this area, and this will be the focus of our attention in the present context.[6]

The discussion of ethnicity and ethnic bias in the foregoing sections suggests that the task of multicultural education is much broader than we have often assumed. In practice, multicultural education has at best involved (a) teaching 'ethnic' students about their own ethnic culture, including perhaps some 'heritage language' instruction; and (b) teaching all students about various traditional cultures, at home and abroad. While such studies can be pursued in a variety of ways, what is usually missing is systematic treatment of fundamental issues of culture and ethnicity. I would suggest, then, that several further elements must be added, notably: (c) promoting acceptance of ethnic diversity in society; (d) showing that people of different religions, races, national backgrounds and so on are of equal worth; (e) fostering full acceptance and equitable treatment of the ethnic sub-cultures associated with different religions, races, national backgrounds, etc. in one's own country and in other parts of the world; and (f) helping students to work toward more adequate cultural forms, for themselves and for society.

It is impossible to separate ethnic education from ethical, cultural and political education in general. If students are to grapple successfully with the difficult problems facing them, they must study such issues as conflict and inequality in society, cultural pluralism, cultural reform, national and regional identity, self-identity and the goals and meaning of life. Obviously, these are of central concern to all students, not simply to those from minority groups. But that is precisely the point: all students are 'ethnics', and ethnic education must be brought in from the periphery of schooling and given a substantial place in the core, common curriculum. All students must learn how to understand and assess the cultural forms of forebears and work out what modifications are needed. In the case of minority groups, including immigrant communities, the need for assessment and choice is more obvious, but a similar need exists for other sub-groups.

If the examination of fundamental issues of culture and ethnicity is not included in multicultural education, there is a tendency to see the task as that of enabling ethnic students to reconcile a largely static traditional culture with a 'given' mainstream culture. Ethnic studies are advocated in order to make students aware of and proud of their roots, enable them to maintain good relations with their family and community, and ease their coming to terms with the dominant culture. However, ethnic cultures are far from static: they are constantly changing, in part to make the most of wider societal relationships. And the so-called 'mainstream' culture, (better described, I believe, as the 'common' culture) is not (or should not be) a given, but rather is subject to constant modification as ideas and circumstances change, with input from all the ethnic groups that comprise the society. For students the task is not one of piecing together components from two (static) sources, but rather of working out a satisfactory communal and personal way of life. Neither study of 'the old culture' nor study of 'the common culture' will be at all adequate to their needs. What is required is a fundamental study of what life and society are all about and how *any* individual or community builds a satisfactory way of life. While some of the value problems and cultural problems that students have are peculiar to their ethnic group, the majority are not; and even the distinctive ones could largely be dealt with in common classes on culture and society, where they would provide extremely valuable perspectives on issues that are of concern to everyone.

Not only does a common curriculum in culture and ethnicity have positive advantages; it also helps overcome some of the disadvantages of alternative approaches. One difficulty faced by traditional ethnic studies programs is that of identifying unified ethnic groups with a sufficiently common culture and background to provide a basis for joint study. We noted earlier the diversity that exists within so-called ethnic groups. Should immigrants from southern Italy learn about the Medici? Should Black immigrants from Antigua learn about life on a Southern cotton plantation or about early civilization in Africa? (And which part of Africa?) What version of modern history should be taught to Vietnamese immigrants? Another major difficulty, closely related to the first, lies in establishing an approach to the subject matter in such courses. What political and cultural stance should be taken? Many instructors feel that their role (and all that they are qualified for) is to teach about ethnic cultures in their traditional form; but this can serve to perpetuate old patterns of dominance, and may offer little of relevance to students attempting to develop a satisfactory way of life in their present situation.

Given these problems, there is much to be said for building ethnic studies into common courses on culture, societal living, politics and values. These can be taught by people qualified to deal with such controversial areas. Within the context of these courses examples, both historical and contemporary, can frequently be drawn from the experience of various ethnic groups — especially those represented in the local community — by way of clarifying and applying general principles. As a result, students may learn a considerable amount about their particular ethnic group while also learning how to engage in culture criticism and development.

I have used the term 'multicultural education' in this section. In drawing our discussion to a close, we should note that many key writers have expressed concern about an excessively cultural emphasis in this field and have questioned the use of terms such as 'multicultural' and 'cultural pluralist'. For example, Sarup says:

'Cultural pluralism' is a term that has become overworked and empty. The main thing wrong with this model is its assumption that all groups within the plural society possess roughly equal amounts of power.[7]

Focusing on racism, Sarup says:

In the current (cultural pluralist) approach in schools it is assumed that racism is merely a matter of individual ignorance, and that racial prejudice and racial discrimination will come to an end through an education in cultural diversity.[8]

Craft notes that there is an ongoing 'disagreement and controversy' between two camps:

Those who focus on cultural diversity have become described as 'multiculturalists' . . . . Others, often termed 'anti-racists', emphasize the need to reveal and combat racist attitudes and practices . . . which result in unequal distribution of opportunities, wealth and power.[9]

While there are legitimate concerns here, given the frequent superficiality of multicultural education, there is a danger that the controversy will force both sides into narrow and inadequate positions. Whatever terminology is used (and any one term, taken literally, will be inadequate) attention must be given *both* to cultural issues *and* to issues of prejudice, power, inequality and the like. As Craft says, 'these are not polar opposites . . . the celebration of diversity is no more than patronizing tokenism unless it is accompanied by a fundamental belief in the equality of individuals from every background:

a multicultural approach must embrace an anti-racist one.'[10] Further, belief in equality is not enough: underlying political and economic problems must be tackled. But so-called 'anti-racists' must, for their part, recognize that people are discriminated against on the basis of religion, country of origin, language and so on *as well as* race; that prejudice against ethnic culture is a significant component of so-called 'racism'; and that a sincere belief in the inferiority of certain cultures, religions, races and nationalities is a *major* contributing factor in ethnic bias, which must be confronted in its own right. Insofar as terms such as 'multicultural education' have been contaminated by a soft, 'liberal' approach to the field, the solution may lie not in changing the terminology but rather in strengthening the approach. However, the terminology is not of crucial importance. Some people may wish for the time being to talk of *both* multicultural education *and* 'multiracial' or 'anti-racist' education in order to ensure that tough issues of political and economic discrimination are not neglected in the schools.

Notes and References

1 Greeley, A. (1971) *Why Can't They Be Like Us?*, New York, Dutton, pp. 51–2.
2 *Ibid.*, pp. 51–2.
3 Greeley, A. (1977) *The American Catholic*, New York, Basic Books, especially pp. 270–1.
4 See Sarup, M. (1986) *The Politics of Multiracial Education*, London, Routledge and Kegan Paul, p. 54; and Hicks, D. and Townley, C. (Eds), (1982) *Teaching World Studies*, London, Longman, p. 29.
5 Kirp, D. (1979) *Doing Good By Doing Little: Race and Schooling in Britain,* Berkeley, University of California Press, p. 110.
6 Some of the comments in this section are taken, with permission and in revised form, from Beck, C. (1975) 'Is Immigrant Education Only for Immigrants?' in Wolfgang, A. (Ed) *Education of Immigrant Students*, Toronto, OISE Press, pp. 5–18.
7 Sarup, M., *op. cit.*, p. 17.
8 *Ibid.*, p. 49.
9 Craft, A. (1986) 'Multicultural teaching', in Wellington, J. (Ed) *Controversial Issues in the Curriculum*, Oxford, Blackwell, p. 75.
10 *Ibid.*, p. 76.

Chapter 11

Sexism

Apart from religious, racial and ethnic bias, people are often discriminated against because of their gender. Sometimes it is males who are the object of prejudice and discrimination; but in most (perhaps all) societies the overwhelming bias is against females.

Gender bias is distinctive in that it cuts across other forms of bias, creating inequities and conflict within the same religion, race, nation, ethnic group and social class. As such, it can bring together people who differ in other respects but share the common experience of sexual oppression.

The term 'sexism' is used to cover both inappropriate *beliefs and attitudes* in relation to the sexes and *discrimination* against people on the basis of sex. The two are closely connected, since sex discrimination usually arises out of sexist beliefs and attitudes. However, discriminatory practices sometimes take on a life of their own and continue despite shifts in outlook. And discrimination towards others is not the only behavioural expression of sexism: one can also do harm to oneself by having a sexist outlook.

Schools promote sexism in two main ways: (i) informally, through organization and atmosphere, comments and gestures; and (ii) through formal curriculum and instructional activities. Accordingly, attempts to overcome sexism in schools must address both these dimensions of the life of the school. In the past there has been a tendency to focus almost exclusively on the 'hidden' curriculum of the school. However, increasingly today attention is being given to the formal curriculum, to the biases inherent in our intellectual traditions and passed on quite directly (though often unconsciously) through subject teaching.

Much of the writing on sexism in schools and in society generally simply assumes that sexism is wrong. While I agree with this assumption, I think the case for it must be made explicitly and systematically, both to specify more clearly the harm that sexism does and to try to win over the large number of people (of both sexes) who still have doubts on the matter. Sexism is very often based on sincerely held beliefs; and while this cannot be offered as an excuse, being aware of it will affect how we go about trying to reduce sexism. If we assume that sexist people are simply wilfully rejecting a position the merits of which are clear to them, we will not approach them in a way which is likely to change their point of view.

The harm sexism does to females and males[1]

Sexism is harmful in three main ways. First, it promotes a stereotype of females and males which is in fact inaccurate and hence results in inappropriate expectations and behaviour. Secondly, it (usually) fosters the view that females are inferior to males, a view which, once again, leads to inappropriate attitudes and actions. And thirdly, sexism (usually) involves discrimination against females in favour of males, a practice which is harmful both to females and males. As Paulo Freire and other theorists of oppression have pointed out, those who oppress are negatively affected (to a degree) by their exploitative practices. Life is not a zero-sum game in which benefits denied one segment of the population go automatically and fully to the other.

The following is a sampling of forms of disadvantage typically experienced by women and girls:

– inferior jobs in terms of status, pay, conditions, interest, enjoyment
– less access to public office
– less access to headships and board memberships in corporations and other institutions
– inferior status in all major religions
– less money to spend in early adulthood, and higher incidence of poverty in middle and old age
– less sexual freedom: a double standard for males and females
– higher incidence of sexual harassment as a child, as a student, at work and elsewhere
– higher incidence of sexual abuse, rape
– less freedom of movement (partly due to threat of sexual abuse)
– name change with marriage
– higher incidence of physical abuse in marriage
– necessity to humour males and make compromises in dealing with them
– necessity to put up with condescension from males
– bias against females built into everyday language
– lower level of attention and respect in a wide range of situations
– lower sense of self-worth and of the importance of what one does
– lower sense of self-confidence in various fields of study and work
– smaller range of options in life generally

As we have noted, while males are less harmed by sexism than females, they too are negatively affected by the stereotyping and discrimination involved. The following are some examples:

– Although males have greater freedom of choice, their options are also limited by sexual stereotyping. There are certain roles and activities from which they are largely excluded because of their sex.
– While males are privileged, they often suffer as a result of the pressure to live up to the male image: to earn well, to achieve status, to be physically strong, to be brave, to avoid showing certain emotions, to 'perform' well sexually, to have 'male' interests, to have a 'male' job.
– Because males typically have such a different way of life from females, it is often difficult for them to have full and satisfying friendships and love relationships with females.
– A specific example of the above is that of heterosexual 'love making' where an intimate experience is sought between two people who, because of their upbringing, may not understand or appreciate each other, may have different kinds of sexual ideals and pleasures, and have been cast by society in problematic roles (dominant-submissive, active-passive, etc.).
– In cross-sex relationships males are often adversely affected as a result of the resentment females feel because of the discrimination practised against them.
– There is growing evidence that males are socialized into a distinctive form of morality and decision-making which in key respects is dysfunctional.
– In general, sexual stereotyping is inefficient for society in a way that affects the welfare of males (as well as females). Many people are forced into roles which to a greater or lesser extent do not suit them, rather than being free to perform those tasks in which they will be optimally productive members of society.

The inappropriateness of sexual bias

We have briefly reviewed the harm sexism does to both females and males. This in itself constitutes a powerful argument against sexual bias. However there are several further issues that must be addressed.

To begin with, some people believe that the differential treatment of females and males is necessitated by differences in inherited characteristics. Females constitute both the 'fairer' and the 'weaker' sex. Even if we regret the limitations placed on women in terms of desirable occupations, positions of power, freedom of movement and personal assertiveness, there is nothing that can be done about it. Women by nature are not as well suited as men to a dominant role at either a personal or a societal level.

As with race and ethnicity, however, so with sex, genetic explanations of differences should be a matter of last rather than first resort. There is considerable evidence that most of the differences between females and males, insofar as they exist at all, are in fact culturally determined. Historical and cultural studies, for example, show that in some societies 'female' and 'male' characteristics and roles have largely been the opposite of those considered typical in Western societies.[2] It is true that the great majority of societies have been patriarchal; but the existence of even one matriarchal society where women have traits and functions widely regarded as 'male' in other societies should make us question biological explanations of sex differences.

Psychological studies, too, suggest that most sex differences may be culturally determined. It has been observed, for example, that there is an enormous difference in the way male and female children are treated from birth onward: the way they are handled physically, the way they are dressed, the toys they are given, the activities to which they are introduced, the comments made on their physical appearance, the conversations engaged in with them, the behaviours praised and discouraged.[3] It has been noted also that from a very early age children begin to reinforce their own sexual socialization: they become aware of their sex and the role associated with it by society and learn to live up to it and apply it in complex ways to influence others.[4] Further, it has been found that sex differences in behaviour in infancy and early childhood increase with age, suggesting that they may be learned rather than inherited.[5]

Many of the differences between females and males which are assumed to be 'natural' can in fact be explained in terms of differences of *power*. The typical (though not invariant) tendency of females to try to work things out by compromise and adjustment, to avoid confrontation, to appeal to people's sense of compasssion, to persuade rather than stand on principles and rights, to hide anger and shun assertiveness, to avoid competition, to value family and communal ties, to proceed by 'networking' rather than rugged individualism: all of these characteristics are what one might expect of people who are in a position of lesser power, who must follow an indirect route rather than simply assert (as males frequently do) what must be done. These are traits seen frequently in peasants, servants, recent immigrants, minority groups and subject peoples generally. They have also been noted among males in matriarchal societies. This does not mean, of course, that if women were to gain power they would or should begin to behave in a typically 'male' manner. Because of their situation, females may have hit upon ways of interacting with people that are preferable even among equals. However, an explanation of current female behaviour in terms of power raises further doubts about biological theories of female characteristics.[6]

But even if it is agreed that we should not see sex differences (apart from physical ones) as biological in origin, the debate may continue. Some people (both males and females) genuinely believe that the typically male way of doing things is superior to the typically female approach. Males are seen as more logical, decisive, principled and impartial, less inclined to be diverted from what has to be done by petty emotions and personal ties. As Gilligan points out, while some of the disadvantages of the rugged individualism of males are acknowledged, women are commonly seen as 'mired in relationships', incapable of the kind of separation and objectivity that life requires.[7] Accordingly, the argument runs, whatever the reason for current sex differences, until women develop more appropriate outlooks and patterns of behaviour they cannot be entrusted with greater power and authority in society.

The immediate objection to such a view is that if, as I have suggested, males and females are largely the way they are for cultural and political reasons, then the so-called 'irrationality' and 'indecisiveness' of women can be quickly cured by giving them equal power and status in society. If the forthright male way of doing things is better, women will quickly acquire it when they no longer have to be so wary of bruising male egos and incurring male wrath. But secondly, and just as importantly, we must question (as Gilligan does) the notion that the female way of handling relationships and enterprises is inferior to that of males. On the one hand, the emphasis on discussion, compromise, feelings and small-group loyalty attributed to females seems well suited to those smaller family and communal settings to which women's influence is largely restricted. It is a sign of moral intelligence — not inferiority — that females have adapted to the distinctive context in which they live. On the other hand, there is growing evidence today that a more 'female' approach is needed, at least to a degree, even in those larger societal and global settings where males are dominant. Males are handicapped by their traditional distaste for losing face, delaying, compromising and recognizing the complexity of situations. It seems that they have been spoiled over the centuries by an excess of unchecked power. There is a fine line between decisive behaviour and ruthless behaviour, between acting 'on principle' and acting without regard for contextual considerations. As I argued in Chapter 1, there is much to be said for a less rigid and more reflective approach to decision making. I am not at this point claiming that typical female morality is superior, on balance, to that of males; only that it is certainly not inferior.

Some people argue against treating women and men equally on the ground that, whatever the capacities of males and females may be, the difference between the sexes adds a very important dimension to life and society. They invoke slogans such as 'variety is the spice of life' and 'vive la différence!'; and they worry that if women and men came to have similar roles and personality characteristics a valuable division of labour in performing society's tasks would be lost and also much of the magic would disappear from male-female relationships. The claim here is not that women would be incapable of performing traditional male tasks but rather that, for other reasons, it is important to keep the male and female worlds distinct. Often associated with this point of view is a feeling of nostalgia for a bygone era when differences (it is thought) were even greater than at present, when 'men were men and women were women'.

But, of course, there are many problems with this position. For one thing, as we noted in the previous section, the differences between women and men appear on balance to do more harm than good. They reduce the range of opportunities open to both women and men, and create many difficulties in female-male relationships. The 'magic' based on ignorance and distance so often dissipates, and is followed by either simple non-communication or constant and damaging conflict. Further, the so-called 'division of labour' has in the past been almost invariably in men's favour. While this *need* not be the case, it seems that a policy of 'different but equal' is difficult to implement. Especially where there has been a long history of preferential treatment, there needs to be at least an interim period of equal access to all positions in society if equality is to be achieved. And as I have argued, there are additional reasons for making this period of equal access permanent. Division of labour is indeed an important principle in human enterprises, but it is generally damaging to make the division along sex lines.

Should we be willing to accept the possibility of women's and men's roles and personal characteristics becoming so similar that there are virtually no generalizable differences between females and males (apart from physical ones)? Personally, I cannot see why not, and I am puzzled when non-sexist people resist such a notion. Kathryn Morgan in her article 'The Androgynous Classroom: Liberation or Tyranny?' objects to the ideal of an 'androgynous' society, one in which there will be minimal sexual differentiation, and where traits which are now typically male or female will be found equally in both sexes; a society in which 'when a child is born, no longer will its genitals determine what his or her parents expect in terms of personality, behaviour and work.'[8] But in my view, while such a society may be difficult to attain, or even to envisage at this stage, it is precisely what we should work toward. Why ever *should* one's genitals determine one's personality, behaviour and work?

Morgan's main arguments against the androgynous ideal are as follows: first, 'a sexually dichotomized society' gives people 'at least two' personality options, whereas androgyny leads to 'a monolithic pattern of human development:' secondly, if we substitute an androgynous ideal for the present male and female ones, almost everyone will fall short of it and develop a poor self-image; and thirdly, if everyone is a 'whole' person, warm, sensitive and compassionate, having both 'female' and 'male' virtues, there will be a shortage in society of 'persistent and single-minded' individuals who are 'creative and theoretically inventive.' But none of these arguments seems to me at all plausible. To begin with, if a society needed sexual dichotomization in order to offer 'at least two' personality options for people, it would already be in deep trouble. Clearly there is at present in existing societies enormous room for personality differences even within a given sex, and the demise of sex-linked personality traits would not change that situation. Indeed, as many people claim, it would open up a wider range of possibilities for everyone. With respect to the second argument, the issue here is simply one of the *manner* in which we move toward an androgynous ideal: obviously, people should not be pressured and pushed in such a way that they are ashamed of their present female or male characteristics. But if human beings are to have any ideals at all (including the ideal of being non-sexist), there must be some tension between what is and what ought to be. Turning to Morgan's third argument, we see that it involves the highly dubious assumption that being a sensitive, compassionate, 'whole' person means that one is less fitted for playing a creative and inventive role in society. Surely the problematic state of the world today shows what can happen when 'non-whole', 'single-minded' people are in charge of our creations and inventions. The pooling of distinctive 'female' and 'male' virtues (insofar as they exist) would not reduce creativity; rather it would establish a more satisfactory set of value parameters within which creation would take place. These values certainly should be subjected to constant scrutiny; but it is absurd to suggest that abandoning values we believe to be sound is a necessary condition of being creative.

There is, obviously, one area in which females and males inevitably have different roles, namely, procreation. Men cannot bear children. However, apart from the biological process of pregnancy, giving birth and early nourishment, men are typically welcome to participate as fully as they wish in the 'reproduction' and rearing of children. In this task there can be — and, I think, should be — a full sharing of labour (as distinct from a division of labour). Further, men's inability physically to bear children is simply no basis for maintaining that women should be excluded from various roles and positions in society. Certainly sheer time is not a consideration. Throughout the history of humankind, so far as we know, women have worked considerably longer hours than men; and today, in wealthy countries at least, women not only work longer hours but also on average live several years longer than men. Accordingly, women clearly have the time to bear children *and* pursue the same occupations as men. Even if, one day, women's hours of work (including child bearing) were reduced to equality with those of men, child bearing is such an important function in society that women should be rewarded for engaging in it rather than penalized with decreased access to interesting, lucrative jobs.

But how is it that such a marked male hegemony has arisen in all corners of the earth? One may be inclined to feel that nature could not have made such a huge mistake; that such a widespread, natural dominance cannot be disregarded: that it possibly points to a greater vitality, aggressiveness and practical wisdom among men which society ignores at its peril. However, I would suggest an alternative explanation. It seems entirely possible that the edge which males had in physical strength and freedom from pregnancy and early nurture (and from the psychological attachment to their infants that mothers almost inevitably have but which fathers can more easily avoid) enabled men, in eras when physical dominance was so decisive, to secure a position of control which became established in intellectual, moral, religious and social life. A physical advantage was translated into a cultural advantage and through vested interest was steadily increased. A study of 'primitive' societies reveals that male hegemony has typically been related to power rather than usefulness or productivity: basic livelihood has usually been provided for by the steady domestic activities of women rather than the more spectacular hunting and plundering feats of men. Women have a long history of being able to ensure that there is productivity and welfare in society. On this analysis, then, there would not be any 'peril' involved in women having power and authority equal to that of men. On the contrary, there might be considerable gains in well being for societies which moved in that direction.

Sexism and the school

At an earlier stage, in wealthy industrialized nations, the pursuit of sex equality in relation to schooling focused on ensuring that girls had access to schools. Now that this fight has largely been won, we are aware of the limits of the achievement.[9] Girls are often subjected to sexual bias while at school;[10] they frequently do not select the courses which are most conducive to career advancement; and schooling does not result in career advancement for females to the degree that had been expected. As Judith Byrne Whyte observes, 'educating girls and boys under the same roof (does not) guarantee that they will receive equal educational benefits'.[11] There is a parallel here with the case of social class and schooling: greater educational access for lower class children has not had the result wished for, and attention has now shifted to ways of achieving more equal educational (and other) *outcomes*.

Girls (unlike lower class children) do relatively well at school. Indeed, in some countries the higher performance of girls is creating a 'problem' at the university admission level. (It is ironic that it was not seen as a problem when more boys than girls met university entrance requirements). But in Britain, for example,

> While boys get qualifications in maths, the physical sciences, technology and computer studies, girls typically leave with a group of exam passes in arts, languages, and subjects like religious studies, art and home economics. These are not the sorts of subjects which lead into well-paid employment, nor . . . do they offer many routes into higher education.[12]

Further, even in cases where girls do take the 'right' subjects and gain access to higher status professions, the rewards are limited. As Whyte notes, 'in every area of life, even where females predominate numerically, men are to be found in positions of power and responsibility, with women in subordinate roles.' There is in the larger society a 'sexual division of labour which is a major source of sex inequality.'[13]

In response to the challenge of continuing sexism in schools and in the job market, some writers are inclined to see teachers as 'both a major obstacle to change and yet the means by which change might be achieved.'[14] They envisage teachers giving greater attention to girls in class (at present boys typically dominate classroom discussions),[15] spending more time counselling girls in choice of subjects and careers, and attempting to teach science and technology in a less male oriented manner, so that girls find them more interesting.[16] However, while these are indeed important lines of action, I believe we must avoid placing *too* much emphasis on the role of the teacher — or even the school — in redirecting the career paths of girls. Just as 'the lads' in Willis' *Learning to Labour* have a realistic understanding of how far society will allow people of working class background to go, so girls often have a better sense than their advisers of how to achieve well being in society *as it is currently constituted*. The goal of changing society in the future must be balanced against the goal of living well in society in the present. In counselling female students we must employ a dialogical method which helps each student determine what is the most satisfactory study and career path for her. At the same time, we must work to change society so that the careers and modes of life *genuinely* available to women are extended. To a degree, female students may be willing and able to be the 'shock troops', so to speak, who open the way for others; but we must not unduly pressure them to fulfil this role.

Part of the difficulty here is that the emphasis on mathematics, science and technology as entry qualifications for various occupations — medicine, engineering and business, for example — is not in keeping with the broad range of insights and abilities actually needed in those occupations. The admission requirements have an unfortunate and unnecessary steering effect on high school education. It seems a great pity to direct female students, often against their inclinations, towards specialization in 'hard' subjects in order to gain access to occupations which in fact could greatly benefit from an infusion of people with a humanities background. Accordingly, once again, our efforts both inside and outside the school should be focused as much on changing the nature of the work world and the requirements for entry to it as on changing the interests and course selections of girls.

As well as attempting to improve the career expectations of female students, a major role of the school should be to teach against sexual prejudice and discrimination in general. At present schools largely reinforce sexist outlooks through both their practices and their formal teaching. At the level of practice, it has been noted that schools are usually biased toward males in staffing (in seniority, if not in numbers);[17] stream girls and boys into different subject areas (as we have seen); pay greater deference to boys than girls;[18] emphasize differences between girls and boys;[19] and condone a degree of sexual harassment toward girls.[20] These elements in school life should be strongly opposed not only because of the direct harm they do but also because of the sexist messages they convey.

In their formal teaching role, too, schools currently promote sexism. Whyte observes that 'analyses of children's reading books and school texts has shown how women and girls are stereotyped, ignored or undervalued.'[21] Morgan comments that females 'are characteristically portrayed as involved in such activities as babysitting, sewing, cooking, shopping, and buying ribbons,' while males 'are portrayed in a variety of activities such as building, earning money, hiking, camping, planting, driving cars, and travelling.'[22] In general, according to Whyld, men are shown in 'work roles' while women are 'limited to the roles of wife and mother.'[23] But, Whyld goes on, 'the most subtle way in which the inferior position of women is "taught" in educational material is by simply ignoring them and their contribution to life . . . . Women are severely under-represented in most areas of school study.'[24] Whyld advises that 'although it is quite impracticable to think of ridding the classroom of all sexist material,' teachers should 'avoid the worst examples' and, in other cases, use such materials 'as consciousness-raising devices with their pupils.'[25]

As in other areas of bias such as racism and ethnocentrism, I believe that the school should engage in explicit, systematic instruction with respect to sexism. Whyld, in a sensitive concluding section on 'surviving' as a feminist in an educational institution, seems to place the main emphasis on 'providing a role model' for one's students, and says somewhat enigmatically: 'Do not expect to change your pupils' ideas.'[26] However, I believe that the school as an educational institution is in a peculiarly strong position to change students' ideas: and since, as I stated earlier, so many sexist beliefs are sincerely held, this is a crucial area in which to work. Whyld speaks quite correctly of the 'snubs and ridicule in the staffroom, and hostility from parents' that a feminist working toward a non-sexist education may encounter, and she counsels: 'do what you feel you can, and no more.' However, it is possible that if teaching against sexism were carried out as part of 'normal' instruction in 'respectable' subjects such as literature, history, ethics and politics, the impact of students would increase without an increase in the fall-out for the teacher from taking a non-sexist stand. Of course, helping people to see that sexual bias is inappropriate is only part of the task of eliminating sexism; but I believe it is an essential task and one to which the school should devote considerable time and resources.

Notes and References

1 Parts of this section are taken, with permission and in revised form, from Beck, C. (1983) *Values and Living: Learning Materials for Grades 7 and 8*, Toronto, OISE Press, section 8.8.
2 Whyld, J. (Ed), (1983) *Sexism in the Secondary Curriculum*, London, Harper and Row, p. 15.
3 *Ibid.*, pp. 10, 13 and 14.
4 *Ibid.*, pp. 10, 11 and 14.
5 *Ibid.*, p. 14.
6 It might be noted that the explanation I have given here of many characteristically female values and behaviour patterns differs from that of Nancy Chodorow (1978) (*The Reproduction of Mothering*, Berkeley, University of California Press) who sees their origin in the close mother–daughter bond, which contrasts with the more distant mother–son relationship. My view is that the nature of the mother–daughter relationship, far from being the origin of female characteristics, is itself dictated by power structures and cultural expectations already existing in society.
7 Gilligan, C. (1982) *In a Different Voice*, Cambridge, Massachusetts, Harvard University Press, pp. 154–6.
8 Morgan, K. (1982) 'The Androgynous Classroom: Liberation or Tyranny?', in Cochrane, D. and Schiralli, M. (Eds) *Philosophy of Education: Canadian Perspectives*, Don Mills, Ontario, Collier Macmillan, pp. 171–81.
9 Whyte, J.B. (1986) 'Gender bias in schools: the controversial issues,' in Wellington, J. (Ed) *Controversial Issues in the Curriculum*, Oxford, Blackwell, pp. 58–9.
10 This is documented, for example, by Maryann Ayim and Barbara Houston in 'A Conceptual Analysis of Sexism and Sexist Education', in Cochrane, D. and Schiralli, M., *op. cit.*, pp. 160–6.
11 Whyte, J.B., *op. cit.*, p. 59.
12 *Ibid.*, p. 60.

13 *Ibid.*, p. 61.
14 Whyte, J., Deem, R., Kant, L. and Cruickshank, M. (Eds), (1985) *Girl Friendly Schooling*, London, Methuen, p. 75.
15 Whyte, J. in Wellington, J., *op. cit.*, p. 63.
16 Whyte, J., *et al.*, *op. cit.*, p. 74.
17 Whyte, J. in Wellington, J., *op. cit.*, pp. 61–2; Whyld, J., *op. cit.*, pp. 42–4.
18 Whyte, J. in Wellington, J., *op. cit.*, p. 63; Ayim, M. and Houston, B., *op. cit.*, pp. 160–6.
19 Whyld, J., *op. cit.*, pp. 28–36; and Morgan, K., *op. cit.*, pp. 171–4.
20 Whyld, J., *op. cit.*, pp. 36–7.
21 Whyte, J. in Wellington, J., *op. cit.*, p. 58.
22 Morgan, K., *op. cit.*, p. 172.
23 Whyld, J., *op. cit.*, pp. 70–1.
24 *Ibid.*, p. 71.
25 *Ibid.*, p. 70.
26 *Ibid.*, pp. 312–13.

Chapter 12

Class Bias

This chapter constitutes in some ways a culmination of the book to this point. In Part 1, I identified equality of well being as one of the main goals of schooling, and suggested some modifications in school practices which would help reduce socio-economic inequality and raise the general level of the school experience for all. In Part 2, in the preceding four chapters in particular, we have been looking at various factors — religious bias, racism, ethnic bias and sexism — which result in discrimination against particular sectors of society. A major consequence of this discrimination, in a great many cases, is a lowering of class or socio-economic level. We must now look in more detail at the nature of class bias and consider what role the school can play in helping to overcome it.

What is class?

The term 'class' in social theory today has a somewhat technical meaning, being roughly equivalent to 'socio-economic status' (SES). People are categorized as belonging to a higher or lower class or SES level using such criteria as wealth, power, privilege and status (or 'social honour', to use Weber's phrase). There is an implication of *advantage* in the word 'class', the assumption being that it is better (other things being equal) to have more rather than less wealth, power and the like. But it is not part of the meaning of the term that those who are of a higher class are better human beings (although, as we will see, some people have gone on to make this claim). 'Class' in this context, then, means much the same as 'category', and does not have the strongly evaluative connotation that it has in such everyday phrases as 'a touch of class' or 'so and so has no class.' Because of the ambiguity of the word 'class' in ordinary language it is often best to talk of socio-economic status instead, as I will frequently do in this chapter.

While wealth is a key criterion of class, its relationship with the other criteria is complex. For example, a person may have considerable wealth and yet lack the connections, skills and life-style that make for a high level of influence and societal regard. And someone may have power and a comfortable, privileged way of life without being wealthy. However, the strong links between the various elements, especially in the long-run, should be recognized. Over time, wealth or at least material security enables most groups to build up power and status; and most people with power and status could rather quickly 'cash them in' for wealth if they chose to do so.

Different class levels are found along a *continuum* from the lowest to the highest. Expressions such as 'middle class', 'lower class' and 'under class' are used simply for convenience. We should not assume a discontinuity between one class and another or a coherent societal sub-group that *is* 'the working class', 'the upper middle class' or whatever. The members of 'class X' may band together on a particular issue; but as one moves on to other issues the patterns of loyalty and cooperation will change. There is no basis for permanent solidarity on all matters. People in a particular segment of the continuum differ from each other in terms of privilege and status and so are in competition; and the appropriate coalitions between different levels shift over time. For example, depending on the circumstances, employed 'working class' people side sometimes with unemployed workers, sometimes against the unemployed and sometimes against each other.

How does class relate to religion, race, ethnicity, gender, age, etc? These attributes affect one's class insofar as they serve to lower or raise one's socio-economic status. Being from a less favoured category tends to lower one's class standing. For example, people of certain religions, races and ethnic groups in a society simply have less access — other things being equal — to lucrative employment and positions of influence. Females, too, in all existing societies, have — on average — less money-earning capacity and less public influence than males, and as a result often pass effectively to a lower SES level: many unmarried, separated to widowed women, for example, are in the 'under class' while men of similar initial background are in the 'working class' because they have a 'real job' and a higher income. It is sometimes suggested that it takes several generations to undergo a class shift, whether up or down, but in many cases it would seem that a significant change of level can happen rather quickly. Finally, age is also, effectively, a factor in class level. Older people, for example, very frequently move to life circumstances below those 'to which they have been accustomed' not long after retirement because of loss of income and association with 'the world of work.'

It might be objected that in defining class I have not given sufficient attention to lifestyle. Many people associate class with a particular way of life and related attitudes and values. However, in my view it is very important to think of class *primarily* in terms of wealth, influence and the like, since it is these which in large measure (though not completely) enable or dictate particular patterns of life. If we conceive of class in terms of lifestyle features, we may lose sight of the advantageous or disadvantageous circumstances which give rise to these features and end up praising higher SES people for their 'fine' ways and blaming lower SES people for their 'limited' culture.

Class prejudice and discrimination

Class bias involves seeing certain classes as superior or inferior to others, and discriminating against individuals and groups on the basis of class. While, as we noted earlier, it is advantageous (other things being equal) to be a member of a higher class, this does not mean that some classes are better than others, or that one is justified in treating people of different classes unequally.

Although it is normally lower SES people who are regarded as inferior (even by themselves in many cases), prejudice is sometimes directed at higher classes. On the one hand, higher SES people are condemned as unusually selfish and callous, when in fact virtually all human beings, in the same circumstances, would behave as they do. (This does not excuse their callousness, but it makes the charge of inferiority inappropriate). And the ineptitude of higher SES people is sometimes exaggerated (as in the British working class caricature of the 'toff'), and many of their cultural pursuits and contributions are undervalued. On the other hand, 'working class culture' or 'the culture of the poor' is sometimes overly romanticized, with glowing acounts of warm family relationships, simple pleasures and the satisfactions of hard, 'honest' work. It would be difficult to argue that higher SES people are very seriously harmed by these unfavourable comparisons with lower classes. Nevertheless, they do constitute a form of prejudice and can lead to unproductive conflict in a society.

Prejudice and discrimination against lower classes — clearly the major form of class bias — are in part defended by reference to the supposed intellectual, moral and cultural inferiority of lower SES people. They are seen as having inherent weaknesses which are the cause of their low level of social and economic attainment. As it is often put, we 'blame the victims' for their plight. I will discuss each of these areas of assumed inferiority in turn, attempting to show in each case that the bias cannot be defended.

With respect to the *intellectual* domain, there is no evidence that a deficit in innate capacity is the cause of lower SES standing. Bowles and Gintis have reviewed the research on this issue, with particular reference to Arthur Jensen's claim that Blacks in the US are at a lower socio-economic level because their inherited intellectual potential is lower. They acknowledge that Intelligence Quotient (IQ) is *in part* a function of one's genes, and also that on average Blacks have a lower IQ than Whites in the US. However, they strenuously reject the claim that Blacks have lower *innate* intellectual capacity. They agree with Light and Smith that 'even accepting Jensen's estimates of the heritability of IQ, the black-white IQ difference could easily be explained by the average environmental differences between the races.' IQ is so much a function of the socio-economic circumstances of one's family and ethnic group that no genetic hypothesis is needed to explain even substantial average differences between lower and higher SES groups.[1]

Bowles and Gintis go even further. Through a series of studies of individuals with the same cognitive ability but differing socio-economic rankings, they are able to show that there is virtually no *causal* connection between cognitive ability and economic success. So that even if the poor (including, in the US, a high proportion of Blacks) *did* have the same average IQ as the non-poor (through inheritance or some other means) it would not significantly affect their chances of economic improvement. It is doubly inappropriate, then, to attribute the poverty of the poor to innate intellectual deficiency: there is no innate deficiency, and even if there were, it would not be the cause of their poverty. Bowles and Gintis concede that there is a strong correlation between years of schooling and economic success, and that cognitive skills increase with additional schooling. But their analysis shows that the greater economic success is the result *not* of superior cognitive attainment but rather of privileges accorded people with more years of schooling and other factors associated with a higher SES level.

Lower class people are often thought to be inherently inferior *morally*, in ways that affect their socio-economic success. They are said to be lazy, hedonistic, lacking in self-control, imprudent and incapable of delaying gratification and pursuing long-term goals. When, for example, it is pointed out that the vast majority of people in jails are from a very poor background, a typical response is that this is a sign not of the unfortunate situation of lower class people but rather of an innate tendency toward undisciplined and unprincipled behaviour that leads to trouble with the law.

Once again, however, one need not hypothesize genetic deficiency in order to explain the behaviour of lower SES people. *If* there is a higher incidence of laziness among such people, it may well be due to their lack of access to interesting, highly rewarded jobs. *If* they are sometimes quick tempered, it may be because of the higher level of frustration associated with their financial and occupational situation. *If* they tend to live in the present, perhaps it is because there is not as much that is secure and exciting in the future for them to look forward to. Indeed, a close examination of the lives of lower SES people reveals that they are remarkably hardworking, patient and accepting, under the circumstances.

The claim that lower SES people are *culturally* inferior is difficult to sustain if what is implied is a genetic deficiency, since cultural differences are not biologically transferred. However, it is sometimes suggested that the poor have become so entrenched in an inferior culture that no matter what opportunities came their way, they could not live like normal human beings. Sarup notes, for example, that in Britain some sociologists describe Afro-Caribbean cultures as 'weak', and refer to ' "culture stripping" or "cultural castration" which African slaves supposedly underwent during slavery'. It is explained that 'the slaves lost their languages, religions and family kinship systems, being left with no alternative but to learn their masters' language and to ape their values and institutions.'[2] As Sarup points out, this account is mistaken in that it overlooks the considerable extent to which slaves did retain elements of their African heritage, including a very strong — though in some cases distinctive — family life. But the extraordinary irony of this analysis is that it describes as cultural deficit forms of behaviour that were forced on slaves by imperious masters. The Africans did not cease to have a culture; rather, they became a culture under siege, and adapted in necessary ways. And the situation is not very different today. Poor Blacks — and other poor people — in Britain and the US still have to live largely by rules laid down by their high SES 'masters.' This does not mean that their culture is inferior; rather, their situation is inferior. If their socio-economic status were suddenly raised, they would be able to handle it: they would quickly build into their culture concepts, attitudes and behaviour patterns suited to wealth and power which at present are irrelevant.

The notion of inherent cultural inferiority is a convenient one for higher SES people. It implies that lower SES people are largely to blame for their current situation, because their culture is too weak to enable them to rise to a higher socio-economic level. Also it suggests that they could not cope with a privileged or equal status even if it were given to them, and so one should not feel guilty about denying them access to it. Thus, while no genetic assumptions are involved, the idea of a deep and unalterable cultural malaise among lower classes is just as effective a medium of class bias as belief in biologially transmitted intellectual and moral deficiency.

Denis Lawton in *Class, Culture and the Curriculum* expresses a concern that full acceptance of the cultural equality of the various classes may involve 'ignoring important questions about the quality of life in certain kinds of urban, working-class sub-cultures.' He states that '*if* an environment is an extremely limiting one, then, to base the whole curriculum on "relevance" to it may be to "sell the children short" in a dangerous way.' He describes as an 'extreme relativist position' the notion that 'any sub-cultural values, attitudes and activities are just as good as any others — they are different but equal.' In this context he asks rhetorically: 'Was the quality of life in ancient Athens really not superior to that in Sparta? Is the quality of life now in the Republic of South Africa really different but not worse than in Tanzania?' And he quotes Morris Ginsberg as saying that 'the attack on humanitarian values made by the Nazis has made the doctrine of ethical relativity, adopted more or less unreflectively by many anthropologists, emotionally untenable and has forced them . . . to examine their attitude to ethical problems afresh.'[3]

While there are important issues here which need to be addressed (and Lawton deals with many of them very well), this way of raising the question of *class* differences seems to me to be unfortunate. It is insulting and prejudicial to suggest that working class culture may be inferior to that of higher SES groups. Working class culture is bound to have its faults, and should be open to critical appraisal. But middle and upper class cultures also have their faults (an obvious one at present being persistent prejudice against the lower classes). The outlook of working class people may be 'limited' in certain ways, but there are also distortions in higher class views of reality. It is true that 'the quality of life in certain . . . working-class sub-cultures' is not high, but on the one hand the same may be said of many middle and upper class sub-cultures, and on the other hand this is in part because of the socio-economic circumstances of the lower classes. Once again, we see how victims are blamed for their ills. Their culture is not primarily at fault; indeed, it is working over-time to make the best of a bad situation. Some of those 'limited' outlooks, for example, are *necessary* in order to sustain a measure of happiness in a world with limited possibilities.[4]

A major focus of Lawton's discussion, it should be noted, is the charge that schools impose on working class students irrelevant 'middle class' subject matter. He is concerned to establish that the various academic disciplines are not the property of any one class, and that lower class students should be exposed to them along with everyone else. However, in order to make this point it is not necessary to suggest that some working class sub-cultures may be inferior to middle class culture: one need only show that working class people can benefit from academic study. Further, Lawton seems to underestimate the extent to which the academic disciplines as they exist today *are* the property of higher SES people, being biased in their favour and largely preoccupied with their life concerns. This *need* not be the case, but currently it is. Accordingly, there is indeed an issue of imposing biased viewpoints and irrelevant subject matter on lower SES students through study of the academic disciplines in their present form.

Class bias and the school

Some of the issues of class and schooling were discussed at length in Part 1, especially in Chapters 1 and 2. It was acknowledged there that the school is just one of many societal agencies which promote inequality, and that it cannot hope to eliminate inequality single-handedly: it must link up with broader societal movements pressing in this direction. It was argued, however, that the school could make an important, distinctive contribution by teaching less biased conceptions of society, politics and culture and by modifying the structure and content of schooling so that harmful divisions and invidious distinctions are reduced. Students of all classes should be brought together in a comprehensive school; instructional groupings should be established on a heterogeneous, mixed achievement basis: 'vocational' schooling should be discontinued; and there should be largely a common curriculum, with any individual choice or individualized instruction being as far as possible *not* along SES lines.

As was acknowledged in Part 1, heterogeneous classrooms present a challenge to teachers since students of different socio-economic backgrounds typically have differences in achievement levels, interests, point of view and learning styles. This point has been emphasized by Lawton:

> . . . even if the content and organization of the curriculum *provided* for the pupils is common, does it follow that the pupils will *receive* this content as common? It is possible that children from different backgrounds and of different levels of ability will receive a common curriculum in a highly differentiated way.[5]

Stephen Ball, also observes (in the context of a particular mixed class study) that:

> The teachers became very concerned about identifying the 'ability' of individual pupils as quickly as possible. In some senses it might even be said that the criteria which were used to evaluate or categorize pupils were narrowed rather than broadened by the introduction of mixed-ability.[6]

Ball continues:

> . . . differences between pupils in terms of social class, linguistic ability, motivation, parental support and encouragement become relevant in terms of differential performance and these are translated into a differential allocation of rewards and status.[7]

However, on the one hand, the difficulties are not as great as we have often assumed. After reviewing the research on leisure activities, reading practices and interest in 'high culture' among the various classes, Lawton concludes that 'despite important differences . . . there does seem to exist a common culture in a very meaningful sense.'[8] And Barker, as we saw in Chapter 2, maintains that there exists today 'a consensus about what is important only partially distorted by the language of class'.[9] On the other hand, insofar as there are problems associated with heterogeneous classrooms, these could be overcome to a considerable extent. A much larger proportion of school time could be spent studying issues which are of importance to all students, and an approach could be taken such that all would contribute from their distinctive class perspectives and all would benefit. Problems of evaluation could be dealt with in part by recognizing the distinctive contributions of different classes to the issues in hand, and in part by reducing the extent to which the life of the school revolves around competitive, university-oriented evaluation.

The nature and use of evaluation is crucial to issues of class. If as I have advocated there were no streaming in schools and students studied common subjects to the end of high school (with modest provision for electives on the basis of interest), grading would no longer be needed for placement in a level or year of study. Its purpose as far as the *school* is concerned would not be for comparison of students with one another but rather, where appropriate, for motivation of students and assessment (for pedagogical purposes) of their mastery of specific material and skills.

But what (if anything) should the school say to the outside world about the abilities and achievements of individual students? In the past, schools have given to employers and to colleges and universities the grades obtained by students in school. However, as Bowles and Gintis and others have pointed out, while academic success is strongly correlated with class, it is not indicative of ability to perform tasks in the outside world. School grades are predictive of college and university grades, but again these are not a good gauge of on-the-job proficiency (except, possibly, as a college or university researcher and teacher). By releasing grades, then, schools are participating in a system whereby young people of higher SES background gain access to more highly regarded, better paying, more interesting occupations. In some ways these privileged young people are more suited to these jobs because they can relate well to other privileged people in positions of power, and so keep the wheels of society running 'smoothly' and 'productively'. However, people of lower SES background could relate better to lower SES sub-groups and could introduce new perspectives which would in their own way promote productivity and well being. Further, it is not only the favouritism of the present system which is problematic but also the way in which it *legitimates* the advantages of higher SES people by reference to supposed superior abilities, thus reducing the self-respect of lower SES students.

The arguments against giving school grades to employers are, I believe, very strong. Employers can devise more appropriate criteria and procedures, tailored to their particular enterprise. Most notably, they can offer a period of probationary employment during which the suitability of the young person for the field of work (and the work for the young person) can be assessed. The introduction of a high school report into this complex and delicate evaluation process usually has a distorting effect, and certainly is not of much help.

What to do in the case of colleges and universities is a much more difficult issue. Most professions which use a post-secondary degree as a basis for certification have already decided that 'academic ability' will be a major criterion for admission. If the school did not divulge grades, professional programs would quickly develop their own academic entrance tests, or would take students largely on the basis of interest and then eliminate those who could not perform well academically (regardless of their possible future ability on the job). It might seem reasonable, then, to provide information on high school achievement, if only to save colleges and universities from extra work and to spare students the disappointment of having their hopes raised and then dashed.

On balance, however, I tend to favour not passing high school grades on to tertiary institutions. There are two main reasons for this. First, it would be symbolically important, constituting a strong statement that the purpose of schooling is to provide a solid, common, general education for all and not merely a screening process for the selection of a privileged few or a training program for the world of work. Secondly, despite its strongly academic emphasis, the university world is sufficiently different from that of the school to justify giving students a 'fresh start'. While academic success in post-secondary institutions tends to correlate with previous school performance, there are many exceptions which should give us pause; and the increased vocational emphasis at the post-secondary level, with professional programs, work–study arrangements and so forth, means that a modified set of evaluation criteria is in order. Particular tertiary institutions are bound to want to be selective, rather than take students on a 'first come, first served' basis (which in any event would not be feasible for the more popular institutions). But then perhaps they should have their own assessment procedures (as many already do to a degree) adapted to particular professional programs and the distinctive ethos of each institution.

Schools face a dilemma in this area: the less class biased their evaluation procedures become, the more they may want to pass on information to post-secondary institutions in order to give lower SES students a break. However, the differences between the two types of institution are such that school information will often be irrelevant and even misleading, no matter how sensitively it is gathered. And so long as universities continue to have such a strongly 'academic' emphasis (despite their major occupational training and selection role), the steering effect of preparing students to satisfy university admission criteria will undermine attempts to make schooling less class biased.

The various measures I have proposed for reducing class discrimination in and through the school can only have a modest effect. Higher SES employers will still tend to prefer higher SES employees; criteria of 'brightness' and 'leadership ability' which are in fact class biased will continue to be used; colleges and universities and professional bodies will find ways of emphasizing class biased 'academic ability'; and young people of higher SES background will continue to gain access to better occupations because of their manners and appearance, their connections, their class-related preferences and so forth. Nevertheless, if school people move to clean up their own act they will make a difference of *degree*, especially in the school itself, and will also be in a stronger position to argue for reforms in other sectors of society which complement efforts at the school level. Perhaps above all, the school can contribute by teaching a more accurate version of the origins of socio-economic disadvantage, so that lower SES students may live their present way of life with dignity rather than self-blame and gain the courage and insight they need to press for greater equality in the future.

Notes and References

1 Bowles, S. and Gintis, H. (1976) *Schooling in Capitalist America*, London, Routledge and Kegan Paul, pp. 117 and 317.
2 Sarup, M. (1986) *The Politics of Multiracial Education*, London, Routledge and Kegan Paul, p. 18.
3 Lawton, D. (1975) *Class, Culture and the Curriculum*, London, Routledge and Kegan Paul, pp. 28–9.
4 At a later point, Lawton says that we should 'avoid ... blanket descriptions or value-judgments and talk, instead, of specific strengths and weaknesses of particular cultures for particular purposes. All cultures, seen from outside, appear to possess certain advantages in coping with some aspects of life and certain disadvantages in other respects' (p. 42). However, while this is a better way of putting the matter, it is inconsistent with Lawton's earlier claim that some cultures *are* better than others; and it still leaves open the possibility that working classs culture, while having some strengths, is on balance inferior to middle class culture. My position is that such a possibility should be explicitly ruled out; and that the weaknesses of middle class culture should be given equal time with the weaknesses of working class culture in any discussion of what should be included in the curriculum.
5 Lawton, D., *op. cit.*, p. 50.

6 Ball, S. (1986) 'The Sociology of the School: Streaming, Mixed Ability and Social Class', in Rogers, R. (Ed) *Education and Social Class*, Lewes, The Falmer Press, p. 97.
7 *Ibid.*, p. 98.
8 Lawton, D., *op. cit.*, p. 45.
9 Barker, B. (1986) *Rescuing the Comprehensive Experience*, Milton Keynes, Open University Press, p. 148.

Part Three
New Directions
for Schools

Many new directions for schools are implied by the discussion in Parts 1 and 2. However, I wish to emphasize in Part 3 the shift in the major focus of schooling to 'personal and social education'. I will concentrate here on moral and values education, religious and spiritual education, and political and global education. A consideration of these curriculum areas will be of interest in itself, will enable us to address several key value issues in schooling, and will illustrate some of the general principles of school improvement outlined in previous chapters.

Chapter 13

Moral and Values Education

If schooling is to become more useful to *all* young people — not just to students of higher socio-economic levels seeking credentials — one of the fields that must be given more attention is values education, including moral education. Everyone, regardless of social class and 'academic attainment', can benefit from and contribute to programs in this area.

Moral education is, I believe, best seen as a sub-area within values education; and later in this chaper I will use the term 'moral/values education' — as is commonly done — to refer to the total field. However, there is not complete agreement on this matter, and we must begin with a discussion of the relation between morality and values.

The nature of morality

In Chapter 1 I said that moral values are part of a comprehensive value system, the purpose of which is to serve human well being. Over the centuries, however, philosophers have often claimed that moral values are in a category of their own, sharply separated from other values. It has been said, for example, that moral values are distinctive in that they have nothing to do with prudence, with what is useful. Further, it has been suggested that morality is concerned only with one's duties to others and not with what is important for one's own well being. Again, it has been asserted (most notably by Immanuel Kant) that moral behaviour, unlike other forms of behaviour, is unconnected with desire: truly moral action springs from a desire-free good *will* guided by a special faculty of moral 'reason'. Even the desire to help others cannot be part of one's motivation in a moral act.

The first two of these claims can be rather quickly rejected since they do not square with a simple review of moral virtues. We commonly think of carefulness and self-control, for example, as moral virtues, and yet these clearly have great prudential value and are of importance in managing one's own affairs as well as in helping others. Robinson Crusoe, alone on his island, had to be careful (e.g. in maintaining a calendar) and self-controlled (e.g. in planting some of the grain he had salvaged instead of eating it) in order to survive and establish a tolerable existence for himself. Most people would say that, in behaving as he did, he was exhibiting moral characteristics.

Despite its widespread acceptance, Kant's notion of a desire-free, autonomous moral will is, in my view, equally implausible. It is not consistent with what we observe in everyday human behaviour. When people act they are typically 'motivated' by a set of wishes, desires, goals, emotions and the like. Sometimes, we do seem simply to 'opt' for one course of action rather than another, in what feels like a pure act of will. However, the choice here is between two (or more) alternatives in an ongoing stream of motivated behaviour without which we could not do anything. Further, it is difficult to see why *morality* should be associated with this kind of minimal, passionless choice. Some non-moral actions also appear to be of this character; and many moral actions are obviously performed out of a strong *desire* to help others or achieve a personal goal.

The simplest and (at present) most acceptable way of identifying the moral realm seems to be to present a list of moral virtues. Being moral, we may say, involves having such qualities as carefulness, responsibility, courage, self-control, reliability, truthfulness, honesty, fairness, unselfishness and kindness. To this 'definition' of morality I would add that the *purpose* of morality is to serve human well being, one's own and that of other people. The above qualities are good because, and only insofar as, they promote 'the good life' for humans. This, of course, brings morality under the general analysis of values which I gave in Chapter 1.

Kant's association of morality with exercise of the will does seem to have *some* basis in ordinary usage. Morality, in the everyday sense, appears to be typically (though certainly not always) concerned with *overcoming inner conflict* or with *making an effort* to do something which one might not otherwise do. Courage and unselfishness, for example, often involve successfully dealing with a conflict between contending desires or tendencies. By contrast, desirable non-moral traits such as intelligence, generosity and sensitivity, to the extent that people have them, seem to come more 'naturally' and easily. (This helps explain the common caricature of morality as concerned with the temptations of power, sex, alcohol and the like, and with the exercise of the will in resisting such temptations.)

However, I believe that the role of the will in enabling people to act morally has been greatly exaggerated. Moral behaviour is like other forms of deliberate action in that it requires a solid foundation in emotions, attitudes, dispositions, knowledge and understanding, and also 'enabling circumstances' which render right action possible. As Durkheim said, Kant's idea of an autonomous, purely rational moral will, unaffected by desire, 'has not and never will have anything to do with reality.'[1] And as Bernard Williams maintains, Kant was mistaken in thinking that morality 'was unconditional in the sense that it did not depend on desire at all'; on the contrary, moral necessity is often 'the expression of desire', desire which is 'essential to the (moral) agent and (has) to be satisfied'.[2] People cannot be moral in a vacuum. While the will (whatever exactly is meant by that term) may play a distinctively larger role in morality than in other value areas, the difference is one of degree and is not sufficient to place moral values outside the general analysis of values presented earlier: like other value domains it is largely desired-based, concerned ultimately with the pursuit of well being, for oneself and others.

The importance of morality

If we are to teach morality in schools we must not only understand what it is but also be assured of its importance. This may appear obvious: what could be more important than morality? But in fact people often joke about morality (in private, at least) as if it were the concern of fanatics and fuddy duddies. And we have no less a person than Nietzsche writing of the need to go 'beyond good and evil.' Also, in the West, we have one major religious tradition — Christianity — which from time to time has raised questions about the importance of rules or 'the law' and suggested that there is really only one rule or law, namely, that of love.

Morality has fallen into disrepute, I believe, through a combination of poor teaching and abuse of authority. We should not be surprised that there is cynicism about it. For example, often moral rules have been presented as if they were absolutes, to which no exceptions may be made, when any humane and sensible person can see the need for exceptions from time to time. Again, morality has often been used by those in authority to force the mass of people to live in ways that serve the establishment's interests. Above all, morality has been taught without explaining its purposes, so that people have not been given reasons for taking it seriously.

In fact, of course, moral traits such as reliability, self-control, honesty and consideration for others are crucial, in some form and some degree, if one is to achieve one's personal goals, have mutually beneficial relationships with other people and live well in society generally. Although the link between morality and 'the good life' has been played down by many philosophers and moralists, it is clearly there. People in their behaviour consistently resist extreme forms of moral obligation, but they typically see the necessity for at least a moderate level of morality. Even among thieves, it has been said, there is honour.

It is sometimes suggested that moral rules and principles are unimportant because we should judge each case on its merits, taking account of all relevant considerations; pre-established guidelines will only bias us in a particular direction, clouding our perception of the unique case before us.[3] In my view, while it is true that each case must be looked at afresh, rules and principles serve a valuable role in summarizing previous insights and experiences and helping to bring them to bear on new cases. As we saw in Chapter 1, there is seldom one right course to take in a situation, but rather a variety of better and worse possibilities. Moral rules and principles, refined and adjusted over time, can 'push us' in an appropriate direction. Without completely determining our judgment, they can give us the advantage of past experience and help us to make better decisions.

Is there a place for moral education in schools?

Morality may be important; but is it something that can be taught? One often hears the comment that morality is 'caught, not taught'. However, while some of the elements of a person's morality are there from birth or early infancy, there is much that can be added through later learning, often of a formal kind. For example, in order to understand the need for religious and racial tolerance, knowledge of other people's culture and point of view is necessary of a type that many people do not 'pick up' through everyday experience. Again, in order to know how to act morally in government positions, or in business, or in the health professions there are facts, not to mention theories, that we must become aware of to help guide our actions. It is true that many of our basic dispositions become established before we begin school, but as David Gauthier has argued, the moral policies we build on these dispositions, and the particular decisions we make, can be crucially affected by education.[4] Even the 'kindest' people can act cruelly if they do not fully understand the consequences of their actions.

As well as making moral mistakes because of ignorance or misinformation, people also make mistakes because they do not have a good sense of how to approach moral decisions. For example, sometimes people see moral requirements in terms of authority; or as absolutes that admit of no exceptions; or as simple when in fact they are complex. Also, some people place too much emphasis on conscience as the source of moral insight and become tyrannized by it, not realizing the extent to which one's conscience is a product of early upbringing and has to be educated along with other aspects of one's being. Young people, then, can benefit from comprehensive study of the nature of morality and moral decision making, together with experience in weighing a wide range of considerations against one another.

Some people reject the idea of teaching morality in schools on the ground that it is too controversial. They argue that there is so little agreement on moral matters that there is virtually nothing one can safely teach. However, I believe that morality is less controversial than we have thought.[5] While religious moralists often maintain that the *ultimate* purpose of morality is to do what is prescribed by the divine order, and Kantians and other deontologists suggest that morality is an end in itself, in fact they show remarkable agreement with other groups, defining doing good in terms of such everyday things as giving assistance, relieving suffering and enabling people to live full, satisfying lives. They even agree to a considerable extent on *why* moral actions are good: they accept the importance of survival, happiness, friendship, freedom and the like, disagreeing rather on just *how* reference to such basic human goods figures in the justification of morality. Given this measure of agreement, then, and also the undoubted importance of the moral domain, it seems appropriate to 'get going' with moral education in schools, presenting various 'wisdom traditions' and other relevant material for discussion and attempting to broaden the areas of understanding and consensus.

A combined moral/values education program

The case made so far for the importance of morality and the place of moral education in schools applies equally, and if anything more obviously, to values and values education in general. Sound non-moral values — personal, social, political, economic, aesthetic, ecological and so forth — are essential for human well being. The neglect of value inquiry in society generally and schools in particular must be seen as a major factor in the problems faced by humans around the globe today.

In most cases it is best to combine moral and values education. This follows from the conception of morality and the relationship between morality and values outlined earlier. If moral values are part of a system of values which together promote 'the good life' for humans and which must be constantly weighed against each other, it is reasonable to include the study of morality within a comprehensive treatment of the value field. To deal with moral issues on their own would be largely unproductive, and would also help perpetuate the belief that morality is a separate domain. Of course, this does not preclude focusing specifically on morality from time to time, as indeed we have done in the early sections of this chapter.

A practical reason for having joint moral/values education is that it is often difficult to separate moral from non-moral value topics within the curriculum. Are honesty and sensitivity moral virtues or social virtues? In which subject area does political corruption fall? Should ecological concerns be dealt with in an ethics course or a personal and societal values program (or in geography, for that matter)? This line of argument is not conclusive, since if followed far enough it might suggest that *all* subject distinctions should be eliminated in schools, something which is not feasible at the present time. However, in the case of moral and non-moral value inquiry, the high degree of overlap seems to require that they be taught together. Even if one gains permission to teach a course called 'ethics' or 'morals', one must in practice expand it to cover a wide range of value questions if it is to go beyond simplistic moralizing or arid analysis.

In moral/values education there are literally hundreds of topics and sub-topics to be covered over the young person's school years. The following list is offered in order to give some specific examples and also to show the general shape of the field. The school should deal with topics such as these:

(i) *Basic human values* such as survival, health, happiness, friendship, love, self-respect, fulfilment, meaning in life;

(ii) *Spiritual values* such as awareness, breadth of outlook, integration, wonder, gratitude, hope, detachment, humility, love, gentleness;

(iii) *Moral values* such as responsibility, courage, self-control, reliability, truthfulness, honesty, fairness, unselfishness;

(iv) *Social and political values* such as peace, justice, due process, tolerance, participation, cooperation, sharing, loyalty, solidarity, citizenship;

(v) *Value centred institutions* such as family, community, school, work, nation, world community;

(vi) *Approaches to life management* (or 'life skills') such as physical and mental health, decision making, coping with change, career choice and change, financial planning, human relations, family living;

(vii) *The value dimensions of school subjects* such as literature, science, social studies, history, geography, art, music;

(viii) *The nature of values,* values and tradition, values and religion, values and the law, how to solve value problems, differences in values, how we get our values, how we change our values;

(ix) *Contemporary value problems* such as poverty, unemployment, racism, sexism, child abuse, wife abuse, ageism, consumerism, ecological deterioration.

Many of these topics, of course, may be considered in traditional school subject areas. Indeed, I have spoken of a moral/values program rather than a 'course' in order to allow for the possibility that *all* moral/values studies may be integrated into other school subjects. I personally favour having separate courses in ethics (broadly understood) or values, both to highlight the importance of the field and because there is so much ground to cover. However, where that is not possible, a considerable amount can still be done in other courses: and even where there are special moral/values courses, they should be seen as complementing the exploration of value issues in other school subjects.

It is important to recognize that the moral/values program of a school should not be limited to formal courses, whether in values or in other subject areas. The whole school experience should contribute to student growth in this area. For example, teachers and school administrators should embody in their behaviour their view of how one should live; and they should continually be engaged in developing that view further. Again, students should be involved in major ways in the governance of the school, participating in decisions about the curriculum, the discipline system of the school, and so on, so that they learn how to make decisions in these domains and also gain a fuller understanding of the values of schooling. The 'school experience', too, should extend beyond the school grounds, with school-sponsored involvement in community and societal development projects. Students will often learn as much about moral/value issues through practical experience as through formal study and discussion.

Whose values?

An objection raised against teaching morals or values in schools is that it involves the imposition of the teachers' values on students. The question 'whose values will be taught?' is asked rhetorically, with the implication that the school has no right or competence to influence the values of students.

Many moral/values educators, in order to avoid this kind of objection, have said that teachers should not promote a particular content. They have proposed for the teacher the role of skill instructor/discussion organizer/devil's advocate (Donald Oliver and Fred Newmann), values clarifier (Louis Raths and Sidney Simon), or stimulator of natural development (Lawrence Kohlberg).

My own view, in line with what was said in Chapter 7 on indoctrination, is that teacher neutrality in values is impossible to attain. Teachers are constantly transmitting values both through their behaviour and through what they teach. Try as they may, they cannot conceal their outlook on life from their students: and the academic material they teach has values embedded in it.

Furthermore, I believe that moral and values advocacy is an essential aspect of the role of the teacher. Certain value beliefs must be promoted by teachers in the daily life of the school: for example, that human relationships should as far as possible be warm and cordial, that students should be treated fairly, that knowledge is important, that a degree of structure and discipline is necessary for learning, and so on. And beyond these 'givens' of good schooling, teachers must present themselves as people of values who have reasons for their convictions. If they do not, why should students respect them or take notice of what they say; and why should they take the study of values seriously?

The strong presentation of value content in schools (including theory about the *nature* of values) is necessary if students are to make progress in this area. An attempted value-neutral approach will help reinforce the currently too prevalent notion that values either are not important or are purely subjective, simply a matter of opinion. Also, without a solid input of ideas and arguments, students will not have an adequate basis on which to develop a sound value system of their own. Pedagogically, too, a neutral approach leaves students wondering what is going on, searching for the hidden agenda and generally becoming frustrated with the enterprise.

The solution to the problem of imposing values on students, then, lies not in refraining from moral and values advocacy but rather in creating a school and classroom atmosphere in which students are genuinely free to disagree, propose alternatives and modify positions under examination. One of the best ways to achieve this is for teachers to show that their views on value matters, though firmly held and supported by reasons, are not *fixed*; that they are willing to modify them in the light of ongoing inquiry in the school and beyond. Thus there should be both a solid input from teachers and very considerable freedom on the part of students. In the end, obviously, students should as far as possible adopt their own values; but they will be aided rather than hindered in this by teachers who are not afraid to reveal and argue for their own value beliefs, while also presenting a variety of other content.

Varying approaches to moral/values education

Most moral/values education programs in the past have suffered from narrowness of focus. So many aspects of the person are involved in the development of an adequate set of values that one cannot hope to succeed by working on just one or two fronts. We have already noted, for example, that attempting to deal with moral issues in isolation from values in general is unproductive; and that moral/values education in schools must be conducted not only through values courses but also through other school subjects, and not only through formal courses but also through practical experience (including school–society projects).

I wish now to review very briefly some of the approaches to moral/values education practised or advocated in recent times. And the main point I wish to make about each of them is that, while it offers some useful insights, it is not sufficiently broad in scope to have a major influence by itself.

Liberal education

Traditionally it has been thought that a study of liberal arts subjects such as literature and history will have a humanizing effect on students, making them among other things more reasonable, tolerant and fair. However, while such an education is obviously important, one should not exaggerate the impact it will have, at least in its standard form. For one thing, as we saw in Part 2, often the writings one has to deal with in literature, history and other humanities areas contain deep racial, class, national, sexual and other biases such that they should be made the object of fundamental moral/values critique rather than straightforward textual analysis of the usual kind. Again, although the systematic study of phenomena of the type explored in the humanities is important for value inquiry, some phenomena and insights are more relevant than others. In order to arrive at conclusions about value issues it is necessary to select and organize the insights afforded by the humanities so that their value implications are clear. Yet another problem with an exclusively liberal arts approach to moral/values education is that it is too narrowly cognitive in emphasis. Deep insight into the human condition and even into what is right and good does not necessarily issue in appropriate attitudes and behaviour, even though it is an essential step in that direction.

Sermonizing and exhortation (sometimes referred to as 'character education')

Perhaps the most widespread type of moral/values 'education' consists in the bald statement of what is right and wrong, coupled with exhortations (perhaps with reference to sanctions) to do the right and avoid the wrong. This approach has been too much maligned in recent decades, since the clear setting forth of the values of a society does have a place, and reference to moral and other virtues should not have been completely replaced by talk of general principles. Within the context of a community which is prepared to back up its requirements with rewards and punishments, this method can have a significant effect. However, the recounting of virtues and vices *by itself* has little if any impact (as Hartshorne and May showed in their studies of Boy Scout and Sunday school classes in the 1920s),[6] since it rarely draws attention to duties that people are not already aware of, and it does not give new insight into *why* one should fulfil one's duties. It is a cognitive approach (except within the context of community sanctions) but offers a minimum of cognitive input. Indeed, to call it 'education' is barely appropriate since it lacks the explanatory and theoretical content which we normally associate with education.

Therapeutic approaches

There are several methods which attempt to overcome the excessively cognitive bias of traditional moral education by the use of psychological techniques. At one end of the spectrum are behaviour modifiers such as B.F. Skinner and Justin Aronfreed, and at the other end are non-directive therapists such as Carl Rogers; in between are a diversity of practitioners including psychoanalysts, transactional analysts, and advocates of transcendental meditation. Now, obviously the psychological perspective is important, both for identifying some of the elements in human attitudes and behaviour and for dealing with particular behavioural problems and 'blocks' in understanding. However, what all these approaches have in common, despite their diversity, is a lack of appreciation of the complex *theoretical* task involved in developing sound values. In each case, it is assumed that the right and the good is known — by society, by the therapist, by the client or by the client's 'inner being' — and what is needed is a psychological technique to establish the appropriate value in the person or clear away the 'blocks', 'scripts' or the like which are preventing the value from emerging or being expressed. But as we have observed before, a large part of the problem in values is *knowing* what is right (and why); and when people behave inappropriately it is often not because they have psychological problems or blocks that could be cleared away, but rather because they do not know what is appropriate behaviour (and neither does their therapist, nor their community). We see, then, that these approaches go to the other extreme of downplaying cognitive factors. In this they are remarkably like the approach of traditional moralists who claim that we always know what is right and merely lack the will to do it.

Stimulating natural development

Jean Piaget de-emphasized the role of the teacher in moral education, stressing that children rather naturally improve the adequacy of their moral judgment as they interact with the world and especially with other children. Lawrence Kohlberg, building on Piaget's ideas, continued to give a central place to natural development but outlines two main ways in which it may be stimulated: by presenting students with moral dilemmas (and related discussion) which reveal the inadequacy of their current modes of moral reasoning, and by constructing a 'just community' in the school within which students have an opportunity to hone their moral outlook and behaviour.[7] The optimism of this approach about the capacity of children to work things out for themselves — Kohlberg refers to them as young 'moral philosophers' — represents a giant step forward in moral education (although it is somewhat undermined by the assumption that children are on average at a lower level of moral functioning than adults). Further, some of the techniques recommended for stimulating development are important additions to the repertoire of values educators. However, the approach tends to be *overly* optimistic about individual moral development (whether in children or adults), underestimating the need for moral theory and the strength of the influence that teachers, the school and society have on people's values. Accordingly, it does not attach sufficient importance to fundamental and systematic moral inquiry (as distinct from discussion of dilemmas and cases) or to factors other than cognitive ones which affect moral formation.

Teaching reasoning skills

As we noted earlier, Donald Oliver and Fred Newmann (and many others following their lead) attempted to overcome the problem of indoctrination in values education by teaching reasoning skills rather than content in value matters.[8] They proposed that the teacher should maintain the stance of a neutral discussion organizer and information source, or at times a Socratic devil's advocate. Instruction should be restricted to factual information, an analytical scheme for clarifying the elements in controversial issues, and reasoning skills for the satisfactory resolution of issues. The main problem here lies in the attempt to teach skills without content, and in the notion that students should not be helped to arrive at viewpoints on substantive values in the classroom but rather be given a set of reasoning skills which they would then go off and use in the real world. While teaching problem solving skills must be a major part of both the aim and process of values education, substantive values must also be taught if students are to develop a more adequate value system for daily living.

Values Clarification (VC)

According to Louis Raths and Sidney Simon (and others in the VC school), the task of the teacher is to help students clarify the nature and consequences of their values and become thoroughly committed to them, without passing judgment on whether or not they are objectively sound.[9] The emphasis here is on developing confident, integrated students with high self-esteem. There is considerable optimism about the desires and values children actually have as distinct from the ones that other people think they should have. Once again, we must acknowledge the positive aspects of this approach, which should be incorporated into a comprehensive values education enterprise. Students *should* have greater clarity about their values and greater confidence in the appropriateness of their values, at least for the time being. However, they must also be introduced to the idea that *one can make mistakes* in value matters, and that today in a great many areas people — individuals and societies, children and adults — have values that stand in need of improvement. Further, they must systematically learn ways in which, at least in the long run, value problems may be overcome, in theory and in practice, at personal and societal levels. This knowledge need not undermine self-esteem, since there are many factors — historical, psychological, cultural, political — that have led to the current state of affairs. Indeed, these factors, too, should be systematically studied, partly to bolster self-esteem and partly to give students a clearer grasp of what must be done to achieve value reform.

In conclusion, then: as we attempt to implement moral/values education in the school we should avoid relying on any one of the various approaches advocated, including the ones reviewed above. Each has much to offer, but the task is so complex that their various insights and techniques need to be brought together in a workable synthesis which makes significant value development possible.

Getting started with moral/values education

In a sense, as we have noted often, the school is already heavily involved in teaching values. But if we are to have moral/values *education* as distinct from inculcation or indoctrination, an explicit program must be established within which teachers and students have, as far as possible, an opportunity to examine value issues in depth and critically evaluate different alternatives.

This should be a very extensive program spread over all the school years, covering a wide range of topics of the kinds outlined earlier.

Dealing with a moral/values 'topic' does not necessarily require formal study or discussion. As Kohlberg and his colleagues have pointed out, questions of justice and fairness, for example, can be grappled with in the context of building a 'just community' school.[10] And as Prakash has argued, greater interpenetration between the school and the community could afford students major opportunities for confronting moral issues.[11] However, formal study is obviously of considerable importance, and is the aspect of moral/values education to which schools — in their present form at least — can perhaps make their greatest contribution.

There is an urgent need for teacher education and the development of learning materials and pedagogical strategies in the values field. People are often disappointed at the unwillingness of teachers to make a major commitment to values education. But apart from the problem that many people still question the legitimacy of values education as a school activity, teachers have far less training and far fewer resources in this area than in traditional school subjects. Until these problems are overcome, we should not be surprised at teachers' reluctance.

Nevertheless, we should try to make a start. Even without courses specifically on values, all teachers are entitled to engage in at least some moral/values education, whether within their teaching subjects or as part of their general leadership and guidance role in the school. Also, as ordinary citizens they are free to become involved in reform movements in the larger society, and may thus illustrate to students what can be done and also have an indirect influence on the school through the community.

To begin with, teachers should identify at least a few value areas to which they are prepared to devote special attention in their own lives, in their thinking and reading and in the life of the school. These should normally be areas which (a) are appropriate given their teaching field(s) and other responsibilities; (b) are of substantial importance and interest to themselves and their students; and (c) are ones which they feel they could talk about with students with confidence and enjoyment.

In connection with these chosen areas, teachers can then proceed to gather topic outlines, study units, textbooks, films, magazine articles, newspaper clippings and so on. They can discuss substantive issues and possible teaching methods with their colleagues and others and attend relevant courses, conferences and workshops (if available). They can identify community resources and plan appropriate activities both in the school and beyond. And of course they should begin to include sessions on the topics in their school classes; they may be pleasantly surprised to find how much they learn about the topics and techniques of teaching them simply by 'getting going'. Initially the time devoted to the areas should perhaps be rather limited; but as experience, knowledge and confidence grows, so can the extent of one's values teaching. And gradually one should add other topics to the original set.

Ideally, the activities of individual teachers should link up with general curriculum reform in the school aimed at increasing the attention given to crucial personal and societal issues. Teachers should both be supported by and feed into an emerging moral/values program. However, this depends partly on schools becoming more communal in nature than they are at present. In the meantime, individual teachers can take the initiative in the gradual way outlined. Any discomfort they feel in the role of 'pioneers' will be more than compensated for by the personal growth they themselves experience and the satisfaction of seeing students enjoy and benefit from these new educational pursuits.

Notes and References

1 Durkheim, E. (1961) *Moral Education,* New York, The Free Press, p. 113.
2 Williams, B. (1985) *Ethics and the Limits of Philosophy,* London, Fontana/Collins, p. 189.
3 See for example Mitchell, D. (1963) 'Are Moral Principles Really Necessary?', *Australasian Journal of Philosophy,* 41, 2, pp. 163–81.
4 Gauthier, D. (1971) 'Moral Action and Moral Education' in Beck, C., Crittenden, B. and Sullivan, E. (Eds) *Moral Education: Interdisciplinary Approaches,* Toronto, University of Toronto Press, pp. 138–46.
5 For an extended account of similarities in morality around the world, see Ginsberg, M. (1956) *On The Diversity of Morals,* London, Heinemann, especially Chapters VII and VIII.
6 See Kohlberg, L. (1981) *The Philosophy of Moral Development,* San Francisco, Harper and Row, pp. 31–2.
7 See, for example, Reimer, J., Paolitto, D. and Hersh, R. (1983) *Promoting Moral Growth: From Piaget to Kohlberg,* 2nd end., New York, Longman, especially Chapters 4–7.
8 Newmann, F. and Oliver, D. (1970) *Clarifying Public Controversy,* Boston, Little, Brown.
9 See, for example, Raths, L. *et al.* (1978) *Values and Teaching,* rev. ed., Columbus, Merrill and Simon, S. *et al.* (1972) *Values Clarification,* New York, Hart.
10 See Wasserman, E. (1976) 'Implementing Kohlberg's "Just Community Concept" in an Alternative High School', *Social Education,* 16 (April), pp. 203–7; Lickona, T. (1977) 'Creating the Just Community with Children', *Theory Into Practice,* 16 (April), pp. 97–106.
11 Prakash, M.S. (1987) 'Partners in Moral Education: Communities and Their Public Schools', in Ryan, K. and McLean, G. (Eds) *Character Development in Schools and Beyond,* New York, Praeger, pp. 126–33.

Chapter 14

Religious and Spiritual Education

Religious education is necessary, as we saw in Chapter 8, in order to help eradicate religious bias from school and society. Students need to understand as far as possible that there is 'no one true way', and recognize that people of different religions are pursuing the same basic human values through their religion. They also need to grasp the point of *specific* religious beliefs and practices in order, where appropriate, to overcome prejudice against them and against the people with whom they are associated.

This, however, is clearly only part of the task of religious education, and focuses on a rather negative goal: to overcome religious bias. In the present chapter we will take a more positive approach, attempting to show in general the importance and legitimacy of religious education (including spiritual education) and how in broad terms it should be conducted, whether in private or in public school settings.

What is religion?

Different people mean different things by 'religion'. In some senses of the word, everyone is religious. For example, Durkheim in *The Elementary Forms of the Religious Life* claims that *all* people use a set of symbols to integrate their beliefs, values and ideals into a total approach to life, and this symbol system is their religion.[1] Paul Tillich in *Dynamics of Faith* maintains that being religious is 'the state of being ultimately concerned', and because everyone has some ultimate concern, even if it be nationalism, success or social status, everyone is religious.[2] And Wilfred Cantwell Smith states that 'any attempt to discriminate between "religion" and "philosophy" is inept';[3] and assuming that everyone has a 'philosophy' in roughly the sense intended by Smith, this suggests that everyone is religious.

On other definitions of the term, however, only certain people are religious. For example, many people identify religion with belief in the supernatural, that which is fundamentally mysterious and beyond all ordinary experience, and would not refer to anyone who did not have such belief as religious. Again, many people associate religion with membership in a specific traditional community, acceptance of the myths and credal beliefs of that community, and participation in related rituals and practices. Yet again, some people use the word 'religious' to refer only to those people who have a certain depth of faith and piety, those who are *really* religious or 'spiritual.'

It is difficult to choose between these usages, and I do not think we should do so *in general*. Each has certain advantages. In everyday situations we will usually be misunderstood if we use the words 'religion' and 'religious' in an unrestricted sense. However, in more specialized settings it is often very valuable to see everyone as in a sense religious, focusing on the characteristics which all human beings have in common rather than those which differentiate us. The important thing is that we make clear how we are using the term on a given occasion, if it is not apparent from the context.

For present purposes, I would like to identify two senses of 'religion': what I will call the 'popular' sense and the 'broad' sense. To begin with the popular sense, by 'religion' most people in the West mean a phenomenon which has features such as the following: belief in the supernatural (or the magical), belief in providence, tradition, community, ritual, interest in profound experiences, an ethical system, a worldview, a preoccupation with the 'large questions' of life. It should be noted that many of these are *typical* rather than necessary features of religion in the popular sense. For example, when a new religion is established the role of tradition (at least the tradition of *that* religion) is minimal. Again, some religions do not have a well developed worldview: their focus is on a limited range of dimensions of reality. However, while not all of the features listed are essential, it is necessary that a phenomenon has *some* of them in order to count as religion in the popular sense; and belief in a supernatural, providential order appears to be essential to religion in most people's thinking.

I would like to propose that, in addition to this popular usage, the word 'religion' sometimes be used in a broader sense to refer to cases where people may or may not believe in a supernatural, providential being or order, but nevertheless embrace a set of ideas and practices tied to a comprehensive worldview and conception of what is ultimately important in life. Such people, while not *necessarily* believing in 'God' or the 'divine', accept the 'transcendent' (as defined in Chapter 8), that is, those phenomena and ideals which extend beyond our present knowledge and attainments and frequently surprise and challenge us. On this definition, many people who are not associated with one of the so-called 'religions' would qualify as religious in a strong and positive sense; and some 'religious' people in the popular sense would not be seen as especially religious.

The popular sense of religion is for many people largely descriptive: it is not necessarily positive or negative, serving rather to identify people who have certain distinctive beliefs, commitments and practices. One often hears comments of the kind: so and so is very religious, but a reasonable person to deal with; or so and so is very religious, but self-centered. No strong connection is seen between being religious and being a good or bad person. By contrast, the broad sense of 'religious' is strongly evaluative: to be religious in this sense is desirable by definition. In this respect, the latter usage is already found among some religious people (in the popular sense) who distinguish between the more and less religious and spiritual members of their community. They may not, however, be prepared to refer to non-religious people (in the popular sense) as religious, as I am proposing, since this implies that one may attain religiousness and spirituality without the aid of religion (in the popular sense). (It should be noted that there are other broad senses of 'religious' that are *not* evaluative. For example, as we have seen, Tillich is prepared to describe as religious anyone who has an 'ultimate concern', even if that concern be materialism or intense nationalism. This is *not* the sense in which I am using the term in this context).

One way of distinguishing the two senses of 'religious' is by means of the concept of spirituality. One could be religious in the popular sense without being particularly spiritual; whereas being spiritual is fundamental to being religious in the broad sense. By spiritual, I mean possessing such qualities as awareness, integration, courage, love and gentleness. Traditionally, spirituality (and religiousness) has often been tied to the notion of being in touch with and perhaps possessed by a divine being or order; but I am proposing a usage which would not *require* this as a component. (We will look at this concept of spirituality more fully later).

The role of religion

Religion in both the popular and the broad sense plays a valuable role in people's lives. However, not *everyone* needs to be religious in the popular sense. As we noted in Chapter 8, one does not have to believe in the 'divine', the 'infinite' or the 'supernatural' in order to live a good, spiritual life, or even to attain 'salvation' in a broad sense of the word. Nor does one have to belong to a religious community (in the popular sense) or practice its rituals and celebrations in order to live 'the good life'. (Although everyone needs to belong to *some* community or communities, and engage in certain 'rituals' and celebrations).

But while not everyone needs to be religious in the popular sense, there are many individuals and groups who do. The fact that religion is not necessary for everyone does not mean that it is not necessary for anyone. To draw an analogy, just because some people do not need to marry and have children in order to live a fulfilled life, one cannot argue that no-one needs to marry and have children in order to be fulfilled. People's needs and circumstances vary. Durkheim was a staunch opponent of religion, and suggested replacing the authority of the Catholic church in France with the authority of the state. Nevertheless, he maintained that the church had played an important moral role in French society, and stressed that one should not dismantle it without putting something in its place. He said:

> . . . due to the close bond established historically between morality and religion, we can anticipate . . . that if we begin to eliminate everything religious from the traditional system without providing any substitute, we run the risk of also eliminating essential moral ideas and sentiments.[4]

The point Durkheim has made here about moral values can, I think, be made about values in general. For many people, religion is an important mediator of a satisfactory way of life. If they were to lose their religious faith, their whole way of life would be negatively affected, in the short run and perhaps permanently.

Religion (in the popular sense) helps many people achieve basic human values: for example, inner peace, happiness, interpersonal harmony, love, companionship, a sense of belonging, wisdom, fulfilment and a sense of meaning in life. Religion has not always promoted these values very well, as we saw in Chapter 8: better and worse forms of a religion emerge over time. But the same may be said of non-religious ways of life; and it is clear that religion has often supported a generally good way of life, well supplied with basic values.

Religion (in the popular sense) is also important because of the questions it raises. It asks about the origin and destiny of things: where have we come from and where are we going? It asks about the nature of reality: its extent, its unity and diversity, its personal and impersonal dimensions, its elements of mystery and transcendence. Religion asks about the nature of human beings: what are the sources of good and bad in us, what is the relationship between body, mind, and spirit? It explores the problem of suffering, of evil in the world, of free will and determinism. It raises the issue of the meaning of life. There has been a tendency in the West in modern times to ignore many of these questions, or even to dismiss them as meaningless in some way. However, people continue to ask them, often unconsciously. And an adequate answer is essential to a full, spiritual way of life for religious and non-religious people alike. If we do not address these concerns, important areas of life are left unexplored, and individuals resort to makeshift solutions to meet needs that cannot be denied.

As well as *asking* the large questions of life, of course, religions also offer their *answers*. While one may not always like the answers, one should not reject them out of hand. Discussing traditional answers is a good stimulus for looking for new ones. And if we do not accept the whole of an answer, we may find insight and inspiration in some part: it may enrich our worldview. For example, the imagery of the action of water in nature found in Taosim and the related principle of 'going with the flow' have been taken over by many people of widely varying belief systems. And even where we personally have no use for a particular religious image or doctrine, it may play a valuable role in the lives of other people.

Another part of the role of religion (in the popular sense) is to give people a community to belong to. Communities are important for many reasons. They help us overcome loneliness; they give us support when things go wrong; they offer a setting within which we can make friendships and learn from each other; they bring people of different generations closer together; and so on. Traditionally, religions have carried a major responsibility for fostering local community life. Most people, of course, belong to several overlapping communities rather than a single one. But for many people, loss of membership in their religious community would seriously affect their quality of life.

While not everyone needs to belong to a religious community, we should note that religions meet some rather distinctive needs that are not met by all groups: for example, they offer answers to the large questions of life, they provide for special kinds of profound experience, and they have time-honoured ways of dealing with life events such as birth, coming of age, marriage and death. People who decide to get by without belonging to a religious community should make sure they have other ways of meeting these needs.

Religious communities are not without their problems. Because they require a degree of compliance with accepted beliefs and behaviour, there is the danger of excessive conformity. Because communal life is guided in part by tradition, there is the possibility of too much reverence for past beliefs and practices. Because a community must have leaders, there may be abuse of authority. However, dangers such as these are found in all communities. There is on average just as much chance of avoiding them inside a religious tradition as outside it.

The importance of the community role of religion has often been underestimated even by religions themselves. Christianity and Islam, for example, have sometimes aspired to a kind of universalism in religious commitment that neglects local community building except as a launching pad for larger scale projects. And the extreme emphasis often placed on *belief* by these religions as the key to religious life also downplays the importance of community. Too often what we believe — what is in our heads — has been seen as what makes us a member of a religious community. But community membership is too important a matter to depend simply on belief. People should not be ejected from their community merely because they do not have orthodox beliefs. The grounds are inadequate and the cost is too high.

I have made a case for the importance of religion in the popular sense in the lives of many people. In closing this section, I wish to note briefly why religion in the *broad* sense is important for *everyone*. In my view, while it is possible to live 'the good life' without being religious in the popular sense, one cannot do so without being at least somewhat religious in the broad sense. Human well being is dependent on having a relatively sound and comprehensive worldview and an openness to 'transcendent' (though not necessarily 'supernatural') realities and ideals. In order to have a satisfactory set of values one must have perspectives, outlooks and attitudes which go beyond what is usually understood by the term 'values'. Another way of putting this might be that one must have a 'philosophy of life', or a 'set of metaphysical assumptions'; but equally, I think, it is appropriate to say that one must be 'religious', in a broad sense of the term.

While the use of the word 'religion' in this way, and the insistence on the necessity of religion in this sense, carries with it certain dangers which we must constantly guard against, it has a number of advantages which, in my view, outweigh the disadvantages. Despite the firm prediction of some great western thinkers of the late nineteenth and early twentieth centuries, religion is clearly not about to disappear, and one must come to terms with it rather than simply reject it. By accepting the legitimacy of religion in some sense, one tends to break down barriers between religious and 'non-religious' people, thus reducing defensive posturing and encouraging all people to work amicably together in developing a more adequate conception of reality and approach to life. One also encourages 'non-religious' people to take seriously many of the large questions asked by religions and often neglected by other systems of thought; and also to examine the answers to these questions given by religious traditions.

But one should not insist too strongly on a particular word usage. If certain people acknowledge the importance of the issues raised by religions but nevertheless do not wish to call themselves 'religious' in any sense, that is their prerogative. And it can certainly be confusing simply to use the word 'religious', without qualification, to refer to matters which are not religious in the popular sense. In cases where one is not following popular usage, it is often best to place the terms 'religion' and 'religious' in quotation marks or use a phrase such as 'religion-like' or 'religion in a broad sense'.

A broad concept of spirituality

I have already introduced a broad, rather unconventional use of the term 'spiritual' which does not necessarily involve reference to a supernatural 'spirit' or 'spirit realm' in the traditional sense. If we are to begin to develop a notion of 'spiritual education', as promised earlier, it is necessary before proceeding further to expand on this conception of the spiritual.[5]

The suggestion that one may be spiritual without being religious may seem startling at first. What we need to do, to begin exploring this issue, is look at the characteristics that are often ascribed to spiritual people (just as, in the previous chapter, we found that a review of moral virtues gave us some access to the concept of the moral). This will enable us to see that, in fact, spiritual traits are ones that could be — and commonly are — found in non-religious as well as religious people (in the popular sense). It will also show the importance of spirituality, since the traits are obviously crucial for any good life.

Spiritual people are characterized, to a greater or lesser extent, by all or most of the following:

(a) *Awareness.* In various religions, the spiritual person is described as 'awake', 'enlightened', open to 'the light'. This does not imply an overly intellectual emphasis, since even the most humble and unschooled person may be 'awake' in this sense.

(b) *Breadth of outlook.* Spiritual people see things in perspective, and have a sense of the extent of reality in time and space. Once again, this does not mean that they must be 'Renaissance persons' with enormous breadth of learning, but rather that they are aware of and take account of the wide range of considerations that bear on their daily life.

(c) *A holistic outlook.* A spiritual person is aware of the interconnectedness of things, the unity within the diversity, patterns within the whole.

(d) *Integration.* Spiritual people are integrated in body, mind and spirit; and in the various dimensions and commitments of their life, including societal ones.

(e) *Wonder.* The spiritual person has a due sense of awe, of mystery, of the transcendent in life. This does not necessariy entail belief in the supernatural, the totally 'other'; but it does mean that we are aware that there is always 'something more', something beyond what we can at present achieve or explain. And it involves marvelling at the complexity and vastness of reality.

(f) *Gratitude.* Sometimes this word is used in such a way that it implies the existence of divine 'person' to whom we are grateful. However, such a belief is not essential; one might conceive of a 'grateful' approach to life rather in terms of attitudes of gladness and humility with respect to the good things of life.[6]

(g) *Hope.* Erik Erikson has identified hope as an important aspect of the human response.[7] Baum defines belief in God in part in terms of having a hopeful outlook and moving confidently into the future.[8] Even without belief in 'providence', a certain degree of hopefulness or optimism would seem to be justified, and indeed necessary for everyday living.

(h) *Courage.* Plato in *The Republic* spoke of the need for a courageous, spirited approach to life. Courage is as basic and important as hope.

(i) *Energy.* Spiritual people, in order to fulfil their many life tasks, must be characterized by energy. Fortunately, their awareness provides a basis for motivation and their integrated life leads to synergy of body, mind and spirit such that they in fact have a high degree of energy.

(j) *Detachment.* The place of detachment has been well elaborated in Eastern thought. The approach of 'going with the flow' does not imply lack of concern but rather a skilful working with the currents of life in order to achieve spiritual goals. It is sometimes called 'active inaction'.

(k) *Acceptance.* Even in popular, non-religious parlance one is encouraged to accept the inevitable 'with good humour' and 'in good grace'. This, of course, is only a virtue in relation to the inevitable and not where one could and should attempt to modify what takes place.

(l) *Love.* To many, love is the paramount characteristic of the spiritual person. From the *Bhagavad Gita* to the Judaeo-Christian scriptures its centrality to the spiritual life is stressed.

(m) *Gentleness.* This characteristic brings together several of the others noted: awareness, detachment, acceptance, love. It involves a sensitive, thoughtful, caring approach to other people, to one's own needs and to the cosmos in general. It is the opposite of a ruthless, exploitative, careless approach to life. It does not imply weakness or indecisiveness, but rather a willingness 'to go with the flow', to act firmly but with kindess and a due sense of what is possible and needed.

A listing of spiritual characteristics in this manner is helpful, I believe, in defining spirituality. But obviously it only takes us so far. Is there anything more that can be said about the nature of spirituality? Why do we include some traits and not others? Can we identify unifying elements which link these characteristics?

A key feature of spirituality is that it is related to what is *inside* a person: it has to do with 'interiority.'[9] Children may show spirit by acting according to forces deep within rather than norms of typical or required behaviour; and yogis similarly plumb the inner recesses of their souls and live in accordance with the resulting enlightenment.

However, there is more to spirituality than interiority. There is also a strong *directional* component, as well as a *procedural* dimension. Spiritual virtues are ones which carry us towards sound ends — toward well being, I would say, for ourselves and others — and in a manner which is appropriate for achieving those ends. They are characteristics of a good person and a good way of life which relate especially strongly to one's inner being. Breadth of outlook is a characteristic of the mind; wonder and hope have a major emotional and attitudinal component; integration refers to a close and appropriate relationship between inner and outer components of the person; and so on.

Spirituality, then, in the sense in which I am using the term, is a complex of valuable personal traits which have a distinctively strong reference to our inner being or spirit. It is important to stress, however, that despite the emphasis on interiority, spirituality has a great deal to do with the outer as well as the inner. Traits such as awareness, a holistic outlook, integration and acceptance (of reality) plant one solidly and soundly in the world, and in the cosmos. Indeed, it is because they serve humans well in the external world as well as within that we see spiritual traits as valuable and spiritual people as good people. While spirituality has special reference to inner being, one cannot have a well developed inner life unless one has a sound worldview (including one that accommodates other people and the ecosphere) and unless the inner and outer dimensions of one's life are integrated with each other. The term 'spiritual' does not point to an emphasis on the spirit to the neglect of other aspects of the person, but rather to a full integration of inner and outer life.

It is obvious that the broad conception of spirituality I have outlined is not precisely the same as the conception religious people (in the popular sense) have traditionally had. Most notably there is no necessary reference to a supernatural realm including, for example, a God or gods, divine or providential forces and a Heaven or series of heavens. A 'spiritual' person has traditionally been understood as someone who is participating in and being affected by this realm.

What I have attempted to do, however, is develop a concept of spirituality which is of value in both religious and non-religious settings.

It seems to me that the difference between religious and non-religious senses of spirituality, while it exists, has often been exaggerated, and we are at a point where we must identify a large area of common ground. How is this possible?

Both groups must make concessions. On the one hand, religious people (in the popular sense) should recognize (as a great many do) that, in order to be spiritual, people must possess a number of virtues that can be clearly spelled out. People who are constantly selfish, brutal and unreflective can hardly be said to be spiritual, no matter how much they claim to be in touch with a supernatural realm or indwelt by a divine spirit. Further, religious people should acknowledge that there are many 'natural' processes at work in producing spiritual traits. Many psychological, social and other conditions must be fulfilled. Spirituality is not achieved simply through supernatural intervention, although that may be part of the story. Even if we use traditional religious language to explain how spirituality is fostered, we must take account of what common experience and social science tell us about the origins of human attitudes and behaviour.

On the other hand, non-religious people should realize that many of the values of interiority and profound experience that religions have emphasized over the millennia are crucial to 'the good life', whether one is religious (in the popular sense) or not. We cannot ignore a whole dimension of human nature and experience without grave consequences. Of course, even religious people have sometimes unwittingly neglected the spiritual dimension, focusing instead on creeds, rituals and spectacular supernatural events. But this does not excuse non-religious people who, in modern times in particular, have often taken pride in reducing human life to matter, physiology, id, ego and super-ego, sociological functions and so on. They have downplayed the spiritual side of life in the name of 'science', 'reason' and 'tough-mindedness', even when spiritual phenomena are staring them in the face. This does not mean that one should adopt an unscientific approach. but rather that one should expand science, or inquiry, to include things which we do in fact experience. The excitement of wonder and the stirrings of love cannot be denied, and our reflection on reality must be extended to accommodate them. Further, non-religious people must acknowledge that there will always be phenomena that lie beyond current theories, and ideals that lie beyond current goals. Insofar as the spiritual has to do with imaginings and aspirations that surpass the actual and that nourish human growth, this too must be accepted. In the terms developed earlier, people who do not believe in the supernatural in the sense of the totally 'other' must nevertheless embrace the transcendent, the 'something more' which is continuous with currently domesticated reality but goes beyond it.

What I am proposing, then, is that there is a spiritual dimension to life which is largely the same for everyone. While religious and non-religious people (in the popular sense) — and people of different paths and different interpretations of particular paths — may differ somewhat in their view of the origins and precise nature of spirituality, they cannot maintain that only *their* 'way' leads to spirituality. They should recognize spiritual qualities in people of other 'ways', and even engage in cooperative inquiry with them into general approaches and specific techniques for achieving spirituality. In this area, once again, there is 'no one true way'.

Religious/spiritual education in schools

We have seen that religion and spirituality are of great importance. In the broad sense outlined, they are essential for everyone; and even in the popular sense, religion plays a valuable role in the lives of a great many people, helping them to achieve individual and communal well being. We come now to the question whether religious/spiritual education has a place in schools, and if so how in general it should be conducted.[10]

I believe that education in religion and spirituality *in the broad sense* can and should be carried out in schools, both public and private. In the previous chapter, an argument was presented for teaching values in schools. Assuming the validity of that argument, it follows that religion and spirituality should also be dealt with in schools. Spiritual virtues are a major sub-category of values and so should be studied and fostered. And in general it is impossible to deal adequately with values without giving comprehensive and sustained attention to religious or religion-like issues. Religion, as we have seen, touches on our overall understanding of the nature of reality and the meaning of life. It is unthinkable that one would be able to resolve value issues, or even come to grips with them, without bringing to bear such perspectives. For example, in considering such issues as the sanctity of human and non-human life forms and the importance of protecting the global environment, one will of course be influenced by conceptions of the nature of the universe, the place of various life forms in the scheme of things, and the relative value of domination and preservation, exploitation and protection. Again, in discussing values such as love and friendship one must consider the extent to which it is the condition of humans to live in isolation, in closely knit communities, or in some fashion in between. To an extent one can settle love and friendship issues in the light of moral virtues such as kindness and unselfishness and other values such as the satisfaction derived from companionship. But perspectives of a religious type about the goals of human life, the place of community and the nature of human nature will very legitimately affect one's judgment.

Not only is religious/spiritual education (in the broad sense) important; it is also feasible. Religiousness and spirituality, in the senses outlined, refer to outlooks and personality traits with which we are familiar and which are not unduly mysterious. They have meaning even to people who are not religious in the popular sense, who do not believe in the 'ineffable' or the 'supernatural'; and we can think of ways in which they could be studied and fostered. The idea of the 'transcendent' which I have proposed is a complex one and requires further elaboration: its meaning may never be entirely clear since by definition we cannot know completely what novelties may arise or where our lives are leading. But it is no more mysterious than other notions already current in schooling theory such as aesthetic experience, moral idealism, and personal fulfilment.

Turning to religion in the popular sense, we see that it too is an appropriate object of school attention. As discussed in Chapter 8, religions should be studied to help students rise above religious bias. Understanding the phenomenon of religion is also important as part of a liberal education, introducing students to a major dimension of human culture and experience. Obviously, too, religious education can help religious students live more adequate lives, by understanding more fully the nature and importance of what they are attempting to do. Too often today religious young people accept (perhaps grudgingly) aspects of their religion which they should strongly reject on moral, humanitarian or other grounds, and fail to appreciate other aspects of their religion which could be a source of great enrichment.

Religion in the popular sense also typically contains a number of elements — tradition, community, profound experiences, a worldview, a conception of the meaning of life and so on — which are important to non-religious people as well. By studying these aspects of traditional religions, *all* students will develop in the religion-like aspects of their lives. Such topics will be approached somewhat differently depending on whether or not one is actually religious (in the popular sense), and depending on the type of religious or non-religious tradition and community one is associated with. But there is sufficient common ground to justify extensive joint study of these aspects of life.

The breadth of the whole field of religious/spiritual education, as I have defined it, means that religious and spiritual issues must be grappled with throughout the school curriculum and the life of the school. However, there is also a place for an explicit program, and the question arises as to the form it should take. The exploration of religion (and spirituality) ideally includes, in my view, the study of a wide range of religions in a 'comparative' or 'multi-faith' manner. This applies to the study both of particular religions in the popular sense and religious and spiritual issues in the broader sense. To try to understand religion by examining only one case — one's own religion, for example — is rather like trying to understand children by studying just one child, or war by studying only one war. Some progress can be made, but not a great deal. This does not mean that we should never engage in specialized study of our own religion or sub-tradition, but in the school setting this is often best handled through special reading and projects rather than separate courses. Where a school is established with reference to a particular religion and is required by its constitution and/or clientele to offer courses specifically in that religion, the content should nevertheless be as broad as the situation will allow. Whenever one approaches religion one must embark on a full-scale inquiry into the 'large questions of life' and how they have been answered in many traditions if one is to enhance significantly the religiousness and spirituality of students. Too often the study of religion is conducted in such a petty way that it does little to answer the very questions or foster the very characteristics with which religions are supposed to be centrally occupied.

Concern is sometimes expressed that the study of many religions will undermine students' commitment to their own (if they have one). The very act of taking other religions seriously may imply that one's own religion is not necessarily the best. Some students, it is feared, may even convert to another religion. However, while it is true (and in my view is to be desired) that many students will conclude that their religion is not superior to others, the assumption that students' commitment to their own religion will be reduced is mistaken. On the contrary, as students come to see that hundreds of millions of other people in the world take religion seriously, they tend to feel less isolated and peculiar as religious persons and become more committed to their religion. Occasionally, students will convert to another religion, but this suggests that their childhood religion was problematic for them in certain idiosyncratic ways, and they would have been likely to abandon it anyway. A well taught course in world religions brings out the fact that all religions are in roughly the same lines of business, and hence there is nothing to be gained by changing: the point is to improve one's religion, not exchange it for another.

An issue often raised is whether religious education in schools should be religious and spiritual *nurture* or simply study *of* or teaching *about* religion(s). Some reject the nurture approach on the ground that the school shold be concerned only with 'education' in an informational, critical, reflective sense and is no place for religious inculcation. Others maintain that teaching 'about' religion(s) cannot possibly capture the essence of religion, and the attempt at a detached, 'objective' religious education will be boring to students and may do more harm than good.

Actual experience with religious education shows that many of these concerns are unfounded: and our previous discussion of religion and spirituality suggests a better way of approaching the issue. On the one hand, if students find anything boring it is dogmatic 'nurture' in their own religion. An open, systematic study of religions around the world is to a large proportion of students fascinating, and also encourages them in their own religious aspirations, as noted earlier. On the other hand, the whole distinction between 'teaching about' and 'nurture' quickly breaks down in practice. Students find the study of religiousness through the ages and across cultures quite inspiring, and pursue various aspects of it out of strong personal interest. Try as one may, the reaction of students makes it impossible merely to dispense information 'about' religion(s). To a very great extent one *is* giving information. But nurture is also involved as students discover that the material has relevance to their lives, enhancing their own religion (if they have one, in the popular sense) and enriching their general approach to life, their religion and spirituality in the broad sense.

The charge of 'secular humanism'

The position I have outlined in this chapter may be seen by some as 'secular humanism', since it allows that one can be moral, spiritual and indeed religious in a strong and positive sense without believing in the supernatural or the divine. In fact, it may be viewed as dangerously and cunningly secular humanist, since it uses the *words* 'spiritual' and 'religious' while deleting aspects of their traditional meaning.

The word 'secular' in popular usage has come to mean 'of this world';[11] hence, a secular outlook is one which focuses on this world or universe and does not acknowledge another realm, notably the supernatural or the divine. The term 'secular *humanism*' simply underscores the point that the outlook in question is from a human point of view alone and does not take account of a divine perspective. People who believe in divine providence and the supernatural make a separation (in varying degrees) between the secular and the divine, and hence find 'secular humanism' problematic. They see it as ignoring a whole aspect of reality and 'lowering our sights' in terms of human obligation and potential.

The charge of 'secular humanism' is effective largely because of the assumption that if one does not believe in the supernatural, one is incapable of spirituality and high ideals. However, as we saw earlier, this is simply not true. Many of the most admirable human beings have been non-religious (in the popular sense). It is possible to reject belief in a supernatural being or order and yet be religious in an important sense and have 'transcendent' perspectives and spiritual values.

Those who are quick to dismiss a position as *mere* secular humanism should be aware of the extent to which religious people (in the popular sense) have often had very 'low sights' morally and spiritually. Belief in the supernatural is no guarantee that one will rise above a narrow 'this wordly' perspective and press toward high ideals and deep awareness. It is simply implausible, then, to maintain that religion in the popular sense is the key to upright living. On the other hand, however, the uncompromising hostility of many 'secular humanists' toward religion is equally unjustified since religious people (in the popular sense) are also often highly moral and spiritual.

But how, practically, should one deal with the charge that one is a 'secular humanist' (if one is)? How can one prevent it from discrediting and undermining one's efforts to teach religion and values in schools? The first requirement is that even if one is not religious in the popular sense, one must show genuine acceptance of people who are, avoiding the stereotypes and respecting their sincerity and spirituality. Hostility toward secular humanism is very often a defensive posture of people who feel that their attempts to live good, upright lives are not being taken seriously. Secondly, one must move as quickly as possible away from abstract arguments to specific objectives which are of interest to both supernaturalists and non-supernaturalists. In this way one will be able to demonstrate that, even if one is not religious in the popular sense, one can attain in one's own life and foster in the lives of students those ideals of human goodness that are held in common by people of all metaphysical persuasions.

The separation of religion from the state

If religious and spiritual education is so important, what is to be done in countries which are committed to the separation of religion from the state? The degree of formality of the separation varies from country to country, but even where it is not an explicit legal requirement it tends to be largely accepted in practice because of the diversity of religious and 'non-religious' outlooks in the society.

The main thing to be said is that insofar as the principle of the separation of religion and state rules out religious and spiritual education in public schools, we must work to change it. It is not acceptable to have a principle of government which prohibits the public schools of a country from helping students learn how to be spiritual and live 'the good life'.

It is perhaps understandable, given the history of religion–state relations in the West, that governments would wish to be free from the direct involvement of organized religions in various state activities. It is perhaps reasonable, then, that religious organizations should not participate directly in teaching religion in public schools (although one can imagine conditions under which it would be acceptable). However, it does not follow that therefore religion should not be taught in public schools. To draw a parallel, if there were various scientific societies advocating different positions in the theory of physics one *might* decide to exclude those organizations from a direct role in teaching physics in schools; but it would not follow that one should stop teaching physics. This would follow only if one believed that physics could *only* be taught by partisan scientific societies.

Of course, many people believe that religion can only be taught by (or from the vantage point of) a particular tradition. However, this is as mistaken in religion as it would be in physics or any other field of inquiry. In the broad sense of 'religion', no one religion or non-religious approach to life has a monopoly on religious insight. And even in the popular sense, teaching *about* religions is possible. It seems clear, then, that religion should be studied in public schools; and this study should include extensive exploration of religions in the popular sense. The only valid implication of the principle of the separation of religion and state would be that such study should not be primarily controlled and conducted by particular religious organizations.

One of the reasons for the exclusion of religions from the public schools was the difficulty encountered in reaching agreement on religious matters. And it is true that the teaching of religion in schools today would require *some* level of agreement in society on which perspectives and values are more worthy of consideration by students. One cannot study everything, and any selection will (and should) show some bias. However, I believe that there is much more agreement on such matters than is usually acknowledged. The era of partisan religious advocacy has encouraged the exaggeration of religious and moral differences in order to convince people that a particular religion is clearly superior. Also, in recent years, religions in certain countries have exaggerated their differences in order to win political and educational concessions; they have played the game Raywid calls 'obtrusive pluralism'. However, as we saw in Chapter 5, such an approach threatens the very pluralism which makes religious freedom and dissent possible, since it obscures the fundamental values such as tolerance, inquiry, freedom and consideration for others to which everyone subscribes at least to a degree.

A standard objection to schools engaging in systematic religious education is that, because of the pluralistic nature of society, the school will only be able to deal with a fairly low 'common factor' of subject matter, that small remainder of relatively innocuous topics which everyone can agree on. However, once again I think this point of view is a product of the 'obtrusive pluralism' which exaggerates differences in order to secure particular ends, in this case, a monopoly on the teaching of religion. There is much to be taught in schools which can be agreed on at least in broad outline; and that which can be agreed on is certainly not trivial. Indeed, many of the things people agree on — the need for love, happiness, knowledge, hope, courage and gentleness, for example — are more important than the things on which they disagree.

But how, in a country where the teaching of religion in public schools is largely excluded, can teachers engage in religious and spiritual education? I think we must simply press the limits of what is permitted, gradually extending the scope of what is studied with topics which people will have to admit *should* be addressed in schools. The law in these matters can be reinterpreted and even changed. Many commentators have already pointed out the inconsistency involved in the present situation in the US, where a country which claims to believe in justice and democracy cannot, strictly speaking, advocate justice and democracy in its schools (although, of course, it does).[12] This debate at the theoretical level must continue. But perhaps more importantly we must advance with greater persistence in curriculum development and in the classroom, opening up new areas of education which are religious and spiritual and of vital concern to students and society as a whole.

Notes and References

1 Durkheim, E. (1954) *The Elementary Forms of the Religious Life*, London, Allen and Unwin.
2 Tillich, P. (1957) *Dynamics of Faith*, New York, Harper and Row, especially Chapter 1. Note that Tillich in this work normally uses the term 'faith' rather than 'religion', but the two words in his usage are roughly interchangeable.
3 Smith, W.C. (1984) 'Philosophia, as One of the Religious Traditions of Humankind', in Galey, J.-C. (Ed) *Différences, Valeurs, Hiérachie: Textes Offerts à Louis Dumont*, Paris, Editions de L'Ecole des Hautes Etudes, p. 275.
4 Durkheim, E. (1961) *Moral Education*, New York, The Free Press, p. 19.
5 Some of the material in this section and subsequent ones is taken, with permission and modification, from Beck, C. (1986) 'Education for Spirituality', *Interchange*, 17, 2, pp. 148–56.
6 See Keen, S. (1973) *Apology for Wonder*, New York, Harper and Row, pp. 206–12. Keen maintains that gratitude may express itself either in worship or in (non-religious) celebration.
7 Erikson, E. (1963) *Childhood and Society*, 2nd ed., New York, Norton, Chapter 7.
8 Baum, G. (1972) *New Horizon: Theological Essays*, New York, Paulist Press, pp. 69–70.
9 See Priestly, J. (1985) 'Religion, Education and Spirituality', in Johns, E. (Ed) *Religious Education Belongs in the Public Schools*, Toronto, The Ecumenical Study Commission, p. 36.
10 Some of the material in this section is taken, with permission and modification, from Beck, C. (1985) 'Religion and Education', *Teachers College Record*, 87, 2, pp. 259–70.

11 Literally, it means 'of this present age'. See Cox, H. (1966) *The Secular City*, rev. ed., New York, Macmillan, pp. 16 and 17.
12 See Sizer, T. (Ed), (1976) *Religion and Public Education*, Boston, Houghton Mifflin, especially Chapters 9, 10 and 16.

Chapter 15

Political and Global Education

Even values education and religious education, we have seen, take us beyond the individual. Value topics include social and political values such as justice and tolerance, and the school religion program deals with questions such as the importance of tradition and community in people's lives and the place of the individual in society. The time has come to address more directly the role of the school in enhancing students' participation in wider spheres. We will focus particularly on political education and to a lesser extent global education; but it should be understood that political education, in order to be effective, must overlap considerably with, for example, economic and cultural studies, and global education, too, must be strongly interdisciplinary in nature.

The case for political education

Some political education is commonly justified on the ground that students should be prepared for 'informed participation in the democratic process'. They should understand 'how democratic institutions work' at the local, regional and national levels, so that they can 'exercise their rights and responsibilities as citizens.' While the programs of civic education based on this rationale are often rather disappointing, being confined to a formalistic, apolitical teaching of government structure and the electoral process, the need for instruction of this kind cannot be denied. Students should indeed be aware of the civic privileges they will have in a *relatively* open society and how they can make a difference through formal procedures of petitioning, presenting briefs, standing for office and voting.

School critics in recent times, however, have stressed the need to go beyond this minimal level and give students a more profound and comprehensive knowledge of political processes. As we have seen in previous chapters, writers such as Apple, Kozol, Sarup and Sharp and Green are concerned that students do not get a clear enough picture of how society actually works. For example, students leave school assuming (mistakenly) that most things happen in society by the will of the majority; that inequalities of wealth, occupational status and power are largely due to differences of merit; and that there is rarely any conflict in society over what should be done. These writers advocate — rightly, I believe — a more accurate treatment of cultural, political and economic matters in schools. In Apple's words, 'we must be honest about the ways power, knowledge, and interest are interrelated . . ., about how hegemony is economically and culturally maintained.[1]

This greater honesty and explicitness is called for not only so that students may be better informed, but also so that they may be politically more active and effective. According to Apple, the lack of attention given in schools to the realities of conflict and power 'can lead to political quiescence and the acceptance by students of a perspective . . . that acts to maintain the existing distribution of power and rationality in a society.' By contrast, an adequate treatment of these realities can develop 'a student's sense of the legitimate means of gaining recourse within unequal societies'.[2] Kozol makes a similar point about the powerlessness engendered by political miseducation. He documents how most references to political conflict are kept out of the social studies curriculum and concludes, as we saw in Chapter 3, that students come to 'look upon historic transformation not as the product of their own intentions, aspirations, dreams . . .'.[3] He tells of a poster he saw in the social studies section of a school which, under the heading 'Occupations To Which Interest in History May Lead', gave the following list: (1) archaeologist, (2) historian, (3) curator, (4) writer, (5) critic, (6) anthropologist, (7) research assistant, (8) librarian, (9) teacher of history. He comments: 'Nowhere in the list do I find two words to suggest the possible goal of being one who *enters* history'.[4] Elsewhere, Kozol talks about the ineffectiveness of apolitical attempts in schools to encourage social action by students. 'The teacher tells the children that the way to deal with problems like bad housing, insufficient heating or excessive rent is by a letter to the landlord'. However, while 'the lesson taught has to do with social change . . . the lesson learned is the lesson of despair and impotence . . . . To suggest to kids that they inform a slumlord of the absence of hot water in the cold of winter is a pre-planned exercise in self-defeat'.[5]

Beyond political understanding and empowerment, a further reason for teaching politics in schools is so that students achieve a better grasp of *other* school subjects.[6] We have already noted how students gain a highly distorted understanding of history and social studies when they are approached in an apolitical manner. In Chapter 7 we referred to Apple's account of the critical misrepresentation of science in schools, as having 'no outside influences, either personal or political'. Literature, too, must be studied in its socio-political context, and seen to be promoting some power and privilege structures rather than others. And even religion, to be fully understood, must be seen as playing a political role in society.

Finally, we should not overlook the importance of political knowledge for self-understanding and personal coping. As Colin Wringe says:

> The political world is a very important part of the environment in which the individual lives. Many of the things (one) undertakes and more especially many of the things that befall (one) will only be fully comprehensive in political terms . . . . If the pupil is later unemployed, sent to fight in distant parts of the world, or arrested, these events may be susceptible of political explanation . . . .[7]

Thus, political knowledge can enable students to grasp more fully the nature of their lives, including their problems. And even when no remedy for the problems is immediately in sight, political understanding can help reduce self-blame.

The issue of controversy and bias

Politics, like values and religion, is seen by many as problematic as a school subject because it is so *controversial*. As David Bridges points out, while controversy 'is a central and dynamic feature of many of the subjects (e.g. the arts, history and science) which traditionally feature in the school curriculum', the treatment of controversy that takes place in these subjects (as far as it goes) does not seem to arouse public concern. Rather, it is the teaching of 'moral, social and political controversy' which becomes 'the focus of wider public and political concern and debate'.[8] The chief difficulty, Bridges maintains, is that the controversies in these areas 'are not resolvable by reference to more factual information or more evidence. Nor will they ever be so, for they are rooted in personal or social values'. This basic problem is exacerbated by the fact that controversies in these areas (unlike in many other school subjects) take place on several different levels at once, engage the emotions and passions as well as the intellect, and affect not only our beliefs but also how we act toward each other.[9]

A related problem is that of *bias*. Because political issues are seen as fundamentally controversial, it is assumed that teachers who advance a point of view are simply imposing their bias rather than engaging in legitimate teaching. And this is thought to create problems in an *educational* institution, whether one agrees with a teacher's bias or not. As Brenda Cohen remarks, 'most parents, whilst agreeing that children should know something about politics . . ., would shrink from the notion of this political initiation being placed in the hands of a teacher known to be of opposing political convictions'. But equally, more 'far-sighted' parents would be 'wary of political instruction placed deliberately in the hands of persons of similar political outlook' since this might well lead to 'political indoctrination.'[10]

The implication of the problem of bias, for Cohen, is that teachers should not try to foster political values or behaviour patterns in students, tempting though it is to want to do so. It is natural enough, she says, for someone to ask: 'Are we not to bring up our children to love freedom and our democratic values?' However, 'it is unfortunately the case that once the principle has been accepted that children in schools are fair targets for the implementation of excellent ideas, or good and valuable ways of looking at life, then the claimants press in from all sides', and there is no way of choosing between them. Rather than attempt to do so, teachers should 'concentrate on equipping (students) with the skills they will need to make their own decisions'.[11]

Bridges is less inclined than Cohen to conclude that the teacher — faced with the issue of controversy and bias — must take a neutral position. He makes a distinction between neutrality and impartiality, and claims that while teachers should be impartial they need not be neutral. Neutrality he defines as 'a strategy through which one either supports alternative points of view equally (affirmative neutrality) or withholds support from any point of view (negative or procedural neutrality).' By contrast, impartiality 'allows or even requires differential support to opinion, provided that the different level of support is related to objective merits rather than any other consideration to do with, for example, one's personal interest, advantage or feeling.' Bridges refers approvingly to Charles Bailey's view that 'classroom discussion . . . should have the objective not just of expressing an interesting range of opinion but of employing rational criticism to try to establish the truth of the matter.'[12] The problem here, however, is that Bridges has previously said that moral, social and political controversies are not ultimately resolvable by means of information or evidence, since they are 'rooted in personal or social values.' He seems to be partly aware of this difficulty, for he goes on to note that 'the critical question here is to what extent ethical questions . . . are amenable to rational argument as against rational preference.' And he concludes with the weaker position that 'the issue between those who defend neutrality and those who argue for impartiality is related to a difference of perspective on this meta-ethical problem.' While appearing to reject neutrality, then, Bridges does not in the end give a full rationale for doing so, stating that he 'will not try to resolve 2000 years of moral argument in a footnote'.[13]

Neutrality versus advocacy

Is there any way out of the problems posed by controversy and so-called bias in political matters? One common suggest.on is that the school should avoid politics altogether and concentrate on its true role of teaching basic skills and liberal arts and science subjects. However, apart from the fact, noted previously, that the study of politics is a necessary aspect of liberal arts education, it is impossible for the school to avoid taking a political stand. As we have seen in earlier chapters, there are a great many political messages embedded in the curriculum, learning materials and everyday conduct of the school. And even the act of excluding politics from the formal curriculum implies in a very strong manner that all is well with the policies and practices of society. When crises arise in other areas — a national shortage of scientists and technologists, a need for greater literacy and numeracy, a herpes or AIDS epidemic — the schools are asked to respond with suitable educational programs. If the school does not teach politics, it is natural for students to assume that the political status quo is unproblematic.

Another solution — the one proposed by Cohen and many others — is to restrict oneself to passing on relevant information and inquiry skills, leaving students to make up their own minds on political matters. And indeed this approach can take us quite a long way, far beyond the point we are at in schools currently. Bernard Crick, while stating that 'the teacher . . . must not advocate one doctrine or another', nevertheless outlines a program of political education which would lead to a high degree of sophistication in students, enabling them to be much better informed and intelligently active in politics than at present. [14]

But in the end, a neutral approach to political education is, I believe, fundamentally flawed. There are several things wrong with it. To begin with, we cannot sit on the fence in the matter of objectivity in politics, any more than in history or physics. It may seem presumptuous to 'try to resolve 2000 years of moral argument' in a chapter or even a book, but we have no choice. For if political questions are not resolvable by reference to facts and evidence (including logical facts and arguments), as Bridges maintains, then it is difficult to see how we can justify political inquiry at all. (And in the present book, we have the advantage that an objectivist approach to values has already been developed).

The type of argument advanced by neutralists is as follows: since politics is a controversial area, in which we can never know who is right, it is irresponsible to influence students to accept certain political views, for these may be no sounder than the views they already have: they are just an expression of our bias. However, a legitimate response to this argument is that if we can never know who is right, surely it does not matter whether we influence students politically or not. We are free to do so; and no harm is done if we do not. Writers who claim that political questions are not objective and then proceed to advocate netural political education have adopted an incoherent position. All the political information and skills training in the world will be pointless if there are no objective questions to address. But if there *are* objective questions, answers must be pursued and taught. It would be irresponsible to do otherwise in such an important area of students' lives.

People who wish to keep politics out of the school entirely are in one respect more consistent than the neutralists: part of their argument is that politics is too controversial to be handled objectively and so should be excluded. However, they have a second reason for their position which is incompatible with the first: they wish to protect certain sacred political assumptions which they believe the school should take for granted and never subject to inquiry. (In this, they are like people who reject religious education on the dual ground that we cannot inquire into religious matters, and that there are religious certainties which should not be questioned). The obvious query to be raised with respect to this position is: if a field is too difficult to inquire into, however do we know with such certainty those things we know?

It is apparent that in politics the truth lies somewhere between the agnostic and the 'certain knowledge' positions. There are many things we do know with a degree of clarity: e.g. that people should as far as possible be consulted on policies which affect them; that 'the rule of law' in some sense is necessary in large, complex societies; that the state has a role to play in protecting people from powerful individuals and special interest groups (although it often does not play the role very well); and so on. However, there are some important matters about which there is considerable uncertainty — presumably because they are so complex — and on which we should not adopt a firm position at present; and even the knowledge we *do* have needs a great deal of refinement: we should not push specific interpretations of political principles too hard at this stage. We need in politics the outlook advocated in earlier chapters with respect to values: our task is to find *better* solutions rather than *the right* solution. Just because there is disagreement over what is the best way to do things, this does not mean that we do not know, and cannot agree, that certain ways of doing things are better than others. Failure to recognize this point has led to exaggeration of the controversy over political matters.

In politics (as in religion) there has been a tendency to assume that ideas and practices come in systems, and that one must accept or reject a whole package. This has increased the sense of disagreement and controversy, since people have overlooked features common to different political systems. And it has confirmed the belief that political inquiry is impossible, since we have not noticed the many examples of procedures which have almost universally been discovered to be sound. A key part of political education should be the study of widely accepted political arrangements, detached somewhat from their official ideologies. This would not only increase optimism about political inquiry, but also have the practical advantage of enabling students of rather different political orientations to work together on common problems. For example, students with different attitudes towards 'socialism' and 'capitalism' could study jointly how to improve bureaucracies, how to enhance worker satisfaction and how to reduce damaging inequalities in society.

But even if there are some things that are known and should be taught in the field of politics, should teachers advocate their *own* views? This issue, it seems to me, has become rather confused. Obviously, in the end students must be allowed to make up their own minds on political matters, as indeed they will. Teachers should not try to *impose* their views on students, either by failing to give them access to other ideas or by forbidding them to entertain other ideas. However, good teachers of politics are bound to have some influence on students in the direction of their own views, both because they will select for major consideration those ideas which they believe to be more fruitful, and because the students will to some extent be convinced by the evidence and arguments they present. But surely this is what we want, on the whole, in politics as in other school subjects. In physics, too, we want well informed teachers presenting sound theories which students to a degree accept because of the sound accompanying evidence and argumentation.

There are, it should be noted, two important differences of degree between politics and a subject such as physics. In the first place, in politics (unlike in physics) the students are likely to know a *great* deal as a result of their own varied experience and reading which they can share with their teachers. Teachers of politics, then, should take special care not to assume that they have superior insight on all matters, and should expect to modify their views considerably as a result of their interaction with students. This does not detract from the objectivity of politics, but rather underlines the extent to which it should be studied dialogically.

Secondly, in politics (unlike in physics) so much depends on where one's interests lie. For example, whereas the socio-economic status of teachers and students will be to a large extent irrelevant in the teaching and learning of physics (although not as irrelevant as we have often thought), in political education it will be of major significance, in terms of the insights people can contribute, the compromises they will accept, and the political strategies and courses of action they will want to adopt. Once again, this does not call into question the objectivity of political inquiry. It simply means that statements about what is good and right in politics must often be qualified with reference to the respective interest groups. As we saw in Chapter 1 with respect to values in general, what is (objectively) good for one sub-group may be (equally objectively) bad for another sub-group, depending on their needs and circumstances. Teachers can be aware of this fact, and teach politics in terms of the varying interests of different sectors of society (including their own). Variety of interests does not in itself undermine inquiry and education; it does so only when the members of a sub-group, instead of looking for compromises, try to promote their own interests by convincing everyone that their interests coincide with those of the sub-group. This, of course, teachers must work strenuously to avoid.

Components of political education

As with values education, so with political education, many of the approaches which have been practised or proposed are too narrow to have a significant impact. It is important, however, not to reject them completely but rather incorporate their strengths into an eclectic, comprehensive program. In this section, I will illustrate how this may be done by reviewing a selection of approaches.

(a) *Inspiration and socialization.* According to Harold Entwistle, much 'citizenship training' in Europe earlier this century consisted in the development of 'civic spirit', 'civic loyalties', 'a belief in the values of democratic institutions, laws and ways of life'.[15] In the United States, too, a similar activity goes on, although with such force that Entwistle is inclined to call it socialization. He talks of 'the unique preoccupation of American schools with daily patriotic rituals,' and quotes R.D. Hess who 'faults socialization, as it has been practised in America, on the grounds that "the schools have contributed to divisions within society by teaching a view of the nation and its political processes which is incomplete and simplistic"'.[16]

Writers in recent decades (including Entwistle) have tended to see largely the negative side of the political inspiration and socialization approach. Kozol claims that schools 'exercise a devastating impact in the realm of moral values and political indoctrination.'[17] He comments that 'the Flat Pledge (in the US) "works", no matter how we smile, judge its syllables or talk about its "meaning" with children. A child cannot swear an absolute allegiance to a single viewpoint, bias, goal or interest, and then proceed into a day or year of honest inquiry and of unbiased disputation.'[18]

However, while we must develop less indoctrinative methods, it is essential that we not neglect the affective dimension of political education. Having sound political ideas is to no avail unless there is emotional attachment to them. As Entwistle himself says, the sociological evidence discourages 'naive assumptions that a rational and altruistic political theory has only to be implanted to take root in the friendly soil of the child's mind.'[19] In Chapter 8 we saw that we may have loyalty to our religion or nation without viewing it as superior to others. Generalizing from this, we may say that spirited commitment is not incompatible with a balanced, moral point of view. And in fostering such commitment we must not *in general* rule out the use of rituals, poetry, songs and the like, in politics any more than in religion and family life.

(b) *Teaching 'political literacy'*. In the '70s, Crick and others in the UK developed the notion of teaching 'political literacy' as the task of political education. Included in political literacy, according to its proponents, are an understanding of political concepts, principles and theories; a knowledge of 'what the main political disputes are about; what beliefs the main contestants have to them and how they are likely to affect (oneself)';[20] and a disposition to pursue political objectives not only along the lines of one's own preferences but also in accordance with certain 'procedural principles' such as 'freedom, fairness, respect for truth, respect for reasoning and toleration.'[21] The approach attempts to avoid favouring a conservative, liberal or radical point of view, giving instruction not only in the value of existing arrangements, but also in the rationales of other alternatives and the ways of working towards them.[22]

There is a danger with such a program that students will become buried in abstract concepts and theories, and lower socio-economic students in particular will not be helped by it: there has been criticism along these lines.[23] Certainly, the conceptual framework for the study of politics outlined by Crick appears forbidding.[24] Further, as we saw in the previous section, the attempt to avoid taking a stand in political education cannot succeed, and it seems likely that the political literacy approach is in fact slanted in a conservative direction.[25] Nevertheless, it is clear that political literacy should be a major component in political education. Students must learn about various schools of thought and acquire the concepts and skills needed to assess them and draw on them selectively.

(c) *Teaching realism*. Entwistle describes traditional civic education as 'utopian': it paints an unduly rosy picture of the status quo, and exaggerates the capacity of individuals to exercise influence through *the vote*.[26] Kozol, Apple and other contemporary school critics, as we have seen, call for a much more accurate explanation of how society works. And Crick states that 'a political education should be realistic and should chasten the idealist.'[27] It must provide what politicians are persistently reluctant to offer, namely, an account of 'the limitations of resources, existing commitment and environment under which any government must suffer.'[28]

There is a tendency to want to keep school-aged young people oblivious of the hard realities of life, lest they become disillusioned and 'robbed of their childhood'. However, Crick argues that, on the contrary, students will become disillusioned if they are ignorant of politics and expect too much. A genuinely informative political education will have a positive effect.

> To give children the 'low-down' on how political institutions work and what political conflicts are about . . . will not feed disillusion: . . . it will encourage ordinary young citizens . . . their teachers and their politicians to think in terms of common problems to be solved, and to talk about them in a common language, not build up protective walls of mutual incomprehension.[29]

(d) *Discussing cases.* In the '60s and '70s considerable effort was put into the production of case study material on public issues for discussion in classrooms. Donald Oliver in the US was one of the chief advocates of the use of this material; and Oliver and Newmann in their book *Clarifying Public Controversy* proposed such discussion as a major component in 'citizenship education'. In Britain, two Schools Council projects (those of Stenhouse and McPhail) employed a similar method (among others); and in Canada it was advocated by the Canadian Critical Issues project under Eisenberg, Levin, Bourne and others. Many of the cases used were historical ones, described in detail on the basis of careful documentation. In other instances they were hypothetical, although presented in realistic terms.

As indicated in Chapter 13, I have reservations about this approach because of its attempt to remain neutral, teaching skills without promoting substantive positions. However, as an element in a political education program, the case study method is valuable. It discourages wild speculation and forces teachers and students to recognize that the accepted idealistic solution to a dilemma is not always an easy one to adopt, or even the right one. It helps show how complex political questions are, and gives students practice in weighing a diversity of considerations.

(e) *Political involvement.* There are in general many advantages to 'learning by doing', and these are to be sought as far as possible in political education. Within the school, students should be encouraged to play a role in decision making with respect to curriculum content, teaching procedures, behaviour codes, recreational activities and many other areas of policy and practice. As they attempt to do so, they will quickly become aware of the political nature of school decisions and will learn how best to try to influence them. Beyond the school, both teachers and students should engage in political action in the wider society. As a result they will learn more about society and how to be politically effective in it, and will also have a greater political influence, both indirectly and directly, upon the school.

Commentators on the whole are not optimistic about the extent to which student political activity will be effective or even possible. Social reproductionists, as we have seen, are impressed with the constraints imposed on the school by the outside world. Crick is of the opinion that 'personal participation in any sense more meaningful than simply casting a vote is plainly impossible for most people'; he places his faith (such as it is) more in politicians being aware that people know what they are up to.[30] Wringe wonders about the extent to which students will be given genuine power in schools, and also queries whether 'the knowledge and skills needed . . . in running the affairs of a modern industrial state are the same as those that can be acquired by participating in the management of limited aspects of a school's life.'[31] With respect to learning through community action, Wringe says that 'at best this must be an essentially one-off experience. Such events depend on happy coincidence of circumstances and staff commitment. They cannot be relied on to provide the staple introduction to the understanding of our society which is needed . . . .'[32] Entwistle argues that we have misunderstood the nature of democratic involvement, and that in fact participation in smaller 'associations' which achieve specific ends and put pressure on formal 'governments' is open to students, both within the school and beyond.[33] However, he does not give much detail on the areas in which victories can be won, and one senses that many important matters lie beyond the sphere of influence to which, in his view, students have access.

The lesson to be learned from this rather pessimistic accounting, I believe, is not that political involvement is unimportant as a means of political education but rather that it faces formidable obstacles. Political influence in general is difficult to achieve, and especially by an oppressed group (children and youth) in a closely governed and highly bureaucratized institution (the school). But even these insights are worth acquiring, at least as a beginning; and so long as we give students some warning so that they are not too disappointed, they might as well learn these hard facts through first-hand experience.

(f) *Developing new visions.* The central task of political education, I believe, is to help students envision (and work toward) better alternative futures for society. All other activities are subordinate to this one. Schools have notoriously focused on the past and the status quo, when the point of schooling is to enable individuals and groups to achieve 'the good life' more fully. Political literacy, a realistic political understanding, and reasoning and discussion skills are important, but the most pressing need is to find a new *content* for our political aspirations. This, of course, is not something to be imposed on students: it is to be developed dialogically with students. But new ideas must be injected into the classroom if students are to make significant progress and contribute substantially to the larger societal quest.

In closing this section, and looking forward to the next, we should note that any adequate political vision in today's world must be global in scope. Problems of nuclear and ecological threat are currently drawing attention dramatically to the interdependence of all human beings. And from a considerably earlier time there have been major cultural, economic and other influences of societies on each other around the world, for good and ill. Political arrangements within nations and communities which do not take account of global considerations are bound to prove inadequate.

Global education

The study of local and national political systems and ways of life in isolation is no longer sufficient (if it ever was). We cannot understand our own society or make rational decisions with respect to it without an awareness of happenings elsewhere in the world. As Graham Pike and David Selby observe in their article 'Global education':

> Global interdependencies . . . affect the purity of the air we breathe and the water we drink; the levels of employment and inflation; the price of tea; the level of taxation; fuel costs; the survival prospects of wildlife; the availablity and subject matter of the books and newspapers we read; the changing roles of men and women in society; our relative peacefulness or unpeacefulness of mind and our image of the future.[34]

Most of the points made earlier about political education apply equally to global education (often called 'world studies'). Understanding the total world context is important for one's general education, for self-understanding, and as a basis for appropriate action. While global issues are often controversial, the school cannot remain neutral with respect to them since in the real world a position must be adopted and action taken. Although we can seldom be sure that we have *the right* solution to a problem, it is possible and necessary to look for *better* solutions. In this search, many different pedagogical methods should be employed, but we must never lose sight of the central task, namely, to arrive at a vision of the world we should be striving for.

Simon Fisher and David Hicks in their valuable handbook *World Studies 8–13* take what I believe is an unduly neutralist approach. They say that 'the key to education is enquiry, rather than knowledge itself,' and accordingly 'the important goals of world studies teaching . . . focus on learning to learn, solving problems, clarifying values and making decisions'.[35] The emphasis is similar to that of several approaches to education in values and politics reviewed earlier and is to be questioned for the same reasons. While teacher authoritarianism is certainly to be avoided, the goal *is* knowledge — of the socio-politico-economic arrangements needed for the modern world — and unless vast amounts of information and theory are brought into the school (in part via teachers) students will make little progress in grappling with the issues.

Opponents of global education — as of political education — often take the strange dual position noted earlier. On the one hand they view some truths as so certain and sacred that they should not be exposed to the vagaries of classroom discussion; but on the other hand they do not acknowledge here a realm of legitimate, teachable knowledge. David Aspin in an article on peace studies quotes Roger Scruton and Caroline Cox as saying:

> Peace Studies is not a genuine educational discipline, and therefore cannot be taught as one.

> The movment for Peace Studies in schools is part of a trend towards the politicisation of education, involving both the lowering of intellectual standards, and the assumption of foregone political conclusions. It is (their) belief that the foregone conclusions in question are immensely damaging to our national interests, and favourable to those of the Soviet Union.[36]

According to Aspin, the claim here is not merely that Peace Studies is taught in a 'biased and irresponsible way' but that it 'could be taught in no other way'. He characterizes their view as follows:

> Whatever else education is about . . . it has nothing to do with the idea of 'relevance'; indeed 'genuine' intellectual disciplines are, for Scruton and Cox, 'respectable' *because* of their irrelevance to the lives of their students and all their main concerns.[37]

The irony is that it is the foregone conclusions of Scruton and Cox about where the interests and responsibilities of Britain and the Soviet Union lie which lead them to oppose the teaching of foregone conclusions in global matters in school. Their mistake is not that they take some things for granted in arguing their case, but that they advocate a form of schooling in which nothing is ever taken for granted. As we have observed often, teachers must make some assumptions, at least for the time being, if they are to teach usefully and effectively. And among the more plausible assumptions, it seems to me, are ones such as that global issues are important to students and peace is worth pursuing.

While accepting, however, that teachers must make assumptions, we should be on guard against questionable ones. For example, it has often been assumed in social studies, history and geography courses that 'development' in the modern Western sense is always a good thing, and that 'Third World' countries should be spurred in that direction as quickly as possible. However, Hicks and Townley argue that insofar as global education includes 'development education' it should not make such assumptions. A distinction should be drawn between 'change' and 'development' (in the sense of improvement), and a range of types and means of improvement should be considered, for rich and poor countries alike. We should not think of improvement simply in terms of industrialization and 'wealth' in the Western sense.[38]

Another dimension of global education takes us back to the issues of religion, race and ethnicity discussed in earlier chapters. Hicks and Townley see 'multicultural education' as a major area within global education.[39] Richardson, too, identifies 'culture and justice' as 'key concepts in World Studies', thus advocating a significant departure from informational, 'value-free' approaches to the field. Richardson stresses the need for in-depth teaching about people of other cultures in order to show that, for example, 'they are not a monolithic, homogeneous mass'; they direct their own lives, being 'moved by anxieties and hopes, and intentions and will-power'; they are 'varied fellow-creatures', not 'wholly evil' or, perhaps worse, 'half-devil and half-child'; they are 'beings with whom one can interact' and from whom one can learn.[40] Thus, while much of the impetus for global education today arises from economic, technological and ecological developments, we must not focus exclusively on these. Cultural study is also urgently needed, both so that we can gain insights from other cultures and so that prejudice and friction between different peoples may be reduced as much as possible.

In concluding this chapter, I wish to emphasize once again how selective I have had to be in discussing political and global education. There is obviously so much more to be said about both content and method in these fields. However, I hope the remarks in this chapter — and the two before it — will help indicate some of the 'new directions' in which schools must go, namely, toward studies of greater relevance to human well being and of greater interest to students of varied socio-economic backgrounds.

Notes and References

1 Apple, M. (1979) *Ideology and Curriculum*, London, Routledge and Kegan Paul, p. 161.
2 *Ibid.*, p. 84.
3 Kozol, J. (1984) *The Night Is Dark and I Am Far From Home*, 3rd ed., New York, Continuum, p. 79.
4 *Ibid.*, p. 83.
5 *Ibid.*, p. 92.
6 On this point, see Wringe, C. (1984) *Democracy, Schooling and Political Education*,

London, Allen and Unwin, p. 92. Wringe argues that, apart from anything else, the teaching of politics may be justified on 'educational grounds'.

7 *Ibid.*, p. 91 ff.

8 Bridges, D. (1986) 'Dealing with controversy in the school curriculum: a philosophical perspective', in Wellington, J. (Ed) *Controversial Issues in the Curriculum*, Oxford, Blackwell, pp. 20–1.

9 *Ibid.*, pp. 21–2.

10 Cohen, B. (1969) 'The Problem of Bias', in Heater, D. (Ed) *The Teaching of Politics*, London, Methuen, p. 164.

11 *Ibid.*, pp. 178–9.

12 Bridges, D., *op. cit.*, p. 31.

13 *Ibid.*, pp. 32–3.

14 Crick, B. (1969) 'The Introducing of Politics', in Heater, D., *op. cit.*, especially pp. 8–15.

15 Entwistle, H. (1971) *Political Education in a Democracy*, London, Routledge and Kegan Paul, p. 1.

16 *Ibid.*, pp. 19–20.

17 Kozol, J., *op. cit.*, p. 2.

18 *Ibid.*, p. 10. Parentheses added.

19 Entwistle, H., *op. cit.*, p. 23.

20 Crick, B. and Porter, A. (Eds), (1978) *Political Education and Political Literacy*, London, Longman, p. 33. Parentheses added.

21 Wringe, C., *op. cit.*, p. 97.

22 *Ibid.*, p. 98.

23 *Ibid.*, p. 99.

24 See the presentation of the framework in Crick, B. and Heater, D. (1977) *Essays on Political Education*, Lewes, The Falmer Press.

25 For discussion of this question see Wringe, C., *op. cit.*, p. 100.

26 Entwistle, H., *op. cit.*, pp. 25–7.

27 Crick, B., 'The Introducing of Politics', *op. cit.*, p. 12.

28 *Ibid.*, p. 9.

29 *Ibid.*, pp. 8 and 19–20.

30 *Ibid.*, pp. 16–18.

31 Wringe, C., *op. cit.*, pp. 102–3.

32 *Ibid.*, p. 104.

33 Entwistle, *op. cit.*, pp. 68–102.

34 Pike, G. and Selby, D. (1986) 'Global education', in Wellington, J., *op. cit.*, p. 40.

35 Fisher, S. and Hicks, D. (1985) *World Studies 8–13: A Teacher's Handbook*, Edinburgh and New York, Oliver and Boyd, p. 15.

36 Aspin, D. (1986) '"Peace Studies" in the curriculum of educational institutions: an argument against indoctrination', in Wellington, J. *op. cit.*, pp. 122–3.

37 *Ibid.*, pp. 123–4.

38 Hicks, D. and Townley, C. (1982) 'The need for global literacy', in Hicks, D. and Townley, C. (Eds) *Teaching World Studies*, London, Longman, pp. 9 and 10. For a critique of Western notions of 'development' see, for example, Esteva, G. (1987) 'Regenerating People's Space', *Alternatives*, 12, pp. 125–52.

39 Hicks, D. and Townley, C., 'The need for global literacy', *op. cit.*, pp. 11–13.

40 Richardson, R. (1982) 'Culture and justice: Key concepts in world studies and multicultural education', in Hicks, D. and Townley, C., *Teaching World Studies*, *op. cit.*, pp. 24–8.

Chapter 16

Conclusion

I will not here offer an overview of what has been said in this book. That is provided in the 'manifesto' outlined in the Introduction. However, some concluding remarks about implementation and about the longer term future of schooling are needed.

While it is important to discuss what should be done in schools, much can change in the attempted implementation. Experience may show that what was recommended either is not feasible or was inappropriate in the first place. I wish to be the first to acknowledge the possible practical and even theoretical difficulties of some of my proposals. There is so much working out yet to be done.

For example, systematic education in 'controversial areas', which we have just been discussing, may prove to be extremely difficult. Teachers may be unable to gain sufficient distance on their own beliefs and values to give an adequate treatment of other worldviews. The advantages of studying other moral codes, religions and political ideologies may be outweighed by the disadvantages of a biased exposition of them. Further, there may be strong public opposition to teaching these subjects in schools.

Again, I have taken a middle position on private schooling. While not advocating a voucher system for education, I have said that it probably does not matter whether schools are public or private: the crucial question is what goes on inside them. However, as we proceed further we may find that a different stance is called for. On the one hand, it may prove advisable to give greater support to private schooling in order to encourage innovation and local community development. On the other hand, if private schools in practice are used mainly to serve adult-dominated interest groups at the expense of student well being, it may be necessary to oppose them, at least when they take certain forms.

Yet again, in practice a compromise position on streaming and common curriculum may have to be taken. There may be *some* academic and skill areas in which classes of different levels of difficulty are necessary, at least until adequate techniques of individualized instruction can be devised. And the degree of individual specialization that is desirable in schools, especially in the senior years, may prove to be *somewhat* greater than I have proposed. As Goodlad says, once the general arguments against streaming and specialization have been accepted, one can proceed to work out solutions appropriate to different circumstances.

I mention these possibilities not to detract from the principles advocated in this book. Every effort must be made to implement them. However, we must be aware of the importance of experimentation in arriving at better forms of schooling. Such an awareness should not cool our ardour for school reform, but rather prepare us to pursue it with flexibility and ingenuity. We must not make absolutes out of particular school arrangements, but rather keep our eyes fixed on the goal of promoting human well being through schooling, a goal which may often be served in unexpected ways.

What of the longer term future of schooling? The recommendations I have made, though drastic in some respects, do not immediately involve dismantling mass schooling. Such an outcome may follow at a later date, if it becomes clear that the reforms needed are thwarted by traditional school structures. But I have not prejudged this issue. Indeed, I have argued against the 'deschooling' option at the present time.

The question of monolithic schooling versus local educational initiative must, however, remain open. It is closely linked to the question of monolithic, top-down, mass society versus local, 'human-sized' communities. Is there something in the very nature of large institutions which undermines human well being and equality, the values I have advocated in this book? If so, then mass education, along with 'big government', must eventually be replaced. The modern industrial-political-educational complex has brought many blessings to industrialized countries, but there is increasing evidence that for the human race as a whole — and even for people in 'developed' countries — it may do more harm than good.

In a paper delivered in 1988 to the American Educational Studies Association, 'American Education: Relevant or Irrelevant?', Madhu Suri Prakash quotes Ivan Illich as follows: '(T)he alternative to the dependence of a society on its schools is not the creation of new devices to make people learn what experts have decided they need to know; rather, it is the creation of a radically new relationship between human beings and their environment'. Extending this point, Prakash goes on to argue that modern education is embedded in a network of 'institutions of development': 'large, hierarchical, bureaucratic, exorbitantly expensive, resource inefficient institutions, designed for the manipulation of humans as well as nature.' She adds that 'the (national and international) scale of these institutions of development destroys the possibilities for community, which depends upon "human scale". (And) their hierarchical structure is at odds with the possibility of equality.'

I believe that this type of criticism of schooling must be taken very seriously. It has special relevance for a book on 'better schools'. Elsewhere in her paper Prakash states: 'professional education and educators, by keeping "the system" alive through offering "treatments" within it, continue to be part of the problem, rather than becoming a part of the solution'. Could an ameliorative approach of the kind advocated in the present book in fact do more harm than good?

The way to come to terms with this nest of problems, I think, is as follows. Yes, we have developed in wealthy industrialized countries a way of life that is completely non-viable in the long-term, and which even in the short-term is so expensive that extreme differences between rich and poor, within and between countries, and extensive ecological damage are inevitable. Further, as Illich has shown at length in *Toward a History of Needs*, so many aspects of this way of life are unnecessary: 'needs' have been artificially created. Finally, modern schooling shares in this manipulative, need inducing, non-convivial, inequity producing way of life.

However, the question is: How do we get there (to the ideal, whatever it is) from here? I am proposing that, first, we must identify the basic human values, the things that ultimately make life good and worthwhile, the things we *really* need (in keeping with what Illich, Prakash and others are saying). Secondly, we must attempt to move the present school system — and, necessarily, the surrounding society — toward these values and away from inequitable, destructive and unduly expensive forms of living and learning. And thirdly, *as we proceed*, we must dismantle those elements of the school system which are inherently incompatible with human well being or 'the good life'.

At this stage, I do not think we can be sure which types and proportions of large-scale and small-scale organization will be appropriate or possible. I believe that we need institutions such as the United Nations and laws such as the Law of the Sea which are global in scope. And equally, national and regional education facilities may always have a major role to play. But it is likely that the eventual ideal society (and schooling process) will in many respects be more decentralized than at present, along the lines indicated by Illich and Prakash.

Meanwhile, there does not appear to be a necessary imcompatibility between promoting personal and social education in existing centralized school systems and working to decentralize schooling in appropriate ways. Indeed, unless the present school system is used to promote sound values, the resistance to developing more human social and educational structures in the future may be insurmountable.

Finally, I want to suggest that we should *enjoy* ourselves while going about our attempted reforms. The contemporary world, while faced with great problems, also presents great opportunities for discovery, fulfilment, friendship, meaningful enterprise and pleasures of many kinds. If we ever lose the sense that life is good, we will not be able to keep going. As we noted in Chapter 4 when discussing the situation of teachers, people must attend to their own well being if they are to have the strength to help others. And we must be constantly exploring how to live 'the good life' ourselves, both individually and communally, if we are to know what it is we are trying to promote through schooling. Enjoying the present is not inconsistent with — indeed, it is an essential basis for — working to improve the human lot in the future, in schools and in the world generally.

Index